THE ARCHAEOLOGY OF THE BOROUGH OF SWINDON

The contents of a Saxon weaving hut discovered in Old Town, Swindon, that burnt down in the seventh or early eighth century, revealing charred timbers, loom weights and other items connected with weaving.

The Archaeology of the Borough of Swindon

Bernard Phillips

THE HOBNOB PRESS

First published in the United Kingdom in 2021

by The Hobnob Press,
8 Lock Warehouse,
Severn Road, Gloucester GL1 2GA
www.hobnobpress.co.uk

© Bernard Phillips, 2021

All rights reserved. No part of this book may be reprinted or reproduced or utilised in any form or by any electronic, mechanical or other means, now known or hereafter invented, including photocopying, or in any information storage or retrieval system, without the permission in writing from the copyright holder or his heirs.

British Library Cataloguing in Publication Data
A catalogue record for this book is available from the British Library

ISBN 978-1-906978-74-7

Typeset in Scala 11/14 pt.
Typesetting and origination by John Chandler

Front cover: Excavation of a second-century Roman pottery kiln at Whitehill Farm, West Swindon, in 1972

Back cover (main image): Parch mark seen by aerial photography in 1976 showing the mansio *at Durocornovium (Lower Wanborough); (inset): Twelfth-century bronze door knocker from Mannington*

Dedication

This book is dedicated to digging friends past and present amongst whom are Roger, Mogs, Jonathon, Bryn, Luigi, Peter, Geoffrey, Mike, Julian, Alison, Lesley, Roy, Claire and Helena.

Fig. 1. Excavation of the Roman Villa at Starveall Farm, Bishopstone

Acknowledgements

The author would like to thank Mogs Boon for her support in the preparation of this book, particularly with regards to assisting in photographic expeditions, and to my wife Andrea who read through the text and made suggestions and corrected my grammar. Also thanks to David Gent for organising access to Wanborough Church and Sheila Passmore to Chiseldon Church.

Fig. 2. Archaeological excavation on the Roman site at Groundwell Ridge in 2005

The Author

The author has been involved with archaeology in the Borough since the mid-1960s. He joined the newly formed Swindon Archaeological Society eventually becoming its Field Director. As such he directed and recorded excavations on Roman villas at Stanton Fitzwarren and Starveall Farm, Bishopstone, other minor research excavations, conducted field walking and rescue excavations notably for the latter during construction of the M4 motorway, Stratton bypass and Lyncroft estate. In 1976 he joined an archaeological team who were excavating in Old Town, Swindon led by the then County Archaeologist Roy Canham. This excavation on the site of Swindon House revealed much about the town's origins that span a period of over ten thousand years. Most important was the discovery of Roman and Saxon buildings. During the summer of 1976 he acted as a supervisor for an archaeological excavation on the Roman town at Lower Wanborough. Returning to the Swindon House excavation he directed its final stages. Two further excavations followed in Old Town with him acting as director and recorder – Lloyds Bank in 1977 and Britannia Place in 1978. The former uncovered a Saxon hut and Roman remains, the latter a row of early nineteenth-century cottages. These excavations were carried out under the auspices of the County Archaeologist and Wiltshire Archaeological Society. Commencement of an archaeological excavation at Littlecote Park near Hungerford, with the author acting as Excavation Director, began in 1978. Open to public viewing this long term excavation (1978-1993) was paid for initially through the estate owner and subsequently became self-financing, having a museum, tearoom, educational facilities and a gift shop. The excavation, initially aimed at a Roman villa discovered in the eighteenth century, revealed the site to be multi-period and resulted in the uncovering and recording of a Roman military invasion road, an early Roman settlement of circular huts, an almost entire Roman villa complex, a third of a medieval deserted village (tenth to fifteenth century) and a mid seventeenth- to late eighteenth-century hunting lodge along with its gardens and river frontage. Following the termination of the

Littlecote excavation the author undertook freelance archaeological work throughout much of Wiltshire but chiefly in the Swindon area. This has involved work for various companies and individuals as well as Wiltshire County Council Heritage and Libraries, and Swindon Borough Council. Amongst these has been work on the Roman villa/temple site at Abbey Meads, the Saxon/medieval town of Cricklade, an Iron Age and Roman settlement at Calstone near Calne, a Mesolithic to Bronze Age occupation site at Kingsdown Crematorium, Neolithic pits at Whittonditch and a walled eighteenth-century garden at Lydiard Park.

Contents

Dedication		5
Acknowledgements		6
The Author		7
Illustrations		10
1	Introduction	15
2	Modern Archaeology	20
3	Geology and Landscape	23
4	Palaeolithic (up to 10,000 years ago)	27
5	Mesolithic (8,000 – 4,000 BC)	31
6	Neolithic (4,000 – 2500 BC)	36
7	Bronze Age (2,500 – 750 BC)	43
8	Iron Age (around 750 BC – AD 43)	52
9	Romano-British (AD 43 – AD 450)	67
10	Late/Post Roman	117
11	Anglo-Saxon (AD 450 – AD 850)	120
12	Late Anglo-Saxon/Early Medieval (AD 850 – 1066)	134
13	Medieval (AD1066 – 1485)	140
14	Post-Medieval (1485 – 1850)	181
Swindon Museum and Art Gallery		199
Bibliography		201
Notes		210
People and Places Index		215

Illustrations

Fig. 1. Excavation of the Roman Villa at Starveall Farm, Bishopstone
Fig. 2. Archaeological excavation on the Roman site at Groundwell Ridge in 2005
Fig. 3. Excavating a Roman pottery kiln, Whitehill Farm, West Swindon
Fig. 4. Swindon Museum, Apsley House, Bath Road
Fig. 5. Archaeological excavation at South Farm, Chiseldon
Fig. 6. Saxon bone comb from Saxon Court, Old Town
Fig. 7. View from Barbury Castle
Fig. 8. View from Wanborough showing medieval fields
Fig. 9. Bishopstone Downs overlooking the Roman villa site at Starveall Farm

Palaeolithic
Fig. 10. Distribution map of Palaeolithic flint artefacts
Fig. 11. Flint tools from Mill Lane Swindon

Mesolithic
Fig. 12. Distribution map of Mesolithic flint artefacts
Fig. 13. Chert and flint tools from Mill Lane
Fig. 14. Flint tools from Kingsdown Crematorium, Stratton St Margaret

Neolithic
Fig. 15. Long barrow, Liddington Warren
Fig. 16. Distribution map of Neolithic flint artefacts and structures
Fig. 17. Flint leaf-shaped arrowhead from Old Town
Fig. 18. Polished stone axe, pottery and flint tools from Lloyds Bank in Old Town
Fig. 19. Flint blades and pottery sherds from Home Farm Blunsdon St Andrew
Fig. 20. Flint arrowheads from: Wanborough; Kingsdown and Fresden
Fig. 21. Sun rise over Liddington Neolithic long barrow
Fig. 22. Stone circle at Day House Lane as drawn by A. D. Passmore

Bronze Age
Fig. 23. Bowl barrow, Gypsy Lane Chiseldon
Fig. 24. Distribution map of Bronze Age artefacts and settlements
Fig. 25. Flint barbed and tanged arrowheads from Kingsdown Crematorium
Fig. 26. Socketed bronze spear head from Coate Water
Fig. 27. Flint tools from Kingsdown Crematorium
Fig. 28. Bronze Dagger from 'The Planks' in Old Town Swindon
Fig. 29. Disc barrow on Burderop Down Chiseldon

ARCHAEOLOGY OF THE BOROUGH OF SWINDON

Iron Age
Fig. 30. Liddington Castle, Iron Age hillfort
Fig. 31. Distribution map of Iron Age artefacts and settlements
Fig. 32. Electrum, gold and silver coins
Fig. 33. Gold stater of the East Wiltshire tribe
Fig. 34. Liddington Castle, ramparts and ditch
Fig. 35. Aerial view of Liddington Castle hillfort
Fig. 36. Barbury Castle's defensive ramparts and ditch
Fig. 37. Final phase plan of the settlement site at Groundwell West
Fig. 38. Hut circles and post pits at Groundwell Farm Stratton
Fig. 39. Reconstruction of the largest hut at Groundwell Farm

Romano-British
Fig. 40. Colt Hoare's 1821 plan of the Roman town at Lower Wanborough
Fig. 41. Distribution map of Romano-British sites and artefacts
Fig. 42. Road construction on the Roman town site at Lower Wanborough
Fig. 43. Extent of the Roman town at Lower Wanborough
Fig. 44. Parch marks of the mansio and bath house, Lower Wanborough
Fig. 45. Plan of the Roman town centre, fourth century AD
Fig. 46. Reconstruction painting of wall plaster from Lower Wanborough
Fig. 47. Artefacts from the Dorcan ford at Lower Wanborough
Fig. 48. Fourth century coins from Lower Wanborough
Fig. 49. Medical implements from Lower Wanborough
Fig. 50. Coin of Magnus Maximus found with a burial at Lower Wanborough
Fig. 51. Stone statue of Mercury found at Lower Wanborough
Fig. 52. Lead sheet incised with cursive script found at Lower Wanborough
Fig. 53. Roundel cut from a samian ware vessel depicting the god Apollo
Fig. 54. Plan of the villa at Badbury
Fig. 55. Bronze figurine of a genius from Badbury
Fig. 56. Drawing the drier at South Farm villa Chiseldon
Fig. 57. Heating chamber of the caldarium at Stanton Fitzwarren villa
Fig. 58. Stanton Fitzwarren, villa bath house
Fig. 59. Buildings and enclosures at Starveall Farm Bishopstone
Fig. 60. Surviving mosaic border, Starveall Farm villa
Fig. 61. Excavated rooms on the villa house at Starveall Farm Bishopstone
Fig. 62. Mosaic fragment from the anteroom at Starveall Farm villa
Fig. 63. Mosaic fragment depicting a hound from the Starveall Farm villa
Fig. 64. A brooch found at Mill Lane Swindon
Fig. 65. Excavating a fourth century AD well at Broome Manor
Fig. 66. Excavated fourth century AD well at Broome Manor
Fig. 67. Prone late Roman-British burial from Whitworth Road Rodbourne Cheney
Fig. 68. Fourth century AD silver hoard found at Groundwell Ridge

Fig. 69. Carved stone water shrine at Groundwell Ridge
Fig. 70. Plan of the shrine/villa at Groundwell Ridge Swindon
Fig. 71. Lead plaque depicting the goddess Isis found at Groundwell Ridge
Fig. 72. Excavation of a Roman burial at Saxon Court in Old Town
Fig. 73. Iron artefacts from Saxon Court in Old Town
Fig. 74. Failed well pit at Lloyd's Bank in Old Town
Fig. 75. Plan of buildings at Haresfield Estate Highworth
Fig. 76. Remains of a pottery kiln at Whitehill Farm West Swindon
Fig. 77. Plan of a potter's workshop and kiln at Whitehill Farm West Swindon
Fig. 78. Pottery vessels from Whitehill Farm West Swindon
Fig. 79. Roman tiles bearing the partial marks of IANVS and IVC.DIGNI

Late/Post Roman
Fig. 80. Late Romano-British belt fitting from Old Town depicting horse heads

Saxon
Fig. 81. Liddington Castle. Site of the Battle of Monte Badonis?
Fig. 82. Distribution map of Saxon sites and artefacts
Fig. 83. Saxon chaff tempered pottery sherds from Old Town
Fig. 84. Saxon gold stud from Old Town
Fig. 85. Saxon settlement in Old Town Swindon
Fig. 86. Plan and section of the hut excavated at Lloyd's Bank in Old Town
Fig. 87. Excavating a sunken floored hut at Lloyd's Bank in Old Town
Fig. 88. Walling daub from Old Town Swindon showing wattle impressions
Fig. 89. Plan and reconstruction of the fire destroyed hut excavated in Old Town
Fig. 90. Loom weights in the burnt hut, Old Town
Fig. 91. Finds from a hut destroyed by fire in Old Town
Fig. 92. Decorated bone pins from the Swindon House excavation in Old Town
Fig. 93. Decorated bone comb from the Lloyd's Bank excavation in Old Town
Fig. 94. Saucer Brooch from Foxhill Bishopstone
Fig. 95. Sixth century warrior burial at Brimble Hill Wroughton
Fig. 96. Silver penny of King Baldred

Late Anglo-Saxon/Early Medieval
Fig. 97. Inscription on an Episcopal ring from Lower Wanborough
Fig. 98. Carving of Madonna and child, Inglesham
Fig. 99. Detail from the font at Little Hinton

Medieval
Fig. 100. Distribution map of medieval sites and artefacts
Fig. 101. 'Ridge and Furrow' in pasture at Liddington
Fig. 102. Plan of the motte and bailey castle at Bincknoll

ARCHAEOLOGY OF THE BOROUGH OF SWINDON

Fig. 103. Bincknoll Castle motte and ditch
Fig. 104. Norman Tympanum in Highworth Church
Fig. 105. Holy Rood Church, the Lawns Swindon
Fig. 106. Excavation at Holy Rood Church in the Lawns Swindon
Fig. 107. St Swithun's Church, Little Hinton
Fig. 108. The 'Green Man' carving on a roof beam in Chiseldon Church
Fig. 109. Window glass in Chiseldon Church
Fig. 110. Thomas and Edith Polton brass, dated 1418, Wanborough Church
Fig. 111. St Katherine's chapel door arch in Wanborough Church
Fig. 112. Numbers 1 and 2 High Street Highworth (the old manor house)
Fig. 113. Lydiard Tregoze House
Fig. 114. Overshot mill depicted in the Luttrell Psalter *c.* 1320–1340
Fig. 115. Overgrown brick channelling of the later mill at Hinton Marsh Farm
Fig. 116. Traces of a stone dam on the Smita stream Little Hinton
Fig. 117. Nineteenth- century print of Swindon Mill, The Lawns Old Town
Fig. 118. Windmill depicted in the Luttrell Psalter *c.* 1320–1340
Fig. 119. William de Valance's shield
Fig. 120. Medieval structures, Market Square Old Town, excavated 1975/6
Fig. 121. Pottery, slag, whetstone and spindle whorl from Stratton St Margaret
Fig. 122. Excavating a building wall near the Market Square Old Town
Fig. 123. Earthworks at Toothill Farm, site of medieval *Mehandun*
Fig. 124. Lead seal from Toothill Farm
Fig. 125. Bronze door knocker from Toothill Farm
Fig. 126. Highworth church, the west porch
Fig. 127. Late 13th/14th century building and infant burial at Bishopstone
Fig. 128. Penned sheep depicted on the Luttrell Psalter *c.* 1320–1340
Fig. 129. Medieval silver pennies and a halfpenny
Fig. 130. Fourteenth- century flask found in Mill Lane Swindon
Fig. 131. Iron working depicted in a medieval manuscript
Fig. 132. Pottery sherds from the a kiln site at Minety

Post-Medieval
Fig. 133. Swindon 1773 Andrew and Dury map
Fig. 134. Reconstruction of a cottage excavated in Dammas Lane
Fig. 135. Silver coin of Louis XIV of France, found at Liddington Wick
Fig. 136. A brick plinth and garden wall revealed at Lydiard House
Fig. 137. Hoard of Civil War period coins from Waterfall Cottage, Wroughton
Fig. 138. Highworth Church, Civil War cannonball shot-hole
Fig. 139. Highworth 1773 Andrew and Dury map
Fig. 140. Tabard worn during the Civil War (Highworth Church)
Fig. 141. River Thames at Inglesham, site of a fishery
Fig. 142. Turner's brickworks in Drove Road Swindon
Fig. 143. Turner's show houses in Drove Road Swindon

Fig. 144. Pottery sherds, including wasters, from a Ashton Keynes kiln site
Fig. 145. Mid seventeenth- to early eighteenth- century clay pipe bowls
Fig. 146. Heeled clay pipe bowl fragment, *c.* 1650, from Old Town
Fig. 147. Brunel statue in Havelock Square Swindon

I
Introduction

Reverend Thomas Cox in his *Magna Britannia et Hibernia* (1720-31) wrote 'Swindon is so inconsiderable a place that our histories take no notice of it'.[1] Though Swindon cannot claim to be a historical borough, unless you count its nineteenth-century industrial heritage, it doesn't mean that there is no history. Swindon and its Borough are built up of many small communities, the stories of which extend far back into the mists of time. It is the people of these communities that have made the Borough of Swindon what it is today. Men and women have toiled, loved, fought and died on these lands for over 10,000 years.

This book presents in words, drawings and pictures our knowledge of the archaeology and a little of the history of the area covered by the Borough of Swindon from its earliest origins till the nineteenth century.

Swindon Borough
Centred on the Wiltshire town of Swindon the Borough of Swindon was formed in 1974 as Thamesdown from the Municipal Borough of Swindon and Highworth Rural District. In April 1997 it became administratively independent of Wiltshire County Council becoming a new unitary authority. Occupying the northeast corner of Wiltshire it is bordered to the north by Gloucestershire and to the east by Oxfordshire. Within the Borough besides Swindon is the town of Highworth and the villages of Badbury, Bishopstone, Broad Blunsdon, Blunsdon St Andrew, Castle Eaton, Chiseldon, Draycot Foliate, Hannington, Little Hinton, Hodson, Inglesham, Liddington, Sevenhampton, South Marston, Stanton Fitzwarren, Wanborough and Wroughton, along with many more small hamlets and farms. Having been swallowed up in Swindon's industrial related expansion of the last hundred and seventy years some former villages have lost their singular identity although their names are retained as areas of the town. They include Eastcott,

Even Swindon, Haydon, Moredon, Rodbourne Cheney, Shaw, Stratton St Margaret and Upper Stratton.

The Archaeological Record
The recording of the archaeology of the region reaches back to the seventeenth century with the observations of John Aubrey (1627-97). Aubrey, born at Easton Pierse in North Wiltshire to a wealthy landowning family, was educated at Malmesbury Grammar School and then Trinity College, Oxford.[2] He spent much of his time in the countryside observing and recording natural philosophy and antiquities. Amongst his writings are *Monumenta Britannica*; *The Natural History of Wiltshire* and *History of Northern Wiltshire*. More antiquarian records were made by Sir Richard Colt Hoare (1758-1838) following his inheritance of Stourhead House in South-West Wiltshire, which had enabled him to pursue his interests in archaeological studies.[3] Amongst his investigations were excavations at Stonehenge and other sites on Salisbury Plain. His writings include the *Ancient History of North and South Wiltshire*. Towards the end of the nineteenth century A.D. Passmore (1877-1958), an antiques dealer who lived at Callas Hill, Wanborough and whose shop stood in Wood Street, began noting and investigating archaeological discoveries in and around Swindon. He recorded these in notebooks and published in the *Wiltshire Archaeological and Natural History Magazine* from 1893 to 1958.[4] Having fallen out with Swindon and Devizes Museums in his later life he bequeathed many of his finds and others that he had collected to the Ashmolean Museum, Oxford in 1955 where they remain today.

Members of the Swindon Archaeological Society, which was formed in the early 1960s by the Swindon Museum curator John Woodward and interested local people, investigated and recorded archaeological remains being uncovered by urban development in and around the town. The society also supported the then Ministry of Public Buildings and Works, and following the ministry's absorption in 1970, the Department of the Environment's excavations on the Romano-British town site at Lower Wanborough from 1966 to 1976, and on a Roman pottery kiln site at Whitehill Farm in 1976/7. It also carried out a number of its own excavations, undertook field walking in the search for new sites and rescue work during road and building construction. Formed in 1972 Highworth Historical Society also supported this work and carried out

INTRODUCTION 17

its own investigations. The resources of the Swindon group, although aided by a professional archaeologist employed through the Wiltshire Archaeological Society, were much stretched during the construction of the M4 motorway. This construction saw the destruction with little opportunity for recording of a huge Roman villa at Badbury, an Early Iron Age settlement at Liddington and a late Neolithic stone circle near Coate.

It was such country-wide destruction that caused changes to planning consent laws and the growth of County Council and freelance archaeological units. Whilst the Ancient and National Heritage Act of 1973, and Ancient Monuments and Archaeological Areas Act of 1979 provided protection (scheduling) to sites of national importance, other archaeological or potential archaeological sites were in need of legislative protection. It therefore became a requirement through planning consent legislation that planning authorities had to take archaeology into consideration when determining development applications. Consequently in accordance with government guidance it became necessary for would-be developers, in some cases, to commission archaeologists to undertake investigations before or during development and carry out post excavation work.

Fig. 3. Excavating a Roman pottery kiln, Whitehill Farm, West Swindon

Swindon Archaeological Society disbanded around 1980, much of its work then being undertaken by Wiltshire County Council and Swindon Borough Council's Thamesdown Archaeological Units and various commercial units. In 1972 Bill Ford had been appointed as Wiltshire's first County Archaeologist. He was followed by Roy Canham MBE and now following Roy's retirement Melanie Pomeroy-Kellinger. An important project carried out by the County Council's archaeological team was the compiling of Archaeological Sites and Monuments Records for the whole County. This is regularly added to and can be accessed online (*Wiltshire.gov.uk/article/889/Archaeology*). It is from this database and personal records that many of the archaeological sites and finds referred to in this book are derived.

It was archaeological excavations in Old Town, Swindon during the latter 1970s, initially under the direction of Roy Canham, then the author and subsequently Julian Heath, that had led to the formation of the Thamesdown Archaeological Unit. This was directed by Julian, H. Digby, and Chris Chandler and supported by the Swindon Borough Council Archaeological Advisory Committee. The unit undertook much of the archaeological rescue excavation and recording in advance of and during Swindon's western expansion.

Amongst the commercial units that have been involved with archaeological work in the area are Cotswold Archaeological Trust, Wessex Archaeology, Oxford Archaeology, John Moore Heritage Services, Foundations Archaeology, Avon Archaeological Unit, Pre Construct Archaeology and Thames Valley Archaeological Services.

Swindon Museum and Art Gallery
Numerous archaeological finds and records require the establishment of a museum to provide storage, facilitate research and present a place for public display and education. Swindon Museum and Art Gallery began its life in Victoria Hall, Regent Circus in 1920 due to the geologist Charles Gore offering the town his collection of geological specimens. As a result Gore became the museum's first curator. Through many gifts the museum's collection rapidly outgrew its premises and in 1930 it was transferred to the imposing late Georgian stone-built Apsley House in Bath Road where it remains today. Archaeological records and finds from the Borough obtained through excavation prior to development,

INTRODUCTION 19

Fig. 4. Swindon Museum, Apsley House, Bath Road

rescue excavation and watching briefs during construction, as well as chance discoveries, gifts and purchases, continue to add to the museum's collection. This collection has grown so much that the museum's reserve and research collections are now stored in several buildings, and only a small fraction can be conveniently displayed. It has been proposed that a purpose built museum and art gallery will be erected in the town with adequate storage and education facilities in the near future.

2
Modern Archaeology

Our past is evidenced through two main branches: archaeology (study of human life through excavation and the examination of artefacts), and the historical documented word. Unfortunately the latter, apart from a few references by Roman and Greek geographers and historians, has not survived, or did not exist prior to the Roman invasion of Britain, and after that not until the medieval period in any quantity. Previous to this we have to rely solely on archaeological evidence to provide a picture of our early ancestors and the facets of their daily lives. In the later periods archaeology and historical documents go together to provide a more exact insight into people's lives and the landscape they dwelt in.

Site Recording
Archaeology has become very technical, a far cry from just digging a hole in the ground to uncover and retrieve ancient remains as the antiquarians of the nineteenth century did. It must be remembered that excavation is destructive as it involves removal of soil and other materials that cannot be replaced as uncovered, hence careful observation and recording is of vital importance for the understanding of an archaeological site. Archaeological sites are made up of deposits or structures that may have built up over hundreds of years. Archaeologists call these 'contexts' which are either layers such as floors or road surfaces, negative features like pits or ditches, or positive features such as walls or banks. Detailed records of their make-up, location, relationship to each other and artefactual content has to be made. This is achieved through drawing, photography, surveying, soil sampling, finds retrieval and detailed note taking.

Archaeology nowadays includes non-destructive methods (geophysics) which can provide a picture of what lies below the surface without digging, including resistivity, magnetometery, magnetic susceptibility and ground penetrating radar. When conditions are

Fig. 5. Archaeological excavation at South Farm, Chiseldon

right, aerial photography is also capable of revealing hidden remains as crop, parch or soil marks. Aerial Lidar mapping, a remote sensing technology that measures distance by illuminating a target with a laser and analysing the reflected light, is also used by archaeologists. It can reveal minute earthwork features in the landscape hidden by vegetation or even beneath forest canopies. Field-walking, that is looking for ancient artefacts on field surfaces following ploughing, also provides indications of former human activity, as does the use of metal detectors by responsible users who record find locations accurately and report them to the appropriate authorities.[5]

Artefact Research

Research on objects recovered is also constantly developing. Incorporated are aspects by researchers who specialise in individual find types which may be: pottery, glass, brooches, coins, animal or human bone, plant or insect remains, wood, leather or cloth remains, etc.. Particularly important amongst these are the plant and insect remains, which reveal details of crops grown and the surrounding environment and changes over time.

Dating methods previously reliant on coinage, pottery or historical documentation, now involve scientific techniques that come under the headings of potassium-argon, thermoluminescence, paleomagnetism, archaeomagnetism, isotopic, dendrochronology (tree rings) and carbon-14. When employed on artefacts made of wood, bone, stone and fired clay these provide accurate or relatively close dating, even on events that happened many thousands of years ago.

Fig. 6. Saxon bone comb from Saxon Court, Old Town (scale 4cm)

It is now even possible to determine a person's likely birth location by using oxygen isotope analysis of dental enamel, or through facial reconstruction to get a glimpse of what our ancestors actually looked like. Even information on a person's or animal's diet can be determined through difference in carbon-13 and nitrogen-15 content within bone collagen and by food particles trapped in teeth tartar. Through recent developments DNA can now be extracted from ancient human bone enabling information such as sex, appearance, ancestry, and lineage to be determined.

Another important facet of archaeology is conservation of artefacts recovered. Involvement by conservators can start with on-site retrieval of fragile finds and through skilled investigative conservation to preservation for public display.

Experimental archaeology is another important aspect, which employs various methods to test ideas regarding how objects or structures were used or made in the past, based on the archaeological and material evidence revealed. It can involve aspects such as building and firing ancient pottery kilns, erecting structures, or using various ancient implements, sometimes in association with re-enactment societies.

3
Geology and Landscape

The landscape of the Borough is varied, ranging from riverside gravel terraces to flat clayland, rolling chalk downs to steep chalk and limestone escarpments. The latter, composed of Upper Corallian limestone, lies at the southern edge of the Thames Valley. It is cut by three main watercourses that head northwards feeding into the River

Fig. 7. View from Barbury Castle

Thames – the Rivers Ray and Cole and the Bydemill Brook. Fanning out from these are numerous watercourses fed from springs that chiefly emerge from the edges of the chalk escarpment and Swindon Hill. On the chalk a single watercourse – the River Og – surfaces near Draycot Foliate and flowing southwards it eventually joins the River Kennet near

Marlborough. This varied geology undoubtedly had a profound effect on the nature and variety of human settlement in the region, and the resources available to them throughout the passage of time.

Swindon and Highworth

At the heart of the Borough successive exposures of Purbeck and Portland stone beds form the ridge that is Swindon Hill. The 2.25km (1.4 miles) long and 0.97km (0.6 mile) wide ridge rises to 146m (480 feet) above Ordnance Datum (mean sea level) and 53m (175 feet) above the surrounding Kimmeridge Clay. At and towards the west end, the land falls sharply whilst at the other end less so. On the southeast corner of the ridge a spur of outlying Swindon Clay and Pectinatus Sand extends for 1.6km (1 mile) towards Coate. These layers of sand and clay also form narrow exposures around the main ridge and from these emerge several copious springs.[6]

Fig. 8. View from Wanborough showing medieval ridge and furrow

Likewise, the neighbouring town of Highworth stands on a hill. This rises to a height of 133m (436 feet) above Ordnance Datum from the Corallian limestone escarpment and is composed of fossiliferous rubbly limestone (Coral Rag) with some clay, silt and sand. Here also a number of springs emerge and as at Swindon, these have evidence around them of human activity from very early times.

Settlement Pattern
West of Highworth on or close to the Corallian escarpment edge lie the villages of Hampton, Hannington, Stanton Fitzwarren, Broad Blunsdon, Blunsdon St Andrew and the former villages now incorporated in

Fig. 9. Bishopstone Downs overlooking the Roman villa site at Starveall Farm

Swindon, of Haydon Wick, Moredon and Rodbourne. To the north adjacent to the Thames and lying on gravel terraces, are the villages of Castle Eaton and Hannington Wick, whilst Inglesham is on Oxford Clay. To the east of Swindon and south of the Corallian escarpment lies South Marston on silt and sand; Sevenhampton lies on sand and Oxford clay and, on the eastern edge of Swindon; Upper Stratton and Stratton St Margaret lie on Coral Rag. Wroughton lying at the foot of the

Marlborough Downs escarpment is located on Kimmeridge Clay and Gault. On the top of the escarpment are the spring-line villages of the ancient Icknield Way – Bishopstone and Little Hinton which lie on Head (sediments formed by slope erosion) and Greensand; Wanborough located on Gault, Head, Greensand and silt; Liddington on Head and Lower Chalk; Badbury on Greensand and Upper Chalk and Chiseldon on Lower Chalk. Further to the south, also on Lower Chalk, is Draycot Foliate.

4
British Palaeolithic (800,000+ to 10,000 years ago)

The *Pleistocene* – the Final Great Ice Age – is an era that began 2,588,000 years ago and it spans the World's recent period of repeated glaciations, when ice sheets up to two miles thick covered much of Europe and North America. The presented image of endless ice is not a true picture, as the era in these regions was punctuated by warm periods when the ice sheets contracted; at least nine major episodes (*interglacials*) and many minor (*interstadials*). Some lasted thousands of years and conditions varied from arctic to warm, and occasionally temperatures were higher than today. Currently we live in the following *Holocene* era which began around 10,000 BC.

The earliest known use of stone tools is around 2.6 million years ago. This heralded the Palaeolithic period which is divided into Lower (245,000 years or more ago), Middle (245,000 to 40,000 years ago) and Upper (40,000 to 10,000 years ago). In Britain the latter is further divide into three sub-periods: Early Upper, Middle Upper and Later Upper.[7]

Connected to Europe and Ireland by land bridges the record of intermittent human occupation during the British Palaeolithic period is divided by episodes when the country was largely or wholly abandoned due to advancing ice sheets. Open tundra dominated by herbs, sedges and grasses with only minimal forest development was grazed by horse; red deer, mammoth, rhino, reindeer, arctic hare, saiga antelope and wild cattle; and was hunted over by brown bear, lynx, hyena, red and arctic fox, and wolf.

The Earliest Britons
The earliest appearance in Britain of humans (*Homo antecessor?*) was over 800,000 years ago and is evidenced by flint cores, flakes and flake tools discovered on the Norfolk coast near Happisburgh.[8] By 500,000 years ago another group of humans (*Homo heidelbergensis*) had occupied

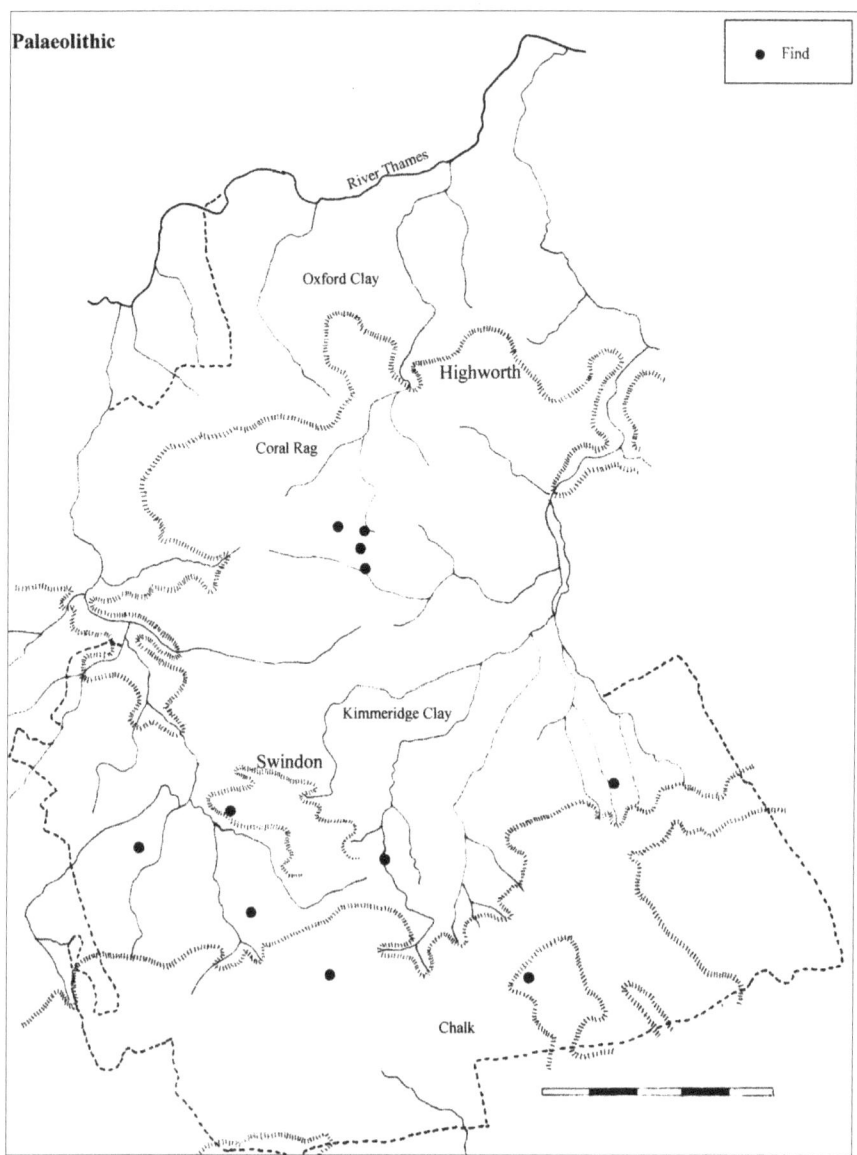

Fig. 10. Distribution map of Palaeolithic flint artefacts (scale 5km)

Boxgrove in West Sussex. Archaeological finds there include: a human shin bone and teeth as well as characteristic Acheulean oval and pear-shaped flint hand axes and bones of: horse; giant deer (*megaloceros*); woolly rhinoceros; vole and wolf.[9] Neanderthals who had intermittently occupied Europe for at least 130,000 years disappeared about 30,000

BC when signs of modern human (*Homo sapiens*) began to appear. Only recently has stratified evidence been found of early Neanderthal activity within Britain. Dating to around 100,000 BC the sealed deposit at Dartford in Kent produced struck flint flakes.[10] Neanderthal occupation sites dating to 65,000 to 30,000 BC include remains found in a gravel quarry in Norfolk that comprise finely-fashioned, elongated D-shape flint axes and the skeletons of several mammoth.

These early inhabitants of Britain were highly mobile, roaming over wide distances hunting migrating animals for food and clothing, and sourcing stone and other materials to make tools. Rough temporary shelters were made from animal skins, wood and bone, or accessible rock shelters and caves were occupied.

Besides axes, tools made from stone flakes included spear heads, backed knives, saws, side scrapers and notched flakes. Characteristic of the Early Upper Palaeolithic period long narrow blades were struck from carefully prepared cores. These were then made into a wide range of tools including leaf-shaped and tanged points, end and nosed scrapers, burins and piercers.

Fig. 11. Flint tools from Mill Lane Swindon

During the Later Upper Palaeolithic the spread and numbers of occupation sites found in Britain increased greatly. Tool making in this period revolved largely around smaller stone implements within which two different technologies are identifiable, Late *Creswellian* and Final *Creswellian*.[11] Use was also made of bone, antler, shell, amber, animal teeth, mammoth ivory and wood, which were fashioned into items such as awls, harpoons, needles and jewellery, as well as rods thought to be batons symbols of authority. Artistic expression seems to have been limited although a remarkable engraving of a horse on a rib bone and cave art at Creswell Crags[12] and the Mendip caves are notable exceptions.

About 11,800 years ago as the climate became cooler and drier, woodland began to appear as revealed by birch and willow pollen samples. As a result the traditional types of animal hunted declined, bringing about a need to adapt flint-knapping techniques to produce new tool types that enabled the hunting of the different incoming animal species.

Palaeolithic Evidence

It is within the Upper Palaeolithic period that human activity is first evidenced in the Borough. As can be expected, finds are scarce and are limited to flint tools and residue from their manufacture. These artefacts are restricted to the higher ground: the chalk downs, the Corallian Limestone to the north of Swindon, Swindon Hill and the Kimmeridge Clay in the west. Recent development at Kingsdown Crematorium has produce the largest total being: a scraper, three backed knives, two possible cores and a few flakes. Close to a spring near Mill Lane in Swindon two large core scrapers, an end scraper and a backed knife were recovered during building work. Field walking near Little Hinton produced a core that had been subsequently used as a hammer stone and then re-worked to provide a cutting or scraping edge. A combined drill and scraper was found nearby and at Little Hinton Manor excavation produced a scraper[13]. More noteworthy though are single finds of hand axes at Burderop Farm, Liddington Castle and St Andrew's Court in Wroughton.

The flint used locally in the manufacture of these tools and throughout the following prehistoric periods would have been largely sourced as nodules from chalk bed exposures on the Marlborough Downs and occasionally from river gravel deposits.

5
Mesolithic (8,000 – 4,100 BC)

Around 8,000 BC with temperatures rising to those like today, the tundra and lightly wooded landscape gradually turned to thick deciduous forests that stretched from one end of Britain to the other. Composed of birch, hazel, oak, elm, lime and alder, and interspersed with pine, the forests were only broken by river and stream courses, lakes, marshland and mountain tops. These 'Wild Woods' were inhabited by red and roe deer, *aurochs* (wild cattle), boar, wild pig, elk, beaver, wolf, wild cat, brown bear, otter and pine marten, along with a variety of bird life. Glaciers melting due to the higher temperatures resulted in escalating sea levels so that Britain became separated from Ireland around 9,500 years ago and about 1,000 years later from Europe.

Groups of hunters and gatherers would have been small, perhaps no more than thirty of all ages and confined most likely to kinship or intimate union. A Mesolithic cemetery excavated in Skateholm, Sweden,[14] included burials accompanied with dogs. Seemingly they had become domesticated due to their hunting abilities amongst reeds and dense undergrowth. Stone tools developed to accommodate new hunting techniques needed within the forest and wetland environments. Tiny microliths were formed from small bladelets struck from flint cores using punches and hammers of antler, bone or wood. Combined, these tiny flints set into wood and secured by resin and fibre created harpoons, barbed arrows, reaping hooks and grating blocks.[15] Most tool types of the Upper Palaeolithic continued to be made, but two large implements appeared – the pick for digging and the adze for woodworking.

Recent archaeological discoveries have shown that Mesolithic people were not as previously considered entirely nomadic, as besides overnight or seasonal encampments they occupied long term residential bases with fairly substantial timber-framed circular buildings. Each site may have been re-visited regularly over a considerable time span. The seasonal camps were probably linked to specific requirements sourced at relevant

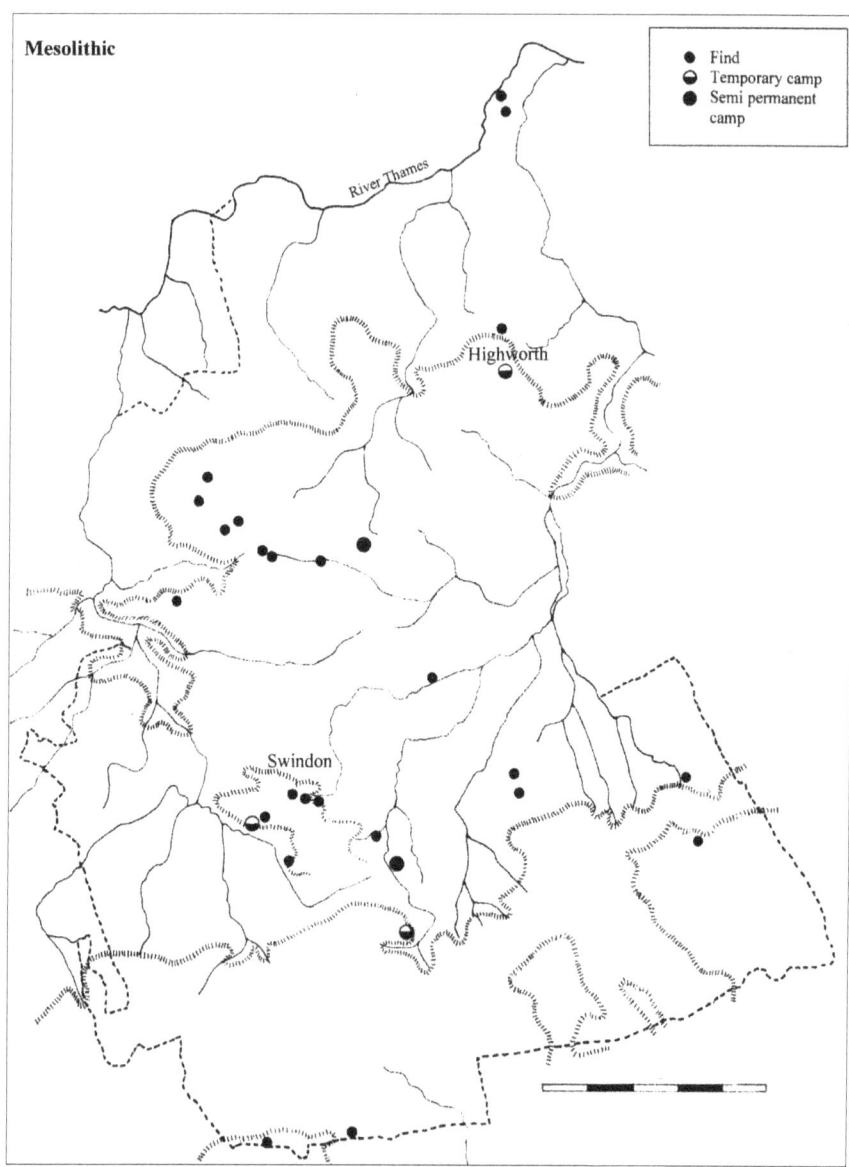

Fig. 12. Distribution map of Mesolithic flint artefacts (scale 5km)

periods of the year that may have included access to manufacturing materials, various food types and traditional or spiritual events.

Specific site activities are seemingly demonstrated through the range and number of tools found. Small concentrated groups with a

MESOLITHIC

majority of microliths hint at temporary foraging/hunting camps, while a wide variety of tools spread over an extensive area indicate a semi-permanent occupation.

Mesolithic Activity

Prior to the 1970s signs of Mesolithic activity in the Borough comprised a few flint tools: a pick; a saw; an adze and a pebble mace head. Archaeological excavation and observation of construction work has since resulted in the discovery of major and minor occupation sites along with numerous artefacts. Most of these sites are located beside springs or streams which offered a ready source of water, an identifiable location, as well as the watercourses providing easier access through dense woodland.

Hunting/Foraging and Seasonal Camps

Found during construction work from 1975 to 1985 likely examples of temporary or seasonal camps are evidenced on Highworth Hill by the discovery at Priory Green, Spa Spring and The Willows of flint tools.[16] Concentrated around springs the flints included cores, blades, a backed knife and manufacturing waste. These came from silt layers on an old land surface and also at The Willows in a watercourse bed. Two similar sites were evidenced on Swindon Hill, one at its east end close to a spring known as Church Well during archaeological excavations from 1975 to 1977,[17] and the other during house construction on the hill's western end adjacent to a spring by Mill Lane in 1976. Struck flints from these sites included a fabricator, cores, borers, microliths, scrapers, an adze sharpening flake and waste material. Also from Mill Lane came a small axe made of black chert. Tools in this material are scarce in this part of the country. In a

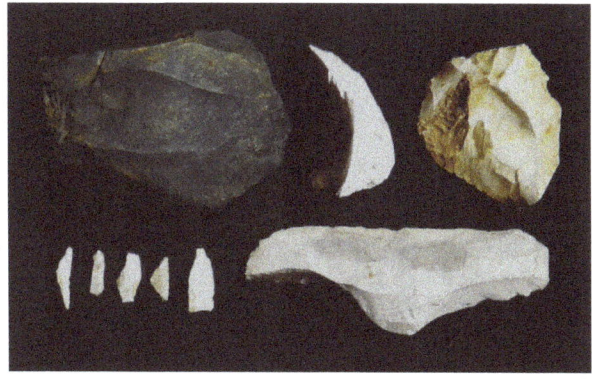

Fig. 13. Chert and flint tools from Mill Lane

ploughed field situated north of Chiseldon, on a ridge that overlooks a small stream valley, an overnight camp was identified by the discovery of struck flints within a fairly small area. Finds there included microlith cores, a hammer stone, retouched flakes, a saw and debitage. Another camp site lies high up on the northern edge of Russley Down, Bishopstone where discoveries included a scraper, a core, a saw blade, a notched blade and numerous flakes.

Long Term Residential Bases
Adjacent to the Bydemill Brook at Kingsdown Crematorium, and near to the sources of the Rivers Ray and Dorcan at Coate Water, long-term bases are indicated by the discovery of extensive spreads of struck flints. At the former site observation of the construction of a cemetery's access road, paths and car-park, and also field walking, resulted in the finding of over two and a half thousand struck flints. This number only represents a tiny fraction of the total that must exist, as the spread extends into surrounding farm land and covers an area of at least 1.4km by 0.5km. Here it would appear that settlement gradually shifted location as land clearance took place for dwellings and work-related areas each time it was occupied. The variety of tools, and techniques used in their making, show occupation on the site first occurred around 8,500 years ago and they continued to be used for several hundred generations into the late Bronze Age period.[18] Amongst the Mesolithic flint tools are: numerous scrapers and microliths

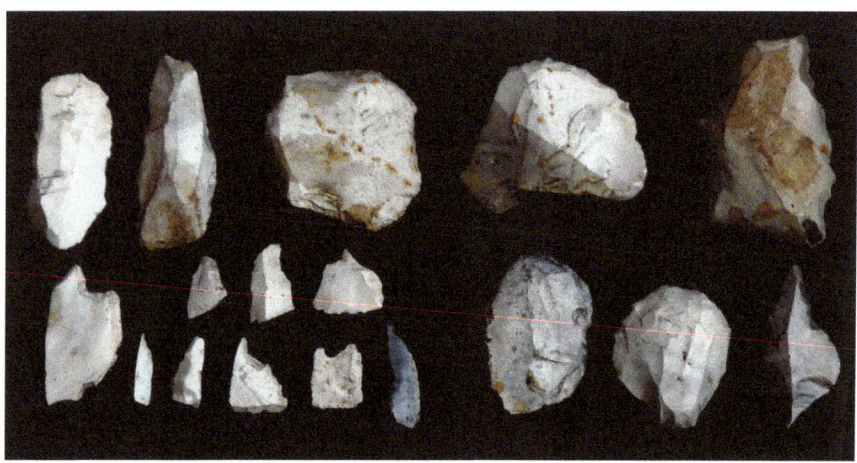

Fig. 14. Flint tools from Kingsdown Crematorium, Stratton St Margaret

as well as knives, burins, borers, saws, piercers, notched flakes, utilised blades and combination tools. Evidence of tool making is provided by cores and core rejuvenating flakes as well as debitage comprising waste flakes and un-utilised blades and bladelets. Some flint nodules and tools, chiefly scrapers, were excessively burnt, each exhibiting signs of crazing, discoloration and fragmentation. This seemingly occurred through their being discarded into fires and cooking pits or through their use as 'pot boilers'. The latter are fire heated stones placed into wood or animal skin vessels to heat liquids.

It is likely, as indicated by the underlying geology and the present water table, that the land on either side of the Bydemill Brook which flows through the site was marshy and cloaked with reeds, whilst the shallow valley's lower slopes with its sandy soil was chiefly open heath. The thin soil overlying the natural stone and clay on the higher ground may have been scrubland whilst further south on the clay there may have been deciduous woodland.

Evidencing a similar scenario at Coate: struck flint flakes, blades, microliths, scrapers and cores, cover an extensive area that extends either side of the present day reservoir, eastwards up to Marlborough Road and westward into farmland.

Other Sites

Struck flints have also been evidenced during archaeological evaluation excavations in Blunsdon St Andrew parish at Abbeymeads in 2003 prior to construction of the Blunsdon bypass in 2009, and also they were found at Groundwell Farm in 1999, Groundwell Ridge in 2003, Moredon Bridge in 2011, and Lower Tadpole Farm where finds include a hand axe, and also near Kingsdown Nursery during fieldwork in 1975 by Swindon Archaeological Society. East of Foxbridge in Wanborough parish, the cutting of a pipe trench revealed a deeply buried ash- and loam-filled pit which contained a microlith. Bordering the Thames on the first river terrace, struck flints were recovered during renovations within Castle Eaton's parish church and nearby, following deep ploughing. In Bishopstone close to a stream at Cue's Lane an excavation in advance of construction work discovered further struck flints.[19]

6
Neolithic (4,100 – 2500 BC)

An improving warm climate saw a reduction of pine and an increase of deciduous woodland. Within it an increasing population, and consequently a shortage of hunting and gathering resources, heralded the need for alternate methods of obtaining food. Farming techniques introduced from the continent made an appearance in Britain around 4,100 BC, firstly in the Greater Thames Estuary, then gradually spreading to other parts and reaching the Upper Thames Valley around 3,900 BC.[20] As a result woodland was rapidly cleared to provide arable land for the growing of barley and emmer wheat, and pasture for domesticated herds of cattle and pig. Recent archaeological work has shown that within the clearings substantial post-built rectangular houses were erected. Surrounding woodland continued to be foraged for timber and

Fig. 15. Long barrow, Liddington Warren (middle of photo)

NEOLITHIC

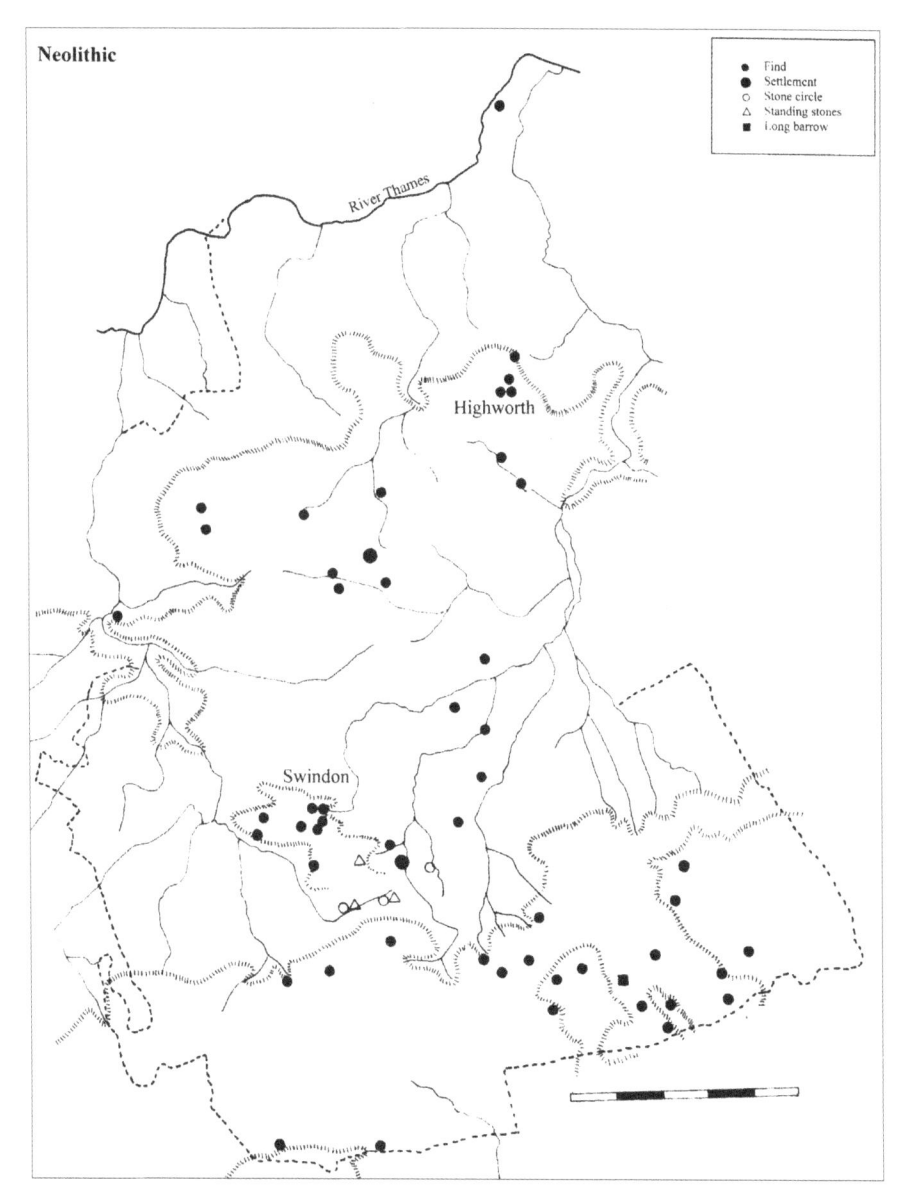

Fig. 16. Distribution map of Neolithic flint artefacts and structures (scale 5km)

food such as hazel nuts, edible roots, berries, fungi, tubers and crab apples. Settlement became more permanent, moving only being a necessity when cleared land became unproductive or resources in the neighbouring woodland were exhausted.

Distinct tribal territories appear to have been established, marked by earthen monuments which were ditched enclosures that defined special places for ritual, trading or multi-tribal gatherings as well as earthen burial mounds being places of transformation, a connection between the living, the spirit world and mother earth. A hierarchy and priesthood now clearly existed which was capable of organising the manpower needed for monument construction. Such structures evoked a sense of belonging, identity, veneration for the dead and spiritual belief.

Other major changes are apparent, notably the making of pottery vessels, leaf shaped flint arrowheads, flint mining and the polishing of stone axes to turn them into desirable symbols of wealth and power.

Neolithic Burial

Within the Borough, only one earthen Neolithic monument exists. Mutilated by ploughing, haphazard digging and the insertion of boundary fence-posts the monument, a long-barrow, stands on top of a natural rise east of Liddington Hill. Its ovoid mound is orientated WNW to ESE and survives 42m in length, 30m wide and 1.5m high. Twelve sarsens have been noted protruding from the mound evidencing burial chambers. Although no longer visible at ground level, 3m wide flanking ditches from which chalk was quarried for the mound's construction run parallel to both long sides. Three human skeletons were found about 1890 and a further adult male skeleton was found later. It is likely that these burials were inserted into the mound at a later period, as Neolithic burials within long barrows are normally disarticulated, since bodies were normally left in the open until only bones remained. In Salisbury Museum records indicate that another long barrow existed nearby in Bishopstone parish but it was apparently destroyed in 1870. Its mound measured 135 feet by 30 feet (41.1m x 9.1m) and three skulls were found in it.

Fig. 17. Flint leaf-shaped arrowhead from Old Town (length 3.3cm)

NEOLITHIC

Neolithic Settlement

Both the former Mesolithic long-term residential bases at Kingsdown Crematorium and Coate Water continued in use throughout the Neolithic period. Finds from the Kingsdown site include flint leaf and triangular shaped arrowheads, scrapers, knives, borers, cores, a hammerstone and a few fragments of pottery. Following

Fig. 18. Polished stone axe, pottery sherd and flint tools from Lloyds Bank in Old Town

ploughing of fields at the southern end of the flint spread where the B & Q warehouse now stands, over the years a farmhand had picked up many arrowheads and several axeheads.[21] Similarly, surface examination at Coate Water has produced flint scrapers, blades, cores, part of a polished axe and pottery sherds. Struck flints of the period demonstrate continuation of sporadic activity on the former Mesolithic overnight or seasonal camp sites on the hilltops at Highworth and Swindon. At the latter, archaeological excavations on the east end of the hill to the rear of the Market Square from 1976 to 1977, at Lloyds Bank in 1977 and the Hermitage in 1994 have produced a diversity of flint tools, including arrowheads, a polished stone axe head and pottery fragments. More flints were discovered during archaeological investigations nearby at Penfold Nurseries in 1977, Evelyn Street in 1978 and Croft Campus in 1989.

From pits at the hill's western end came a polished flint axe head, an arrowhead and a sarsen hammer stone.

A seemingly short-lived camp site was evidenced in 1969 during observation of the cutting of a gas pipeline trench east of Blunsdon. Sectioned in the trench side a cooking pit, lined

Fig. 19. Flint blades and pottery sherds from Home Farm Blunsdon St Andrew

with fire blackened stones, contained ash and burnt stone chippings in its lower part. From an upper soil infilling came a few flint blades and fragments of a whipped cord and bird bone impressed pottery bowl datable to around 3,000 BC. Adjacent a posthole which slanted towards the pit was also partly filled with ash.

Fig. 20. Flint arrowheads from: Wanborough; Kingsdown and Fresden (longest 4cm)

Other occupation sites are indicated north of Hodson in the parish of Chiseldon where a flint-working site produced part of a flint knife, also on Liddington Hill where pottery fragments have been found and east of Popplechurch in Wanborough parish. A trial excavation north of Bishopstone Church produced two pottery sherds and struck flint tools. Whilst near Gore Lane Farm, Bishopstone, an extensive scatter of struck flints include: scrapers, a borer, blades, a hammer stone, a core and flakes.

Fig. 21. Sun rise over Liddington Neolithic long barrow

Single flint arrowheads, perhaps lost during hunting trips, have been picked up close to Blunsdon St Andrew's Ordnance Survey obelisk, at the bottom of Plough Hill in Chiseldon parish , from near the River Ray at Moredon and close to Moon Plantation in Wanborough parish. Finds of polished flint axeheads are more numerous ranging over much of the Borough's higher ground. Besides flint, some of the axes are made of Rhyolite – a stone sourced in North Wales or Cumbria, and Dolerite – a stone sourced in South Wales. Such finds are indicative of trade over long distances during the Neolithic era.

The Later Neolithic

Towards the end of the Neolithic period much of the higher ground within the Borough had been largely deforested owing to extensive cultivation. Around this time (2,500 BC) communal burial within chambered long barrows ceased and the monuments were deliberately sealed up. In their place, burial of the individual occurred either inhumed or cremated and as recent evidence suggests placing of cremated remains in water took place.

Northwest of Barbury Castle a crouched burial of a young adult female excavated in 2004 by the author had been badly disturbed during the cutting of a field boundary ditch.[22] She had been buried with a Neolithic flint scraper. Multiple pitting in the upper part of her eye sockets caused by excessive bone resorption (*cribia orbitalia*) probably resulted from the lack of the normal amount of red blood cells. This is thought to have been acquired through either a combination of iron deficiency, insanitary living conditions, diets deficient in nutrients, or

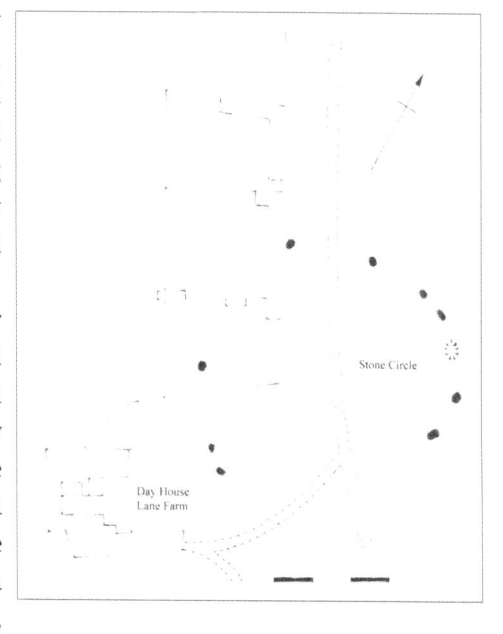

Fig. 22. *Stone circle at Day House Lane as drawn by A. D. Passmore (scale 30m)*

infectious disease. A misshapen third molar on the *maxilla's* left side was likely to have been due to heredity or environmental factors. Likewise, a crouched skeleton of a young man whose skull had been fractured prior to death, was buried in a flat oval grave in front of Liddington Castle. Excavated by Passmore in 1916, the grave also contained ox bones and flints.

By the very end of the Neolithic period, introduced from the Continent, metallurgy is evidenced by the appearance of copper knives and axe heads of flattened form.

Stone Circles and Stone Alignments
Having an obvious ritual significance, standing stone circles, stone alignments and avenues were constructed in the Neolithic period. In southeast Swindon the area around Coate and Broome appears to have been a special place during the late Neolithic, as it was a focus for a number of such monuments. Close to Broome Manor Lane a large standing stone is recorded as having smaller stones extending from it, unfortunately these were broken up for building material. Not far away, as noted by Richard Jefferies *c.*1867, nine recumbent stones formed part of a circle adjacent to Day House Farm. Today seven stones remain, of which four form an arc which if projected give a monument with an original diameter of around 70m. Passmore later drew and published a plan of the stones and following a drought he also recorded a double stone circle (one within the other), beneath the south end of Coate Water with a 400 yards long double line of stones leading up to them.[23] Nearby, two concentric elliptical stone circles were later discovered at Fir Clump. A survey, prior to their destruction during the construction of the M4 motorway, showed that the outer ring measured 107m by 86.5m and the fragmentary inner ring 86.5m by 73.7m. About 125m to the west a single row of stones aligned NNW to SSE measured 102m long.

7
Bronze Age (2,500 – 750 BC)

The Early Bronze Age
Recent DNA evidence strongly points to incoming people from across the channel who in a short period of time wiped out the indigenous Neolithic population. These newcomers have been given the name 'Beaker people' due to the highly decorated vessels found in their graves.

Fig. 23. Bowl barrow, Gypsy Lane Chiseldon

Around 2,150 BC metal-workers discovered that by adding a small amount of tin to copper a much harder material – bronze – was obtained. This enabled the manufacture of a greater range of weapons and tools that included axes, daggers, awls, gouges and scythes. Flint though, continued to be used for the making of scrapers, awls, knives and arrowheads. Also a wider range of pottery vessel types were now made: beaker; urn; food vessel; cup; storage and serving pot. Clothes were produced in leather, wool and possibly linen. This period saw the creation of long-lasting settlements since food supplies were assured through the efficient cultivation of cereals and the husbandry of animals.

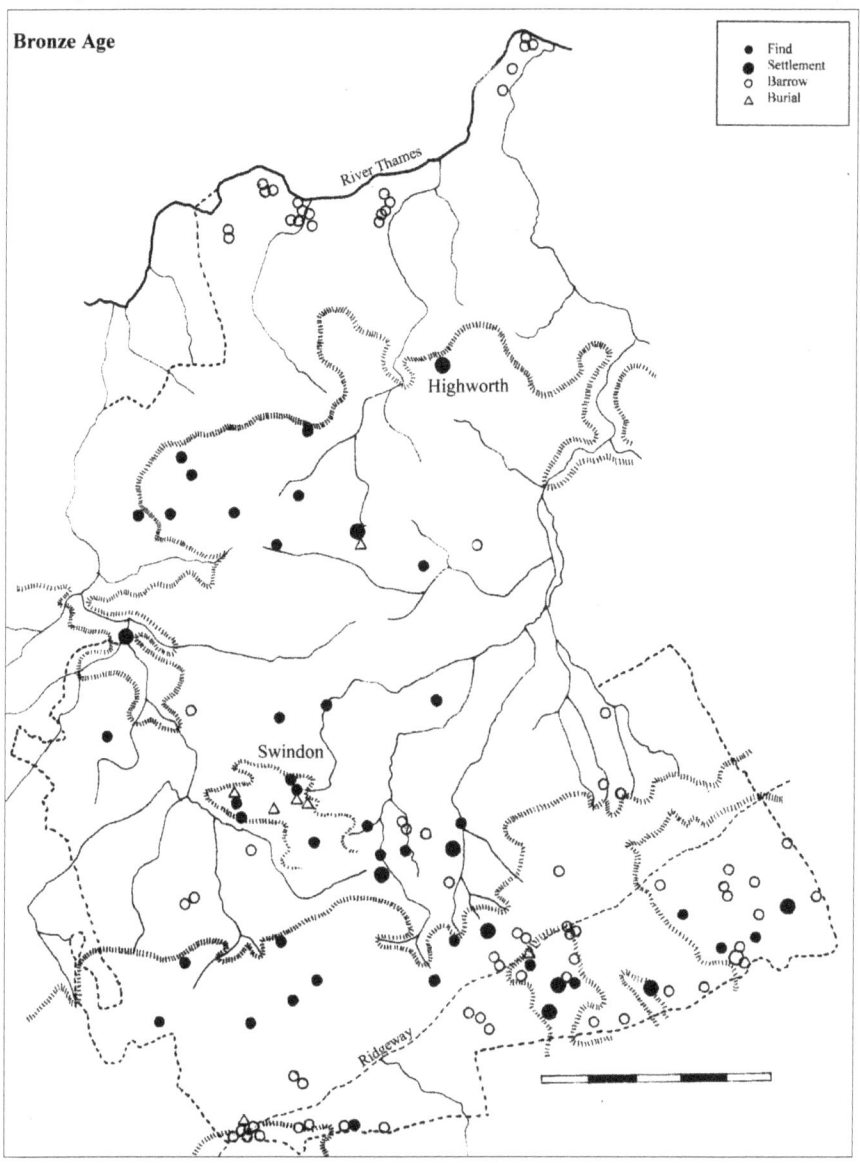

Fig. 24. Distribution map of Bronze Age artefacts and settlements (scale 5km)

Settlements though were small and the circular houses built were of slight construction. A wealthy hierarchy is indicated by the use of gold as jewellery and ornamentation. Additionally and perhaps indicating the need to defend territory and position bronze weapons for warfare rapiers, swords and spears were now used.

The Later Bronze Age

Commencing around 1,200 BC this period saw the erection of substantial roundhouses in bigger enclosed settlements with clearly defined fields and circular burial mounds erected on land borders, so demonstrating concepts of domesticity, identity and property rights. Fields were small and rectangular and can be seen preserved as cropmarks or earthworks, such as those overlooking Burderop Down, Chiseldon. Divided by trackways, enclosures and settlement areas they formed a patchwork that covered substantial areas. Further evidencing territorial boundaries and a desire to increase control over wide-ranging land are the arrival of long ditches, some many miles in length, often associated with fortified hilltop enclosures.

Bronze Age Settlement

Evidence is emerging of a rapidly increasing population indicated by the growing number of settlement sites being discovered through ploughing and construction work. Like during the preceding periods, these sites and other finds are largely confined to the higher ground in the southern part of the Borough. This would suggest that much of the low-lying clay land of the Thames Valley apart from the gravel terraces adjacent to the river, were still largely forested.

Occupation, presumably now permanent, is evidenced at Kingsdown Crematorium by pottery fragments, a loom weight and flint tools, including barbed and tanged arrowheads, and small discoidal scrapers. During the recent construction of a grounds

Fig. 25. Flint barbed and tanged arrowheads from Kingsdown Crematorium (longest 3cm)

Fig. 26. Socketed bronze spear head from Coate Water (length 12.8cm)

maintenance depot at the crematorium, several small pits, scoops and stake holes were found containing burnt clay, ash and a fairly small amount of burnt human bone associated with a Late Bronze Age pottery sherd. Clearly from the remnants of a cremation and its associated rites it is likely that a funeral pyre site and an urned cremation awaits discovery in the vicinity.

Flint tools and pottery confirm continuing occupation at Coate Water. In addition, a bronze looped spearhead and part of a stone mould for socketed axe manufacture were discovered and, at Day House Farm, a socketed bronze arrowhead. Most likely dating to this period a possible enclosure, penannular and annular features, pits, ditches and areas of burning were evidenced during a geophysical survey carried out in the field between the lake and Day House Farm in 2004/5.

Found during archaeological excavations and attesting to sustained activity at the eastern end of Swindon Hill are pottery fragments, a clay loom weight, flint tools and a barbed and tanged arrowhead. Nearby, a similar flint arrowhead was discovered during the construction of the Burmah Oil offices at Piper's Corner. Elsewhere in Swindon investigations have revealed likely settlement sites beneath the former GWR sports field in Shrivenham Road, in Shaw at Ridge Green, southeast of Groundwell House and west of Blunsdon St Andrew. The latter comprised pits containing pottery, animal bone fragments, an antler tine and worked flint. Close to the Great Western Hospital archaeological evaluation

BRONZE AGE

trenching in 1999 and 2002 located ditches and pits containing sherds of Middle Bronze Age pottery. Similarly dated pits and postholes associated with pottery and struck flints were discovered during archaeological investigations in advance of the Blunsdon Bypass in 2006-2007.[24]

Fig. 27. Flint tools from Kingsdown Crematorium

A settlement on Hampton Hill, Highworth is evidenced through finds of worked flints including two arrowheads, a looped socketed bronze axe, hammer-stones and burnt flint; whilst slag and bronze fragments found hint at metal working.[25] Most likely from this site two bronze axes and a socketed chisel are part of the Passmore collection in the Ashmolean Museum.

Likewise bronze working is revealed on Burderop Down Chiseldon, as well as the manufacture of sarsen quern stones (implements used to grind grain into flour). Excavation here by Chris Gingell in 1977 and 1978 also found hut traces, Late Bronze Age pottery, flint cores,

Fig. 28. Bronze Dagger from 'The Planks' in Old Town Swindon (length 8.7cm)

scrapers, flakes, hammer-stones and bronze artefacts comprising an axe fragment, a rivet, a ring and dress pins. Within the Borough at least ten other settlement sites are discernible on the chalk downs, as evidenced by pottery spreads and struck flints. Whilst burnt clay, fire cracked flints and charcoal associated with pottery sherds found by the Cotswold Archaeological Trust provide evidence for a possible Late Bronze Age/ Early Iron Age pottery production site at Commonhead.

Burials

In 1906 Passmore recorded that during stone quarrying at the western end of Swindon Hill an inhumation associated with a sarsen hammer-stone and many flint flakes was found. Over the following two years he noted a further three Early Bronze Age burials accompanied by decorated pottery beakers – a 22-25 year old female, a 12 year old child and a 15 month infant.[26] While in 1908 at the east end of Westlecott Road, stone quarrying revealed a family group – man, woman and child – interred in crouched positions within a pit. During alterations to the Masonic Hall in 'The Planks' in 1973 a crouched adult burial with an archer's polished stone wrist guard and a bronze dagger was uncovered.[27] This may well have been interred beneath a round barrow as around two thousand five hundred years later the area became a focus for a small, late Romano-British cemetery. A barrow may have also covered the interment of two adult female cremations uncovered in Bouverie Avenue during the cutting of a sewerage trench in 1935.[28] Accompanying these were five Late Bronze Age pottery urns and three small, knobbed cups.

Bronze Age Barrows

A diversity of funerary practices had evolved, with inhumations and cremations being placed within round earthen mounds (barrows) which often became a focus for further interments. Many of these distinctive features of the Bronze Age are still visible in the landscape. These burial mounds come in a variety of shapes – saucer, pond, bowl, bell and disc. Commonest is the bowl barrow that comprises a hemispherical mound of earth surrounded by a ditch. The similar bell barrow has a berm between the mound and ditch and sometimes a bank external to the ditch. Saucer barrows feature a low, wide mound surrounded by a ditch

BRONZE AGE

Fig. 29. Disc barrow (centre) on Burderop Down Chiseldon

that also may have an external bank. A rarer kind of burial mound is the disc barrow which comprises a circular or oval flat platform, occasionally raised above the surrounding ground level, on which are one or more small mounds. The whole is enclosed by a ditch and an outer earthen bank. Also rare is the pond barrow that has an embanked rim formed from earth taken from the interior.

Within the Borough many bowl barrows are known but no bell or pond, and only single examples of saucer and disc. All extant barrows bar one lie in the south, however aerial photographs have revealed others surviving as ring ditches on the River Thames gravel terraces, their mounds having been ploughed out over the following millennia. Many are closely grouped, creating barrow cemeteries which are features apparent on the chalk downs. Clearly settlements must exist nearby that demonstrate both the fertility of the soil overlying the gravels and that the Thames served as a major route into the heart of Britain.

Nearly all the barrows on the chalk downs have been dug into in the past, mainly during the nineteenth century. This includes the digging by Sir Richard Colt Hoare into an incredible 378 burial mounds on Salisbury Plain during his lifetime.

The single saucer barrow existing within the Borough is located immediately west of Barbury Castle. It survives as a mound 21m across and 0.2m high and it is surrounded by a 0.4m deep ditch and a 0.5m high outer bank both 3m wide. Not far away on Burderop Down the single disc barrow lies slightly west of the settlement excavated by Chris Gingell. Inside this is a single 1m high elongated mound excavation of which revealed a cremation in an urn. On Hinton Down in Bishopstone parish a primary cremation associated with a bronze dagger was found in an oval grave beneath a bowl barrow dug into in 1889. North of Downs Barn in the same parish Passmore, in about 1922, excavated a bowl barrow wherein he discovered a cremation and a sherd of thumb-nail marked pottery. He also excavated an adjacent barrow finding a further cremation. Two more barrows were excavated by Passmore in the neighbouring Liddington parish at Shipley Bottom. One contained a primary cremation and part of an incense cup, the other a cremation in a cist below a cairn of stones was accompanied by the rim of an urn and a conical shale button. At Coate east of Day House Lane slight earthen mounds are the remains of two or three bowl barrows; others have been identified by geophysics close by. To the West of Barbury Castle two barrows survive as earthworks of what were until recently a group of three, the other having been levelled by vehicles using the Ridgeway. The largest is 15m in diameter and 1m high. Both are surrounded by ditches 2m wide. East of Barbury Down a bowl barrow is situated north of Gypsy Lane and, although this is much disturbed through tree and bush growth, rabbit burrowing and cattle tread, it stands to a height of 4m and is around 25m in diameter. It had a surrounding ditch 3m wide, but this is now infilled. Many ploughed-out barrows have been identified as circular crop marks on aerial photographs within the southern part of the Borough. Two have been recently noted close to Little Hinton. At City Corner a small trench excavated across the ditch of one showed it to be 3m wide and 0.8m deep and dished in profile. From the overlying plough soil came a Bronze Age flint fabricator.

Artefacts

Amongst chance finds found within the Borough there are three bronze swords. The first recovered is a *c.*700-500 BC leaf-bladed sword with its grip missing and was discovered in an old stream bed at Commonhead, north of Moor Leaze Farm.[29] Not far away prior to development excavation revealed the second in a terminal of a ring ditch which confirms, along with other discoveries, the importance of the area around Coate during this period. The third a bronze rapier datable to 1050-600 BC was recovered near Flaxlands Cottage, Lydiard Tregoze, by a metal detectorist during 2003.[30]

Bronze axe heads were found at Upper Burytown Farm, Broad Blunsdon in 1906, Okus Quarry and Broad Street in Swindon, whilst spear heads came from Cricklade Street and Coate Water in Swindon and from Liddington.

Single flint barbed and tanged arrowheads have been found at: Mays Lane in Chiseldon, Marsh Farm in Lydiard Tregoze parish, Elcombe and Red Barn Field in Wroughton parish and by Liddington Castle. Part of a finely worked flint knife was also discovered on waste ground behind Lennox Drive in Walcot.

8
Iron Age (around 750 BC – AD 43)

Although introduced into Britain from Southern Europe around 750 BC iron working technology which marked the beginning of the Iron Age was not commonly employed until around 500 BC. Iron ore was plentiful in Britain and easily obtainable. The resulting metal being much stronger than bronze revolutionised many aspects of daily life particularly iron tipped ploughs that could turn up even clay soils quicker and deeper than those of wood or those tipped with bronze. Woodland could be cleared faster with iron axes enabling much more farmland to be created for an ever growing population. Within the Borough this encroachment into forested land is evident with the beginning

Fig. 30. Liddington Castle, Iron Age hillfort

of settlement on the fringes of seemingly previously uninhabited clay lands between the Corallian escarpment and the River Thames gravels.

Settlement and Agriculture

Ruled by chieftains, the population lived mainly on isolated farmsteads spread across the tribal territory. Around these, the inhabitants in the Early Iron Age grew crops and raised animals. According to the fourth century BC Greek geographer and voyager Pytheas, Iron Age Britons were famed wheat farmers. This is clearly shown in the preserved flora and fauna remains found. Cattle, a major investment, were a source of portable wealth as well as providing useful domestic by-products like milk, cheese, meat and leather. In the later Iron Age it appears that cattle ceased to be the main animal reared, giving way to the less labour intensive rearing of sheep, which besides mutton provided wool for clothmaking. Pig, horse, dog and less commonly chicken, are also widely represented in the osteo-archaeological record.

Pressure on land available for cultivation invariably resulted in warfare between adjoining tribes over boundaries. This undoubtedly was the chief reason for construction throughout the Early Iron Age and into the Middle Iron Age of fortified enclosures and hillforts, some of which were on a massive scale. The latter would have served as centres where tribal groups could retreat in times of threat as well as a place for tribal gatherings, trading and religious activities. However in about 350 BC they largely went out of use. Those remaining though were substantially reinforced,[31] perhaps indicating the merger of existing tribes into larger and consequently stronger groups.

Religion and Death

Various religious practices revolved around offerings and sacrifices which were sometimes human but more often involved the ritual slaughter of animals or the deposition of metalwork below ground or in water. Also disused storage pits and the terminals of ditches occasionally produce deliberate offerings. These ritual events would have been largely carried out or overseen by an order of priests known as druids. A number of buildings used for spiritual purposes have been located within hillforts and as separate complexes identifiable largely by offerings, location and ground plan. To a great extent however, religious ceremony could have

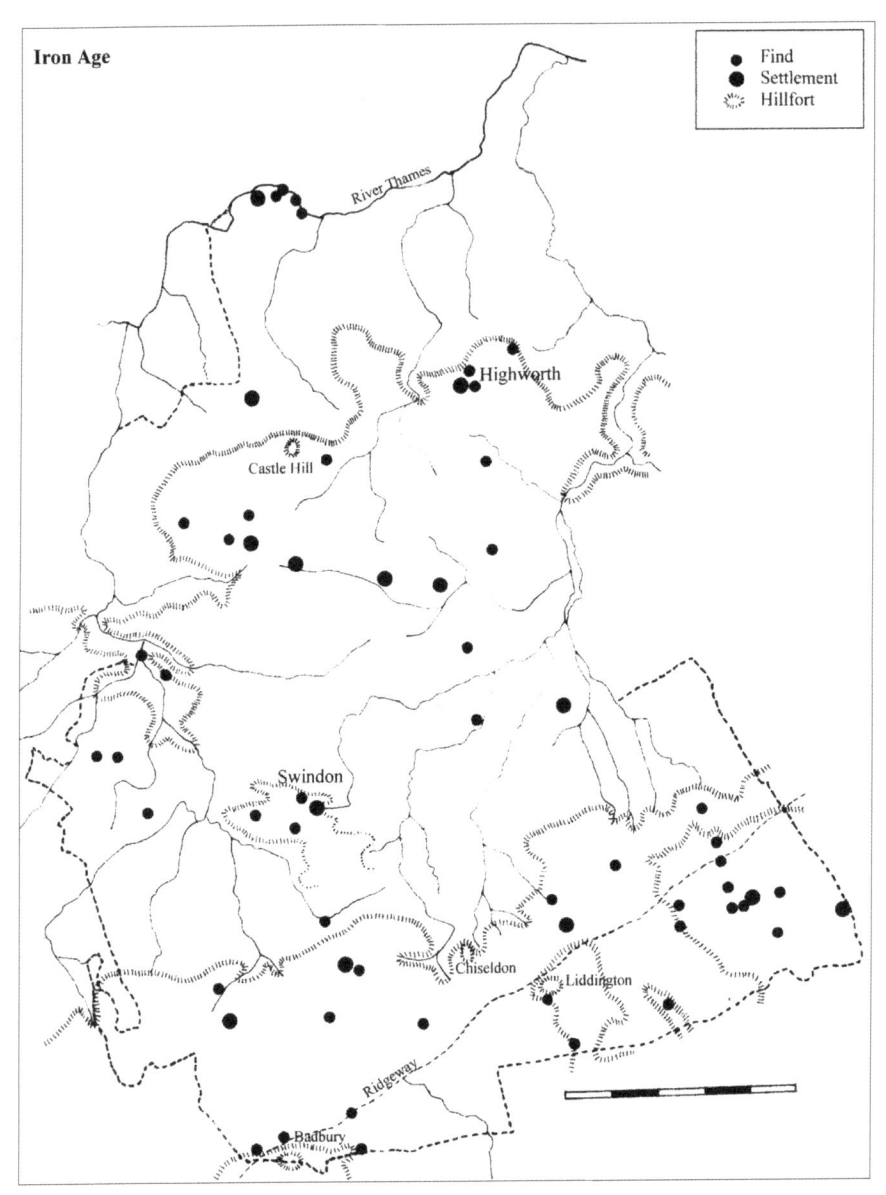

Fig. 31. Distribution map of Iron Age artefacts and settlements (scale 5km)

been undertaken in sacred groves which would have left little evidence for archaeologists to find.

One ritual deposit representing the importance of the occasion and wealth of the participants had taken place west of Chiseldon close to the Ridgeway. Here, in 2004, Peter Hyams, a metal detectorist, made a nationally important discovery. What Peter found comprised a large group of extremely rare Late Iron Age (200 BC-50 BC) copper-alloy and iron constructed cauldrons. It is a unique find, the largest group ever to have been discovered in Europe. In 2005 an archaeological excavation conducted by a team of specialists from the British Museum, Wessex Archaeology and the Portable Antiquities Scheme took place.[32] This revealed twelve globular shaped cauldrons, varying between 60cm and 80cm in diameter at the rim. They had been buried together in a large circular pit with around half being upside down, whilst the others were either the right way up or on their sides. A small quantity of pottery fragments and two cattle skulls were also present. To ensure the fragile cauldrons were disturbed as little as possible they were lifted by conservators in soil blocks wrapped in cling-film. Following the cauldrons' official acquisition by the British Museum in May 2007, one was carefully excavated from its block of soil. Buried upside down, it had been crushed due to the weight of the overlying soil. Repairs to the rim show that it had been used for some time prior to its deposition so it was not made specifically for the burial event. Recent examination of a second revealed just below the rim, raised decoration in the form of opposing stylised oxen heads face on with their long curved horns extending around the vessel with suspension rings above the heads. Each cauldron will eventually receive similar treatment – careful excavation from its block of soil, and thorough recording using drawings, photography and laser scanning. This will provide valuable data enabling both a virtual three-dimensional reconstruction and the rebuilding of the actual vessels if found sturdy enough. Soil excavated from within the cauldrons will be sieved to obtain potential bone, plant and pollen remains analysis, which may provide evidence of the cauldrons contents at their time of burial. They will then be stabilised and prepared for long-term storage or public display. Being substantial vessels used in the preparation of large quantities of food or liquid, they were probably used communally or at large social gatherings of people during festive or ritual events.

Evidence for the disposal of the Iron Age dead is virtually non-existent in the region, pointing to the likelihood of excarnation (leaving the bodies exposed for birds and animals to scavenge) or cremation, with the ashes being scattered on the land or in water, a spiritual return to the resources that had sustained them.

Coinage

The first British coinage in gold and silver appeared in Southern Britain around 150 BC and later on bronze coins were struck. Designs were initially based on continental coin types bearing stylised horses and disjointed heads. Some of the later examples bore the names of tribal leaders and displayed a diversity of figures, animals and motifs.

Fig. 32. Electrum, gold and silver coins (largest 19mm diameter)

Trade

Trade with Europe which had developed in the Bronze Age increased dramatically following Caesar's conquest of Gaul (58-51 BC). Strabo, a Greek geographer (c.64 BC-AD 24), records pottery and glass vessels, olive oil, wine, ivory, amber jewellery and other petty wares being imported into Britain; whilst exports comprised grain, cattle, gold, silver, iron, hides, slaves and hunting dogs.[33]

A Tribe with no Name

Based on the distribution of coins, recent research shows that the

IRON AGE

Borough of Swindon occupied the northern half of a territory ruled by an Iron Age tribe whose name is unknown (see in chapter 9 'The Town's Name'). Designated the 'East Wiltshire' tribe it appears to have held an area that stretched from the River Thames to a little south of the River Kennet.[34] It is thought that their tribal centre lay southeast of Marlborough at Forest Hill on the edge of Savernake Forest and that their civitas capital in the Roman period was *Cvnetio* (Mildenhall near Marlborough). To the south were the *Atrebates*, to the east the *Catuvellauni* and another unknown tribe who, seemingly, was eventually annexed by the *Atrebates*. The East Wiltshire tribe's distinctive gold and silver coinage minted for a short period (50-35 BC) was influenced by coins of the *Dobunnic* and *Atrebatic* tribes. The coins depict horses, solar spirals and solar wheels.[35] It would seem from the lack of later coins that they were annexed by a larger tribe, probably the *Dobunni* who bordered to the north and west, whose territory extended over an area that included West Oxfordshire, Gloucestershire; North Somerset, Northwest Wiltshire; Avon and the Southern parts of Herefordshire, Worcestershire and Warwickshire. The *Dobunni* tribe's people lived on very fertile land in farms and small villages. They did not resist the Roman conquest of AD 43 and may have submitted to the Romans even before the legions reached their territory. Bagendon in Gloucestershire was one of several important centres for the tribe. It is possible that following the conquest its inhabitants were relocated adjacent to a newly established military base a few miles to the south which was to become the *Civitas* of the *Dobunni* – *Corinium Dubonnorum* (Cirencester). Their early coins are not inscribed with rulers' names but some of the later ones are, and through coin styles a sequence of sovereignty can be assumed – *Bodvoc* 25-5 BC, *Corio* 20 BC-AD 1, *Commux* AD 1-15, *Catti* AD 1-20, *Inamn* AD 1-20, *Anted* AD 20-43 and *Eisu* AD 20-43.[36]

Fig. 33. Gold stater of the East Wiltshire tribe

Hillforts

Four substantial hillforts lie within the Borough. Having a substantial single defensive ditch (*univallate*) Liddington Castle and the hill that it is located on dominate the view to the south of Swindon, and as it is 277 metres high this is the Borough's highest point. Enclosing 7.5 acres (3 hectares), the scheduled oval earthwork has a simple causewayed entrance around 3m wide on the east side with an opposing western entrance that was eventually blocked. Built in four phases, the fort's inner timber revetted turf rampart is dated in its earliest form to the Late Bronze Age or Early Iron Age. The second and third phases date to the fifth or fourth century BC and the final phase dates to the post Roman period. Geophysics carried out by English Heritage in the interior identified the existence of pits and gullies and at least three round-houses, the largest being 19m in diameter.[37]

To the west, visible from Liddington Castle and south of Wroughton, lies Barbury Castle, which is an impressive scheduled hillfort having two defensive ditches (*bivallate*). Its inner rampart's platform stands around 3m above the interior surface and encloses 11.5

Fig. 34. Liddington Castle, ramparts and ditch

IRON AGE

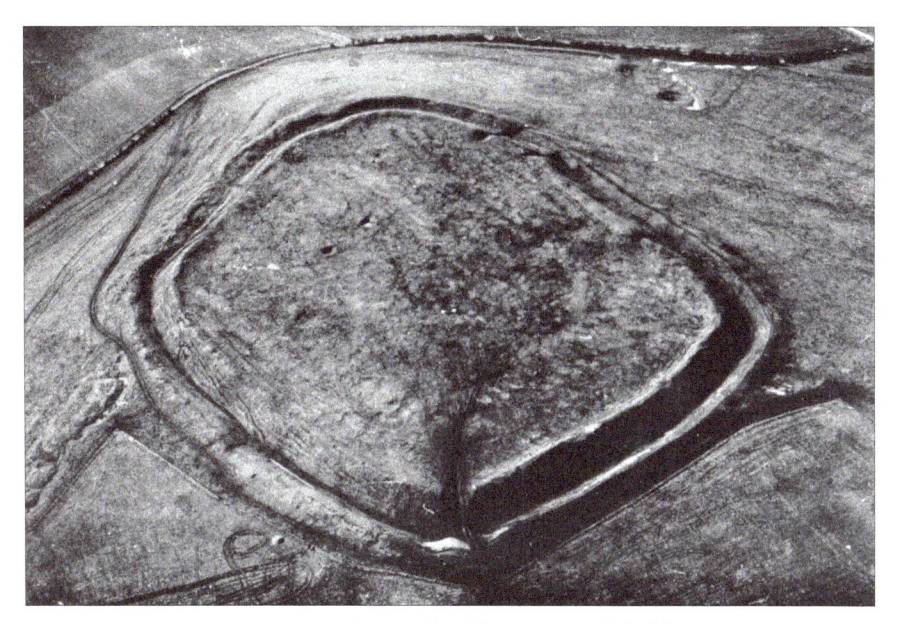

Fig. 35. Aerial view of Liddington Castle hillfort

Fig. 36. Barbury Castle's defensive ramparts and ditch

acres (4.65 hectares). Entrances to the east and west are 10m wide with, at the eastern entrance, a defensive banked and ditched outwork that faces level ground. The inner ditch is about 24m wide at the top and is up to 10m deep from the rampart's summit, whilst the outer ditch is roughly 10m wide and 3m deep. A geophysical survey in 1996 and an earthwork survey in 1998 by the Royal Commission for Historical Monuments recorded forty hut circles and numerous pits within the hillfort.[38]

Further discoveries within the hillfort include a blacksmith's hoard of: knives, sickles, awls, spearheads, an anvil, a chariot fitting, and pits containing pottery and skeletons.[39] The combined evidence points to this hillfort having been dominant in the region and to having had domestic, agricultural, trading, military and religious functions throughout the Iron Age.

Little known Castle Hill, the third scheduled hillfort, is located to the east of Broad Blunsdon. Thought to have been constructed c.600 BC, the earthwork has a single ditch with a strong counterscarp bank to the southwest and southeast, and is roughly triangular in shape. The rampart now largely levelled due to the robbing of its make-up enclosed an area similar to that found at Liddington Castle. Internal features are also comparable in density to that of Liddington, as shown through a magnetometer survey by Oxford University in 2004. Identified were probable pits and a linear ditch.[40]

Ploughing has razed the other Late Bronze Age/Early Iron Age hillfort, recognisable as such through

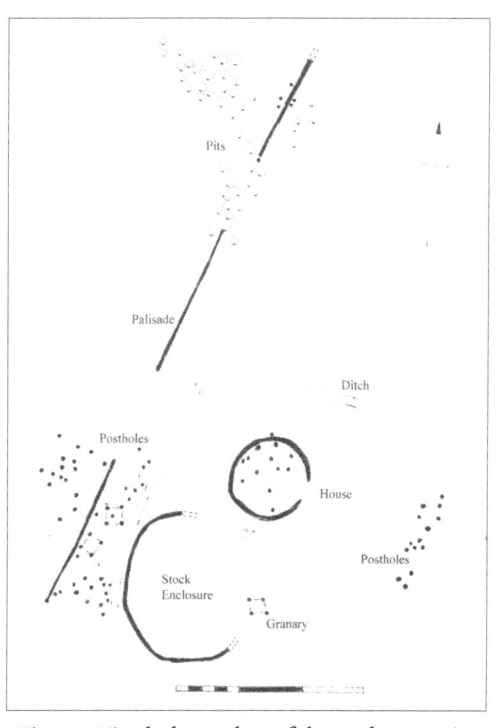

Fig. 37. Final phase plan of the settlement site at Groundwell West (scale 30m)

IRON AGE

crop marks visible on aerial photographs.[41] A single ditch encloses about 8 acres (3.2 hectares). Located at the top of the chalk escarpment north of Chiseldon it is overlooked by Liddington Castle.

Iron Age Settlement
Surface finds from ploughed fields, construction work and aerial photography have revealed many farmstead sites within the Borough particularly between the Corallian and chalk escarpments. In recent years two have undergone major excavation in advance of industrial development and so these demonstrate the archaeological potential for the region. Both lie close to Groundwell Farm in North Swindon.

A cropmark site north of Groundwell Farm at Groundwell West which was excavated in 1995 by Cotswold Archaeology, revealed four phases of activity dating to the sixth and fifth centuries BC.[42] The first phase was an unenclosed settlement that comprised five round houses and associated pits. After abandonment, the focus of activity shifted slightly to the south. Here a large carafe-shaped enclosure was bordered on three sides by substantial ditches and alignments of large posts. A roundhouse was centrally positioned within the enclosure with outside

Fig. 38. Hut circles and post pits at Groundwell Farm Stratton

it, to the north, a second. The third phase saw the enlargement of the enclosure to the north and east. Two roundhouses were associated with this phase – one northwest of the enclosure and the other in the enlarged enclosure's neck. Forming the final phase, a single roundhouse was set within an enclosure that incorporated a stock enclosure and a four post granary. External to the enclosure were further granaries, a fence line and a cluster of beehive-shaped rubbish pits. Carbonised barley and spelt grains were present in samples from the pits. Animal bones found comprised cattle (39%), sheep/goat (43%), pig (13.8 %), horse (3.2%), dog (0.6%) and roe deer (0.3%). Cattle were mature when slaughtered indicating that they had been exploited for use other than meat and skins, such as providing milk or haulage.

East of Groundwell Farm the second site was also initially identified as a cropmark visible on an aerial photograph. Excavation by Chris Gingell in 1976-7 showed that it consisted of a banjo shaped double-ditched enclosure in which a succession of four round houses

Fig. 39. Reconstruction of the largest hut at Groundwell Farm (Swindon Museum)

were defined by shallow trenches.⁴³ Dating to the fifth century BC the earliest hut measured 13m in diameter and had a wide southeast facing entrance. Its replacement, measuring 11.75m in diameter, had an entrance porch on its southeast side and four central roof support posts. With massive post pits on either side of its southeast entrance the following hut, being 12m in diameter, had its roof supported by a ring of eight posts. Three posts set in a triangle had held up the roof of the final hut that had a southern entrance. Inside this 19.5m diameter building a pit containing burnt stones may have been a hearth. Around the various huts postholes set in groups of four, with some containing carbonised grain point to the presence of granaries. Raised above ground these structures were less vulnerable to vermin intrusion and damp. Large quantities of pottery and animal bone along with other finds: iron bucket handle, iron knife, bone needles, bone weaving shuttle and a stone saddle quern are evidence of both the agricultural and domestic activities of a single family unit over a number of generations. The animal bones show that sheep at 48.3% were the commonest, followed by pig at 33.1%, cattle at 14.3% and horse at 2.3%. Pig compared to other sites of the period in Wessex were abundant, this perhaps being due to the adjacent seemingly forested clay vale which would have provided them good autumn feeding. Culling of sheep occurred at an elderly age implying mutton production or more likely a flock kept for their wool.

Positioned on the Corallian limestone and clay plateau, archaeological work at Honda and the B&Q warehouse sites east of Swindon have revealed linear features, pits and postholes, as well as a circular post built house and a four post structure. Associated with these are pottery and animal bone that evidence occupation in the Early Iron Age. Also discovered were two Late Iron Age burials, one female aged 25-40 and a male of 50+years⁴⁴. These burials may relate to buildings, trackway and ditched enclosures, evidenced nearby on the South Marston Industrial Park.⁴⁵ Geophysics and excavation at Moredon Bridge revealed the ring gulley of a house and a four-post structure as well as a ditched enclosure of Late Bronze Age/Early Iron Age date. Dated by pottery to the Middle or Late Iron Age, an unenclosed settlement incorporating a circular hut was revealed during archaeological excavation in advance of construction at Ridge Green, Shaw. Excavation in advance of construction at Ridgeway Farm, Common Platt by Wessex Archaeology uncovered a sequence of at least five round houses and storage pits dating from 700 BC to 100 BC. Finds there comprise pottery, animal bone, weaving equipment and quern stones. Likewise excavation prior to construction and a watching brief during building work at Shaw Ridge Primary School, revealed traces of the circular drip gulley of a roundhouse which had a 2m wide entrance facing east. Internally there were several postholes and pits with associated sherds of pottery and charred grains of spelt wheat and barley.[46]

During excavation in 1975, in advance of an extension to a cemetery on Hampton Hill Highworth, the following were found: a circular hut, pits, postholes, a cremation, pottery sherds, animal bones and bone implements. Further finds in the vicinity including more pottery fragments and a bone weaving comb, point to the site being extensive and that due to its hilltop location it may eventually prove to be the location of a levelled fortified enclosure.

Lying on clay within the River Thames Valley two farm sites were found. At Little Rose Lane in the parish of Blunsdon St Andrew, an extensive occupation layer with pits, gullies and a hearth, as well as sherds and animal bones, was exposed during the cutting of a gas pipe trench in 1969. Whilst at Red Barn, Castle Eaton, a photograph of cropmarks shows an irregular circular enclosure within which is a large hut circle.

On the chalk downs an Early Iron Age farm site was located southwest of Hill Farm in Liddington parish during the construction of the M4 in 1970. Here nine pits and a possible hut site were salvage excavated by members of the Swindon Archaeological Society in very trying conditions. From the pits came pottery and cattle, sheep, horse and dog bones. Much though was lost due to the road construction machines. Finds within the ploughed soil of pottery fragments, part of a weaving comb, a large stone rubber, bronze brooches and an iron ring-headed pin demonstrate the existence of an extensive settlement on Russley Down, south of Bishopstone. Within Wroughton parish two farm sites were found. One was on the Wroughton airfield, where an archaeological evaluation excavation in April 2006 exposed a hut circle and a series of pits; while the other was east of Burderop Camp, where field-walking unearthed pottery sherds after enclosures were noted on aerial photographs.

Single pits containing pottery and animal bone have been found west of Blunsdon St Andrew and northwest of Toothill Farm, whilst at Okus Quarry a pit contained thirteen chalk loom-weights.

Other likely farm sites hinted by the discovery of artefacts include: Old Town, Swindon; several locations on Bishopstone Downs and Hinton Downs; Burderop Park in Chiseldon; north of West Hill near Highworth; southwest of Moon Plantation near Mount Pleasant Farm and southeast of Foxhill House, with the latter both being in Wanborough parish.

Iron Age Pottery

Locally, Early Iron Age pottery was handmade until the introduction of the potter's wheel in the second century BC. A variety of vessel types were made, their form dependent on function – storage, cooking, or consumption. To reduce shrinkage and prevent cracking on drying temper was added to the potting clay. Temper used locally was either sand, crushed fossilised shell, flint, oolitic limestone, chalk, iron oxide, quartz or a combination of the materials that were easily obtainable due to the underlying geological deposits. Many vessels prior to firing in bonfires or pits were hand smoothed, wiped with a cloth, or lightly burnished and some were decorated. The decoration often took the form of horizontal lines of regularly spaced impressed thumb-nail marks on a vessel's side or rim. Most bowls of carinated or tripartite form (vessel's body made in two or three parts) were decorated with multiple horizontal grooving on the shoulder and neck. Rarer embellishment usually on the shoulders took the form of deeply incised patterns composed of angular, triangular, zigzag or wavy lines and stabbing marks. Some were highly burnished and others were coated with powdered hematite prior to burnishing, which produced a red-brown lustre.

Artefacts

Artefacts discovered by chance include: an iron spearhead and a La Tene III bronze brooch from Hinton Downs; a bronze mount in the form of a schematised mask with curved horns and a split flowing beard near the Ridgeway south of Bishopstone; whilst north of Forty Acre Barn, Castle Eaton a bronze toggle or horse's bar bit with engraved decoration and enamelled terminals was found. The commonest recorded finds are coins. Gold coins from Swindon Hill or nearby comprise staters of *Corio* of the *Dobunni* tribe, *Tincommius* of the *Atrebates*, the *Namnetes* (a Gaulish tribe) and two uninscribed. Unlocated apart from being found near Swindon a hoard of eight base silver coins of the 'Upavon' type are attributed to the East Wiltshire tribe. Also issued by this tribe, a 'Wanborough Wheel' type coin came from Wanborough along with seven *Dobunnic* uninscribed coins. Three gold staters of the East Wiltshire tribe were also found at Chiseldon. An additional *Dobunnic* silver coin and a uniface gold stater came from southeast of Kempsford Church in Castle Eaton parish. Both were probably dredged from the River Thames. Also at Castle Eaton near Red Barn a gold *Morinic* stater was found. Further coins have been found west of Wanborough Plain Farm, on Hinton Downs near Bishopstone, Mount Pleasant Farm in Wanborough parish and south of Liddington Castle.

9
Romano-British (AD 43 – AD 450)

Within the Borough, archaeological evidence for this period is the most prolific and densely spread, signifying that during almost four hundred years of Roman rule substantial population growth and prosperity occurred, through successful government and military control.

Invasion
It began in AD 43 with the invasion decreed by Claudius to secure his position as emperor and gain prestige. The eventual aim was to use the country's wealth in land, labour and resources to enrich the Roman state and help support its massive military machine. General Plautius landed, probably at Richborough in Kent, at the head of 40,000 troops with all the necessary equipment, transport, food etc. to keep them supplied during the initial stages of the campaign. They landed without opposition but shortly after fought a two-day battle at a crossing on the River Medway. The main field army of the *Catevaulauni*, the leading force in southeast Britain was destroyed. Then the legions pressed northward and captured the *Catevaulauni* Oppidum (fortified settlement) at Colchester (*Camulodunum*). During this early stage of the invasion it is recorded that eleven tribal kings offered their allegiance to Rome, including the *Dobunni* tribe whose territory incorporated the area in which Swindon Borough lies. The army then split into several groups; the *Legio II* commanded by Vespasian, a future emperor, headed into the southwest. In opposition to the advancing troops, the local population took refuge in hillforts. According to the Roman writer Suetonius, Vespasian's troops fought 30 battles, overcame two powerful tribes, captured the Isle of Wight and took over 20 hillforts. His force seemingly started out from a supply base in the Fishbourne or Chichester area and advanced overland against the *Durotriges*, the western *Atrebates* and the tribes of Devon

and Cornwall. Meanwhile the navy sailed westward taking the Isle of White (*Vectis*) and it established supply bases along the south coast. As the legions progressed they built supply roads and constructed forts at road junctions and river crossings.

Lower Wanborough, a Roman Town

By AD 47 a temporary border had been established extending from Exeter to Lincoln linked by a road now known as the Fosse Way and defended by a line of forts and fortresses backed by a zone of defence up to 30kms wide. It is feasible that as part of this defensive line, as well as protecting a junction of two major roads, a fort had been sited at Lower Wanborough close to a small river – the Dorcan.[47] Evidence for a military presence here is provided by finds of military equipment such as a pilum, spearheads, a caltrop, arrowheads, harness fittings, a helmet carrying handle, an apron stud, Claudian/Neronian pottery and early Roman coinage. The two major roads built to enable swift troop movement and ease of supplies were Ermin Street and Broken Street (Anglo Saxon *Tobrokene Strata*). Commencing at *Calleva Atrebatum* (Silchester), the tribal centre of the *Atrebates*, Ermin Street linked with *Corinium Dubonnorum* (Cirencester) – the tribal centre of the *Dobunni* and then on to *Glevum* (Gloucester). Broken Street passed through *Venta*

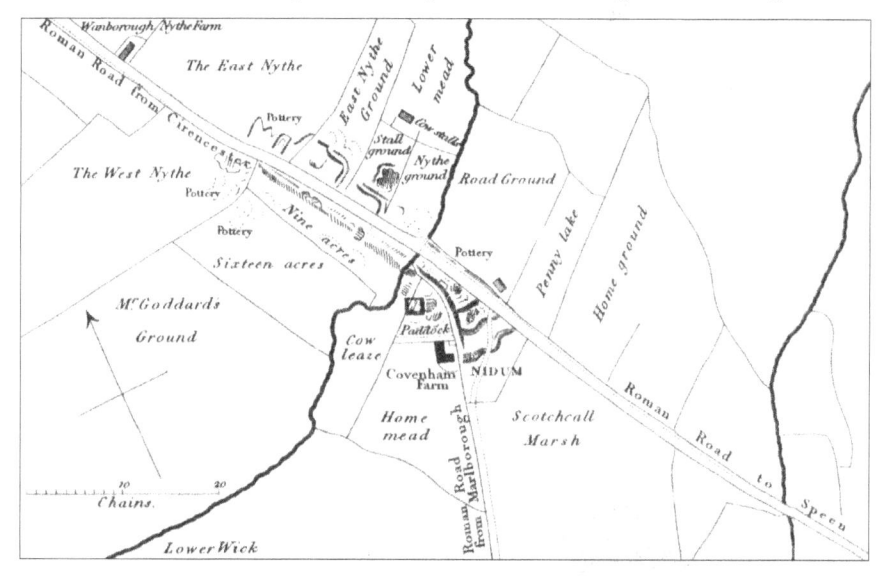

Fig. 40. Colt Hoare's 1821 plan of the Roman town at Lower Wanborough

Belgarum (Winchester) the tribal centre of the *Belgae,* on its way from a likely supply base on the south coast.

Discovery

'At several places hereabout are every yeare digged up Roman coyness, ruines of houses and black ashes especially about the meadow called "The Nigh";' so noted John Aubrey in the late seventeenth century in his *Monumenta Britannica*. It was the first recorded reference to Roman remains at Lower Wanborough. Colt Hoare made further discoveries in the early nineteenth century and published a plan in which he incorrectly named the site as *Nidum*.[48] He wrote that

> Mr Carpenter an intelligent old farmer fifty years at Covenham, eighty-five years of age, had found every mark of Roman residence in coins, figured bricks, tiles, &c but unfortunately had not preserved them. Every heap of earth, every new-made ditch and every adjoining road teemed with Roman pottery of various descriptions from the fine red glazed Samian and thin black to that of a coarser manufacture. There are no regularly raised earthen works or enclosed camp to be seen here but in several of the fields there are great irregularities of ground and excavations which indicate the site of ancient buildings and which if properly examined would doubtless produce much novelty and information. In a meadow on the eastern side of this farm there was formerly a deep cavity which is now filled up. The farmer informed me that he had traced a road paved with large flat stone, leading directly from the Roman road up to it but not extending beyond it. This was probably the site of a temple. On the western side of the 'old Causeway' and in a field belonging to Mr Goddard of Swindon there are some great irregularities in its surface from which many large stones have been extracted and which evidently denoted substructures of ancient buildings. In the modern road which intersects the station of *Nidum* I noticed half a quern and in a heap of dirt I picked up a piece of coral or *Samian* pottery elegantly ornamented with vine leaves, and in no one Roman Station have I ever found so many specimens of Roman pottery without the assistance of the spade as at this place.

In the early part of the twentieth century the antiquarian Passmore

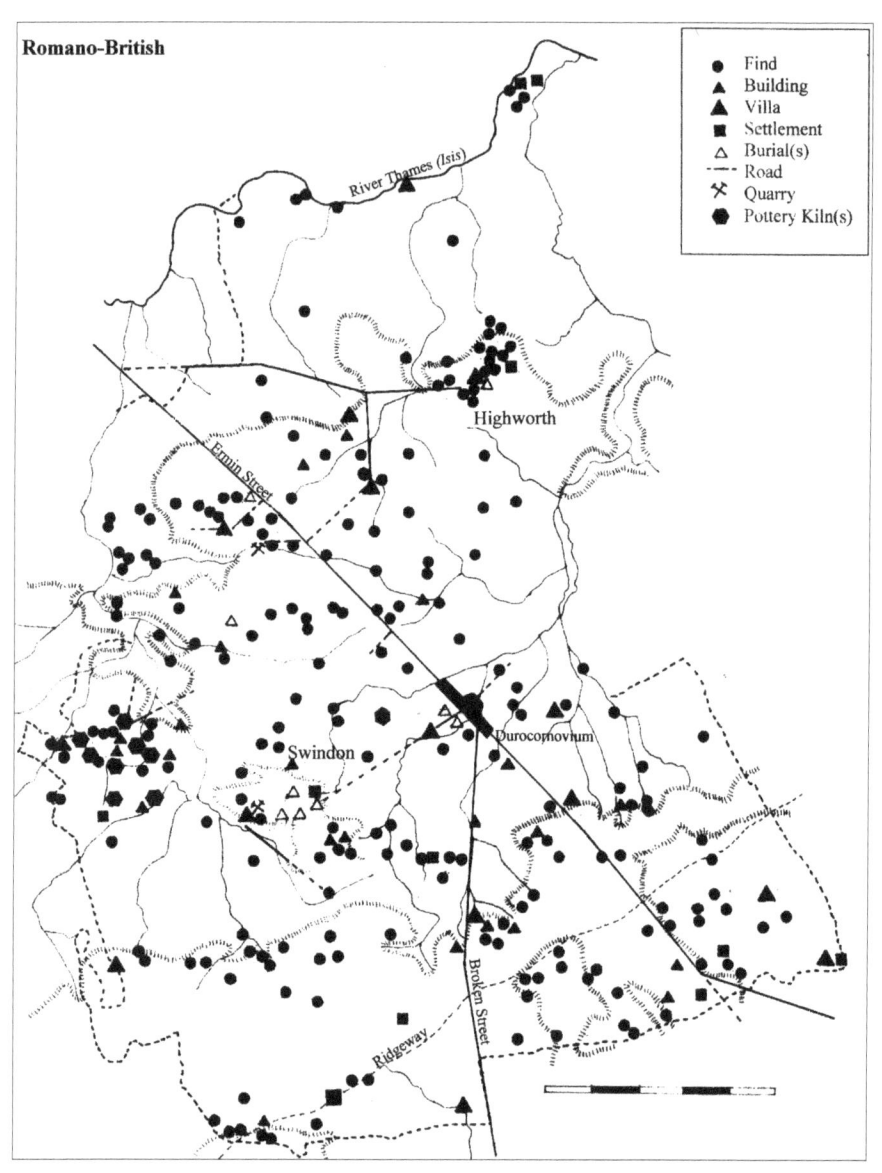

Fig. 41. Distribution map of Romano-British sites and artefacts (scale 5km)

carried out an investigation of the site and established the extent of the settlement. Archaeological test pitting and excavation were undertaken from 1966 to 1976 in advance of road and flood lagoon construction. These were initially directed by Ernest Greenfield from 1966 to 1968 then John Wacher 1969-70 and in 1976 by Scott Anderson. Rescue work

ROMANO-BRITISH

Fig. 42. Road construction on the Roman town site at Lower Wanborough

during the road and lagoon construction, and during the building of the Lyncroft housing estate, as well as small excavations, were carried out by members of the Swindon Archaeological Society from 1965 to 1977.[49]

Early Occupation

Excavation at Lower Wanborough has shown that the early Ermin Street within the settlement, comprised a paved strip set between two side ditches 23m apart. Coral ragstone used to surface the road was probably quarried at Blunsdon. There, extensive Roman quarrying has recently been found close to Groundwell Farm. A crossroad junction with its construction dated by coinage to the second half of the first century has also been located on Ermin Street 370m north of the Broken Street junction.[50] One road heads towards Swindon Hill and the other to the northeast. A further clue to a fort's existence is a stone-walled building revealed as a cropmark on aerial photographs 125m east of Ermin Street.[51] On an alignment different to other identified structures it measures at least 20m by 25m and is discernible from its layout as a bath-house. Those built by the military for their use are usually set just outside a fort's walls to prevent the risk from fire. Following abandonment of a fort they were often retained for public use. Roman bath houses military, public and private, comprised rooms of varying heat through which a person progressed, usually a cold room (*frigidarium*) with a plunge bath; a warm room (*tepidarium*); a hot room (*caldarium*) with hot bath; as well as a dressing room (*apodyterium*); a latrine; perhaps a dry heat room (*laconicum*) and an exercising area.

The military presence would have quickly encouraged the establishment of a civilian settlement (*vicus*) to cater for the soldiers' needs as well as those of travellers on the roads. These early inhabitants, most of whom would have derived from the native populace, were quick to seize the opportunity to make a good living and these included inn-, lodge- and brothel-keepers; metal, wood, leather, basketry and textile workers; merchants and waggoners; bakers and butchers; as well as agricultural workers who cultivated nearby fields, orchards and allotments. It may also have housed other natives removed from their strongholds and homesteads to where an eye could be kept on them and to provide a labour force for obtaining building material (timber and stone) and to carry out supervised construction work.

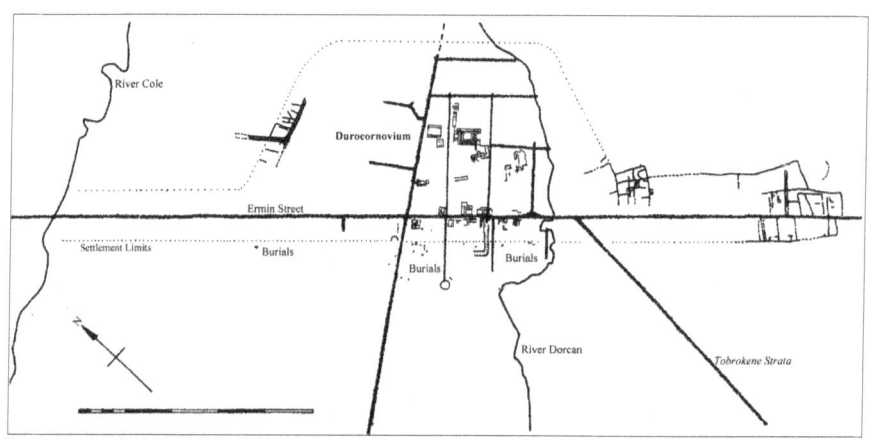

Fig. 43. Extent of the Roman town at Lower Wanborough (scale 500m)

Archaeological excavation and geophysics[52] have shown that by AD 60 timber buildings had been erected on either side of Ermin Street, set within plots bounded by ditches. Such plots and ditched tracks have also been identified by geophysics further east of Ermin Street and beneath Lotmead Fruit Farm[53]. Besides acting as property boundaries the ditches also served for drainage, a necessity due to the surrounding flat clay land which was liable to flooding. As protection from this flooding it is evident that the early buildings, particularly those close to the River Dorcan, were raised above ground on timber stilts. One such building located within a ditched plot was defined by large pits, on the base of which surviving substantial wood boards had clearly supported the stilts on which the structure once stood.

The Town's Name
Dorcan the river's name, recorded as such in a late Saxon charter is possibly a partial survival of the settlement's name – *Durocornovium* – as identified by Passmore[54] from the *Itinerarium Antonini Augusti*.[55] This late second or early third century AD road map gave routes with mileage throughout the Roman empire to enable imperial messengers on horseback and vehicles (*calbulae*) for magistrates or officers of the court to travel quickly to their destinations. At the places named were official buildings, either *mutationes* or *mansiones*, where the traveller under official licences (*diplomata*) issued by the Emperor, could change horses or stay overnight.

It is unclear how *Durocornovium* came by its name *Duro* is a Celtic word meaning fortified place or gateway. *Cornovii* is the name of a tribe whose territory lies to the north of the *Dobunni* and whose tribal capital is *Viroconium Cornoviorum* (Wroxeter).[56] An enclave with the same tribal name was also based in Cornwall from which the modern county obtained its name. That tribal area was recorded in the '*Ravenna Cosmography*' as *Durocornavis*. It is feasible and quite likely that the 'East Wiltshire' tribe (see the Iron Age period, 'A Tribe with no Name') was also an enclave of the *Cornovii* and so then the name of the settlement at Lower Wanborough could mean the 'Fortified place of the *Cornovii*' as first suggested by Rivet and Smith.[57] However apart from a few late Iron Age pottery fragments,[58] there is as yet no evidence for activity let alone fortifications immediately prior to Roman military occupation. It is clear though from 'East Wiltshire' and *Dubunnic* coin distribution, that the settlement had been established on or near the former border between the two tribes.[59] Consequently it is more likely the name meant 'Gateway to the *Cornovii*' and that the settlement was established on a virgin site.

Town Growth

Following pacification of the region and as the Roman military machine pushed on from the Fosse Way into Wales and the north, the likely military establishment at Lower Wanborough would have been dismantled and the troops deployed elsewhere. Such a loss of custom would have had a dire effect on the inhabitants. Some would have followed the troops, confirmed perhaps by the deliberate filling in part of the Ermin Street side ditches with large quantities of pottery, including complete vessels at a date in the mid-70s AD.[60] Some people however undoubtedly stayed to continue serving travellers on the roads and the surrounding agricultural community.

Fig. 44. Parch marks of the mansio and bath house, Lower Wanborough

By the early second century AD a substantial stone walled building revealed as a cropmark in the summer drought of 1976, clearly from its layout a *mansio* (official inn), had been erected immediately east of the bath house and aligned to Ermin Street.[61] Measuring 34m by 48.2m it comprised ranges of rooms, corridors and probable stairwells set around two courtyards with the southern courtyard being open on its south

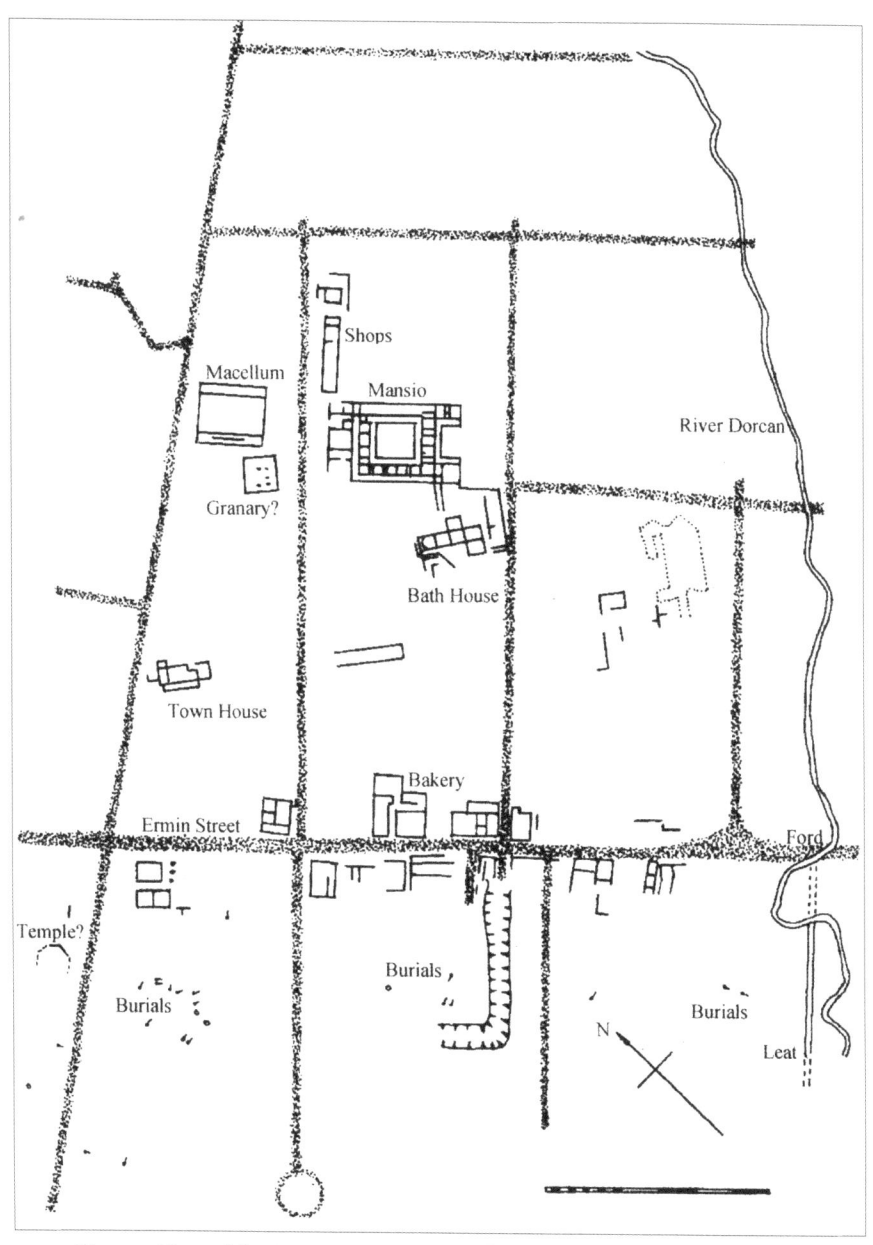

Fig. 45. Plan of the Roman town centre, fourth century AD (scale 100m)

side. At some stage the building appears to have had rooms added at the northern end and was linked to the bath house by a corridor. Another sizeable stone-walled structure measuring 25m by 27m and evidenced as a cropmark to the north of the *mansio*, from its plan was probably a *macellum* (market-hall). It comprised a very large central room flanked on two sides by long narrow single rooms. The central area would have functioned for trading purposes including the setting up of temporary stalls, whilst the flanking rooms would have been divided up by timber screens into shops. To the south an apparent open area between the building and a projected road line could have accommodated overspill stalls or standing for wagons. Three other buildings revealed nearby also as cropmarks in 1976, appear to be a town house, shops and a fairly large square building perhaps a granary with either aisles or having a floor raised on stone piers.

Archaeological excavation has shown that timber- and daub-walled buildings, some with stone foundations, were built on either side of a subsequently narrowed Ermin Street overlying its former ditches. Hearths, ovens and iron slag suggest that some of these buildings were associated with small-scale industrial activities.

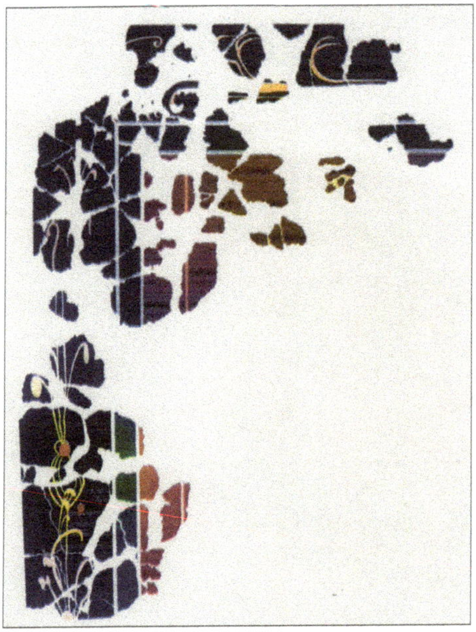

That some earlier buildings had been richly decorated is evidenced by a dump of painted wall plaster found in a side ditch of Ermin Street.[62] Timber impressions and a rolled chevron pattern on its rear show that it derived from a wood-framed and clay-daubed building. A curve to the plaster's upper part indicates that the room from which it came had at least in part a yellow painted vaulted ceiling and below this there are red panels which were framed in green bands and fine white lines. Between these

Fig. 46. Reconstruction painting of wall plaster from Lower Wanborough (Bryn Walters)

black divisions bear an ornate free-flowing pattern of yellow foliage and tendrils interspersed with green, yellow and red buds and leaves. Above the panels a black frieze bears bold yellow tendrils whilst the division below is plain black above a continuous horizontal yellow ochre band edged with vermilion lines. Underneath the band there is a dado which as far as the plaster survival shows, is plain white.

Dating to the late second or early third century AD the cutting of a 9m wide and 1.5m deep flat-bottomed ditch took place on the southwest side of and at right angles to Ermin Street. It had sharpened stakes on its bottom and a clay rampart on its northwest side. Some 70m from Ermin Street the ditch turned northwest to run parallel to the street. It is possible that this was an uncompleted attempt to fortify the central part of the town prompted by barbarians overrunning Hadrian's Wall (Britain's northern frontier) and their ransacking of the northern parts of Britain in AD 180-4. Many other towns have evidenced similar preparations at this time.

Archaeological excavation, construction work and re-cutting of the Dorcan stream have evidenced that a grid system of streets had prior to the third century AD developed on both sides of Ermin Street. Rebuilding alongside the main street continued right through the third and fourth centuries AD. It included several substantial limestone rubble-walled structures, one of which had painted plastered walls in one room and two ovens in another, whilst a further building had a plain stone tessellated pavement. A further building contained a large millstone suggesting that the structure had been a bakery. Limestone used in many of the buildings came from quarries that have been evidenced on Swindon Hill.[63] Closer to the River Dorcan new buildings continued to be timber built but now they were set on sizeable sarsen stone pads to combat the continued threat of flooding.

Geophysics, field-walking and archaeological excavation demonstrate that buildings had ultimately extended along either side of Ermin Street for 1.64 kilometres (1.02 miles). Such an extent clearly indicates the importance of having premises fronting onto the major road, all aimed at accommodating the undoubtedly large numbers of travellers using it. Overall the town eventually covered around 38 hectares (94 acres).

Fig. 47. Artefacts from the Dorcan ford at Lower Wanborough

Artefacts

Finds demonstrate the inhabitants' desire for and ability to acquire the varied produce the Roman Empire could provide and the extent of trade during the period. They included glass vessels from northern France, high quality pottery from France and Germany, a lamp from northern Italy, wine, olive oil or fish sauce shipped in amphorae from Spain and southern France, a bowl from North Africa and millstones from Germany.[64] Pottery vessels manufactured in Britain used in food preparation, eating, drinking and storage comprised products from kiln sites in south Dorset, the Nene Valley, Oxfordshire, Northamptonshire, Colchester, Caerleon, the New Forest, Farnham, and closer to home Savernake Forest and West Swindon. Early *mortaria* (mixing bowls) include some bearing their makers name – *Darrivs, Doinvs, Albinvs* and *Melvs*, potters who worked on kiln sites to the south of *Verulamium* (St. Albans, Hertfordshire).

Other finds point to the trades carried out and services provided by the inhabitants who lived and worked alongside Ermin Street. Shopkeepers are identified by steelyards for weighing produce and writing implements (*styli*) for keeping records, whilst shears, spindle whorls, a bronze thimble, needles and a flax heckle provide evidence of textile workers. Carpenters clearly worked there as saws, an axe, a hammer, chisels, a gouge and drill bits were found and agricultural workers are known to have been there as ploughshares, a sickle, a pruning hook and a spade were unearthed. Butchers worked there as a cleaver and knives were found; and a punch, a hot chisel, a file and a hammer indicate metal workers plied their trade. Further evidence for metal working is provided by large quantities of iron slag. A little slag from glass working demonstrates the manufacture of vessels and perhaps the casting of windowpanes. Off-cuts and shoe fragments from waterlogged deposits, including those from the Dorcan stream bed, point to the presence of leather workers. Linch pins, bridle bits, horse shoes, *hipposandals* (temporary iron shoes for animals) and ox goads provide evidence for the transportation of people and goods and the movement of livestock.

A need for security was demonstrated by the finding of: many keys, locks and latch lifters for doors, cupboards, chests and caskets.

Many items relating to personal adornment, dress and toiletry were found including a wide variety of brooches, rings, bracelets, hair pins, buckles, belt fittings, leather shoes, nail cleaners, tweezers, cosmetic spoons and mirrors

Fig. 48. Fourth century coins from Lower Wanborough

of silvered bronze. Depicting an eagle, shield, standard and helmet, a cornelian *intaglio* (engraved ring setting) found must have belonged to someone with military connections. Another *intaglio* unearthed depicts a deer below a hunting stick. Two more *intaglios* discovered show *cornucopias* (horns of plenty), symbols of prosperity. One has an ear of corn set between crossed *cornucopias* and the other a *Capricorn* (a seagoat) with a *cornucopia* on its back and a steering oar below. Both had presumably come from rings that had belonged to wealthy merchants.

Household items include bronze and bone spoons, an iron candlestick, pottery lamps, pewter bowls, also furniture and door fittings. A find of particular note, found just outside the scheduled area, is a late first-century AD bronze wine strainer with a long handle. It was discovered by Joe Rossi, a metal detectorist, in 2004.[65] Leisure activities are indicated by the discovery of gaming counters of bone and pottery, and bone dice.

Numerous coins recovered during the archaeological excavations, construction work and by metal detecting outside the scheduled area span the whole period, most being made of bronze with a relatively few in silver and a single of gold. Compared to other Roman settlements within the country the trend in coin loss over the whole period is fairly typical, apart from a big drop in the late second and early third centuries AD and a much higher increase in the latter half of the fourth century AD.[66] John Aubrey records a hoard found in 1688 by two workmen digging a ditch at Lower Wanborough. It comprised 1,600-2,000 silver coins (*denarii*), concealed during the reign of Commodus (AD 180-193) in an earthen pot.[67] Recently a hoard of 161 *denarii* was discovered by Peter Hyams at Mount Pleasant Farm not far from the town.[68] These coins ranged in date from AD 68 to AD 158 and so must have been deposited a little earlier than the other hoard. Coin burials like these would have been triggered by some period of uncertainty or threat rather than a religious offering.

People, Health and Burial
The extent of the town and density of buildings suggest that at its height the population could have been of around 1,000 to 1,500 people. Names scratched onto pottery vessels which are

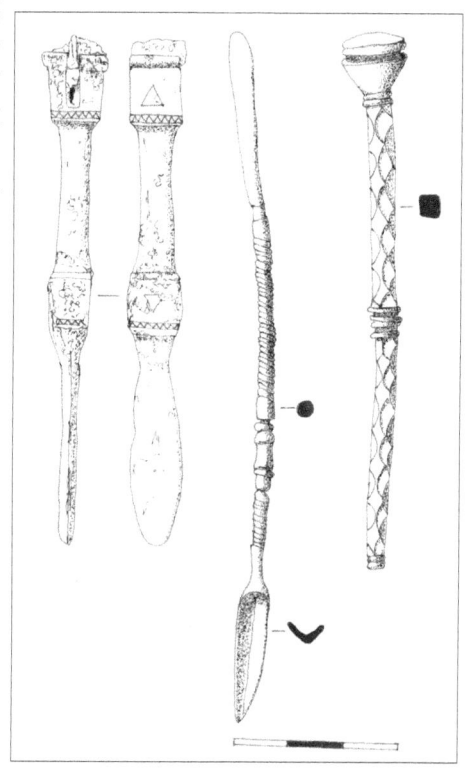

Fig. 49. Medical implements from Lower Wanborough (scale 3cm)

ownership marks show that one of the inhabitants was called *Beliatus*, a Latinised Celtic name, and another seemingly *Sec[undus]*. Two other vessels similarly incised have partial names ...]TIA and TAMM[... .

For most ills people would have relied on herbal medicines. Doctors or surgeons for military personnel and those who could afford their services are indicated by the finding of surgical implements: a spatula, probes, a scalpel and a traction hook.

The area immediately behind the buildings lining Ermin Street's west side had been set aside for burials. These burials revealed during house, flood lagoon and road construction, comprised a scattering of first- and second-century cremations placed within pottery jars and at a later period of inhumations interred within shallow graves.[69] The latter comprised two distinct groups. The earliest group which is orientated from north to south included one grave that contained a denarius of Salonia, wife of Emperor Gallienus (AD 253-68) and aligned from east to west; the later included one burial buried with a worn siliqua of the Emperor Magnus Maximus (AD 380-388). Why and exactly when the change in alignment occurred is unknown. It has been suggested that it was influenced by Christian belief at a time when the religion became dominant in the empire following Constantine I's victory over Maxentius at the Battle of the Milvian Bridge in Italy on 28 October AD 312. Three females had been buried wearing bronze bracelets, otherwise the burials appear to have been unaccompanied by grave goods.

Fig. 50. Coin of Magnus Maximus found with a burial at Lower Wanborough

Examination of the skeletal remains of nineteen individuals has provided an insight into the health of the settlement's inhabitants.[70] Ages at death varied from neo-natal to 45+ with infants forming a high proportion of the total. Arthritis chiefly affecting the spine and shoulders was common even amongst young adults, implying that most had led active and strenuous lives involving carrying heavy loads and with the constant repetitive use of body and upper limbs. Frequent slight trauma had resulted in the bone of the right feet of a male and a female, both young adults, to degenerate, pointing to continuous action such as the working of a treadle. Two people evidenced *cribia orbitalia* (see chapter 6 Neolithic burials) which is thought to have been acquired through either/or a combination of iron deficiency; insanitary living conditions; diets deficient in nutrients; or infectious disease. Illness demonstrated by *periostitis* (new bone growth), existed in four people, including a young girl who had a similarly affected infant cradled in her left arm. She had also suffered a short term illness such as scarlet fever or a deficiency in vitamin D revealed by hypoplasia (pitting or denting in tooth enamel). Poor oral hygiene is evident for most shown through tooth loss, extractions, calculus, abscesses, caries and *periodontal disease* (gum infection). Attrition, the wearing away of tooth material due to abrasion through chewing food containing hard material, notably grit from stone-milled grain, was present in all adults. Skull fragments from one adult cremation showed evidence of anaemia through slight traces of *porotic hyperostosis* (an overgrowth of the skull's spongy marrow space). A concentration of burials lay adjacent to the road leading to Swindon Hill, close to an apparently hexagonal building exposed during the construction of a road bridge which is tentatively identified as a temple. Of this structure only one corner was revealed, it had deep foundations, a flagged floor and white painted plaster on its stone walls. Its remains now lie beneath the bridge's western embankment.

Religion

A 34cm tall carved stone statuette of *Mercury*, unfortunately with its head missing, is fitting for the town's inhabitants, being the god of merchandise and merchants. The figure holds two money bags and a *caduceus* (rod of commerce). Found close to Ermin Street in 1968 it probably came from a roadside shrine or temple. *Mercury* is also engraved on

Fig. 51. Stone statue of Mercury found at Lower Wanborough

Fig. 52. Lead sheet incised with cursive script found at Lower Wanborough

a cornelian *intaglio* from a ring, as is *Ceres* (goddess of agriculture) and *Apollo* (the sun god) on other *intagli*. Seated on a stool a *Muse* (a goddess of literature and the arts), gazes at a theatrical mask held in her right hand. It is cut into a nicolo paste setting of an iron ring. A bronze ring is inscribed 'MANE TERMO VENI' (*Thermodon* come and stay with me). *Thermodon* was a river god of *Pontos*, a coastal region in Anatolia (Turkey).

Dating to the early second century AD and recovered from the River Dorcan a small lead sheet is inscribed with Latin cursive script.[71] Only partially complete, the text – a curse – appears to run on the lines of 'I beg that you do not permit him to drink nor eat nor sleep nor walk and that you do not allow any part to remain of him or the family from which he springs'. The missing part would have borne the name of the deity invoked and the crime involved. Usually this was the theft of an article such as a cloak. Such curses were inscribed by priests and nailed blank side out to a temple wall, rolled up and buried, or broken and thrown into water. This was so that they could be only seen and read by the deities to whom they were addressed.

Fig. 53. Roundel cut from a samian ware vessel depicting the god Apollo as an archer (diameter 4cm)

Found amongst rubbish thrown into the Ermin Street ditch early in the second century AD (based on hairstyle) part of a moulded pottery head of a female appears to be from a seated nursing goddess (*Dea Nutrix*) figurine. Of similar date, part of a naked female pipe-clay statuette made in Central Gaul and representing *Venus* the goddess of love was found. Fired clay figurines like these would have been kept in household shrines. From the River Dorcan ford came a fairly crude pottery figurine of a bird. Such models are rare in Roman Britain and are considered to be votive items. Also unearthed two small hands cut from thin metal sheets are undoubtedly votive. Offerings representing body parts, which the supplicant desired to be cured, are not uncommon and are chiefly found in religious contexts.

Local Government

In AD 197 Britain had been divided into two provinces – *Britannia Prima* and *Britannia Maxima*. Under the Emperor Diocletian (AD 286-305) the country was further subdivided so creating four provinces – *Britannia Secunda, Flavia Caesariensis, Maxima Caesariensis* and *Britannia Prima*. Although the boundaries of the provinces are not recorded, artefactual and documentary evidence points to borders based on former Iron Age tribal territories, the Celtic people still having retained much of their tribal identities despite Roman rule. Apparently included in *Britannia Prima*, in the south western part of Britain were the tribal territories of the: *Dobunni, Cornovii, Durotriges, Dumnonii, Silures, Demetae, Ordovices* and *Deceangii*.[72] *Corinium Dubonnorum* (Cirencester) in the *Dobunni* territory became the province's governmental administrative centre. *Durocornovium* lay on or close to the provinces eastern boundary where it adjoined *Maxima Caesariensis* whose capital was *Londinium* (London). Although the majority of the province's civil administrative work took place at *Corinium,* a town council at *Durocornovium* would have seen to local issues such as policing, refuse collection, and the maintenance of roads and public buildings. This council would have been made up of the more influential, wealthier town inhabitants, and affluent owners of the surrounding villas who had connections to the town.

Road traffic was very important for the town's existence, but it was not the only reason as the settlement undoubtedly served as a market for the surrounding villas, farmsteads, rural industries and minor settlements. Fieldwork, construction work and geophysics have revealed a dense spread of such sites around the town. On market days these rural folk brought their produce for sale in the town and received in exchange the coinage needed to purchase services and goods, including the luxuries that the Roman world enjoyed, and so that they could pay taxes. Taxation in the Roman world took the forms of *tributum capitas*, a poll tax that included property, and *tributum soli* which was a land tax based on productivity.

Villas

Inside the Borough, through archaeological excavation, fieldwalking and construction work, fifteen villa sites and another twenty substantial rural buildings are known to have existed. Some of the latter will, with further investigation, also prove to be villas, whilst others undoubtedly await discovery. Comparable to a modern farmhouse and its associated outbuildings (barns, stables, stores, workshop etc.), a villa was the centre of an agricultural estate. The villa house varied in extent from small buildings having a few rooms, to two-storied palatial establishments, their wealth displayed by mosaic floors, under-floor heating, painted wall plaster, glass windows, bath suites and landscaped gardens. Most developed over time, as their owner's prosperity grew, perhaps evolving from an Iron Age predecessor or from small timber farmsteads of later first or second century AD conception.

A little south of *Durocornovium*, a short distance east of Ermin Street and lying at the base of the chalk escarpment is a substantial villa site. Here, at Upper Wanborough, surface evidence and aerial photographs show this scheduled monument to comprise substantial buildings or wings set around a courtyard. A spring arising just above the site and flowing through it, supplied drinking water, bathing facilities and, perhaps sanitation and garden pools. Finds of mosaic cubes, traces of

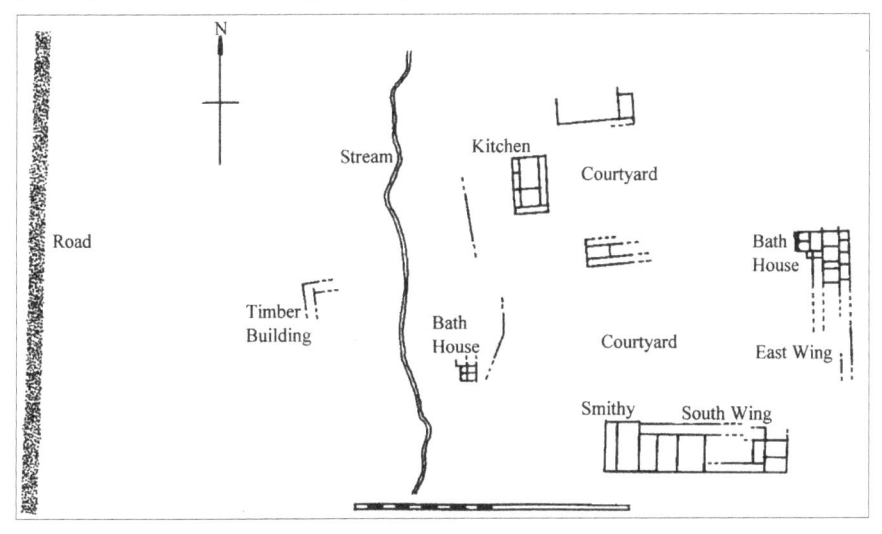

Fig. 54. Plan of the villa at Badbury (scale 100m)

tessellated flooring and *opus signinum* (waterproof plaster), demonstrate the wealth of the structures which lie hidden beneath the ground.

In an identical location, also with a stream flowing through it, a palatial villa was discovered at Badbury adjacent to the Roman road Broken Street.[73] Although first identified in 1956 during construction of houses adjacent to 'Berricot Lane', its full extent was not realised and much of it, including mosaic and tessellated flooring, was destroyed during the building of the M4 motorway between 1969 and 1971. Chiefly due to rescue work by members of the Swindon Archaeological Society, a large part of its ground plan and some dating evidence was obtained. Occupation began shortly after the Roman invasion, as indicated by the extensive wall trenches of a large timber building close to the Roman road. Little of its remains could be recorded prior to obliteration by site machinery. The sequences of stone-built structures including a bathhouse, were erected around several courtyards after the mid-second century AD. Most buildings were clearly residential but the southernmost containing iron slag and an internal drain had served as stabling and a smithy, whilst in its earliest phase the easternmost may have been an extensive barn. This was subsequently turned into residential use with the insertion of internal cross walls to create a range of rooms, corridors and a bath suite. Some rooms were floored with tessellated pavements, and walls had been plastered and then painted. Two or possibly three rooms were also added to the southern building's eastern end and floored with tessellated pavements. Clearly the property was the centre of a very prosperous estate. Part of that wealth may have been gained through the hiring out of oxen teams to assist heavy laden wagons to ascend the road as they climbed the steep chalk escarpment. Due to the nature of its uncovering few artefacts, apart from pottery, painted wall plaster and terracotta tiles (some stamped IVC. DIGNI), were found. Occupation on

Fig. 55. Bronze figurine of a genius from Badbury

the villa complex continued into the fifth century AD. Following the building's abandonment the interment of an adult took place. Concealed beneath a layer of terracotta tiles it lay within the ruins of the easternmost wing at its northern end.

Not far from the villa site a small bronze figurine of a *genius*, a protective spirit of a place, was found in a ploughed field by Joe Rossi in 2002.[74] This was probably from a household shrine in the villa and it portrays a jovial, clean-shaven, cloaked youth who had originally held accoutrements in his hands, perhaps scrolls or a *cornucopia* (horn of plenty).

Fig. 56. Drawing the drier at South Farm villa Chiseldon

Further south and a little to the west of 'Broken Street' a recent excavation directed by Bryn Walters has revealed a fairly substantial villa house incorporating a bath suite at its southern end.[75] Here at South Farm, a small mosaic floor survived largely intact, in a rear room. Coins and pottery show that the stone-walled building was occupied from the early third century AD until the end of the fourth century AD. Residual late first- and second-century AD pottery points to an earlier timber phase. A partially excavated building adjacent, almost certainly a barn, contained a drier. These stone structures had a channelled hypocaust which, when fired, heated an overlying floor on which produce such as grain, flax, beans, and peas could be dried prior to storing, and also for use in the process of making malt. Adapted and enclosed they could have been used for smoking food such as meat, fish and cheese. Following demolition of the house a midden was formed over its remains. Then in the early fifth century AD the construction of a possible small timber shrine took place. In an adjacent field aerial photography has revealed the cropmarks of two aisled buildings and to the west of the excavated house surface debris indicates a further structure.

Fig. 57. Heating chamber of the caldarium at Stanton Fitzwarren villa

Known to local inhabitants, the site of an old building lay at the centre of the shallow valley where Stanton Fitzwarren occupies the upper eastern slope.[76] They had used the site as a stone quarry for many years prior to major discoveries during the construction of the Swindon to Highworth railway in 1879. Then extending over a distance of two hundred yards (183m), coral ragstone walling and several plain stone tessellated floors were revealed. In 1969 excavation by Swindon Archaeological Society adjacent to the disused railway embankment exposed part of a bath-suite constructed in coral ragstone blocks and tiles. The ruins comprised the hypocausts of a hot room (*caldarium*) and warm room (*tepidarium*), a tile-floored cold plunge bath and a furnace room. Debris shows that the rooms had tessellated floors, glass windows and painted, plastered walls. A curved terracotta roofing tile (*imbrex*) found, bears an impressed maker's mark – TPFC (see tileries). Clearly the remains uncovered were part of a much larger structure which is implied by walls extending outside the excavated area and the earlier discoveries around 20m to the north. Such a building may have been the main house of the complex incorporating the bath-suite at its southern end. East facing, its alignment is typical of such a building. A spring arises very close to these remains and probably served the structure before flowing into the Bydemill Brook that passes through the site. Pottery and coins demonstrate that its demolition took place in the early to mid-fourth century AD. Occupation continued, with a timber structure being built over the debris followed by a build-up of very dark grey loam that contained late fourth-century AD pottery and coins. Pointing to the site's abandonment, the Roman drainage systems ceased to function and a thick accumulation of silt occurred which contained no artefacts other than an iron horseshoe. In 1997 a geophysical survey showed ditches and structural remains across much of the field where the 1969 excavation had taken place. It was in this area that Passmore recorded another tessellated pavement close to the brook. Ploughing in 1981 on the opposite side of the watercourse revealed building stones, stone roofing tiles and third- to fourth-century AD pottery fragments spread over a large area. This clearly demonstrated both the presence of a further building and that the complex comprised buildings grouped around an extensive courtyard. The country estate in which the now scheduled site lies was purchased in 1990 by Swindon Borough Council and has been developed as a public amenity with countryside and woodland walks.

Another villa site, scheduled following an investigative excavation by Swindon Archaeological Society in 1972, lies on the chalk downs to the south of Bishopstone.[77] Its unearthing close to Starveall Farm initially occurred with the exposure of a mosaic pavement during ploughing in

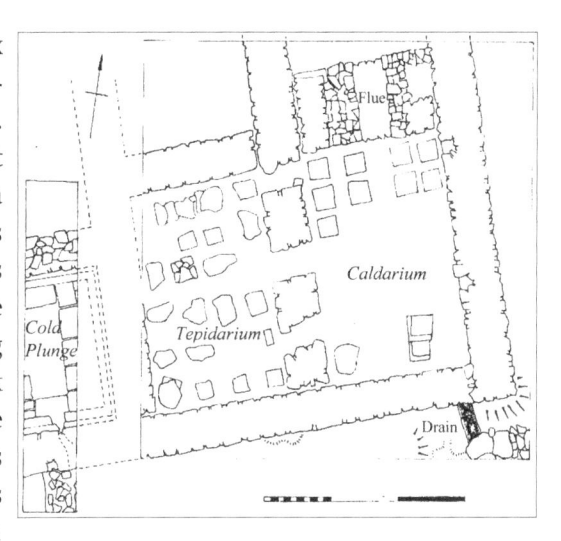

Fig. 58. Stanton Fitzwarren, villa bath house (scale 3m)

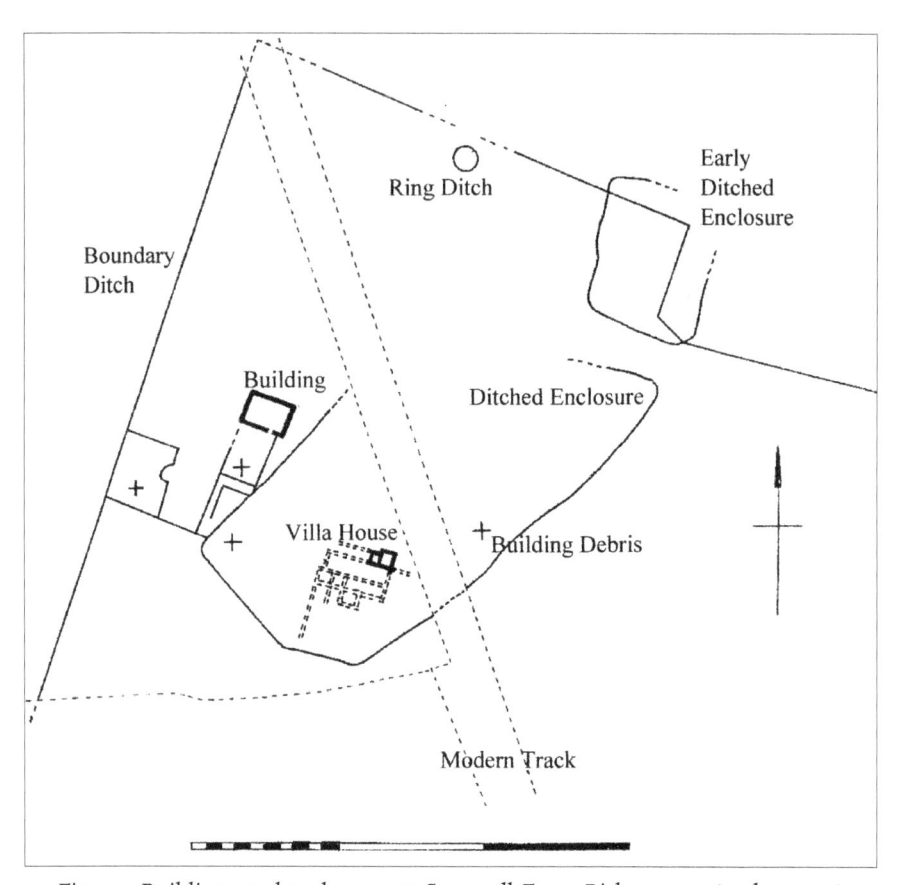

Fig. 59. Buildings and enclosures at Starveall Farm Bishopstone (scale 300m)

1880. The floor was then re-discovered in 1938 by A. D. Passmore. A subsequent geophysical survey undertaken in 1969 located a rectangular building measuring 12m by 17m and aerial photography revealed cropmarks of ditched enclosures that covered an area of 2.25 hectares (5.6 acres). Following ploughing Swindon Archaeological Society members walked the site and identified building debris in six areas, one of which included tesserae and terracotta heating system tiles. In this area, in order to determine the extent of plough damage and to lift any possible surviving pavement remains, an area 9.5m by 11.5m was opened in 1972. Four rooms clearly being part of a domestic building were revealed. One of these was clearly the main reception or dining room as it had a channelled hypocaust, *opus signinum* (concrete) flooring and faced chalk block walls that had been plastered over internally and painted.

Fig. 60. Surviving mosaic border, Starveall Farm villa

Early fourth-century AD refurbishment saw the laying on the earlier floor of a mosaic, re-plastering of the walls and painting them in imitation of marble cladding and a panelled design in purple, red, yellow, white, grey and blue. Due to stone robbing during the late-Roman or post-Roman period and recent ploughing, only part of the floor's tessellated border remained, but enough to show that this was the floor found and photographed by Passmore. Small fragments of its central panel, broken up in antiquity, did survive amongst the destruction debris infill of the

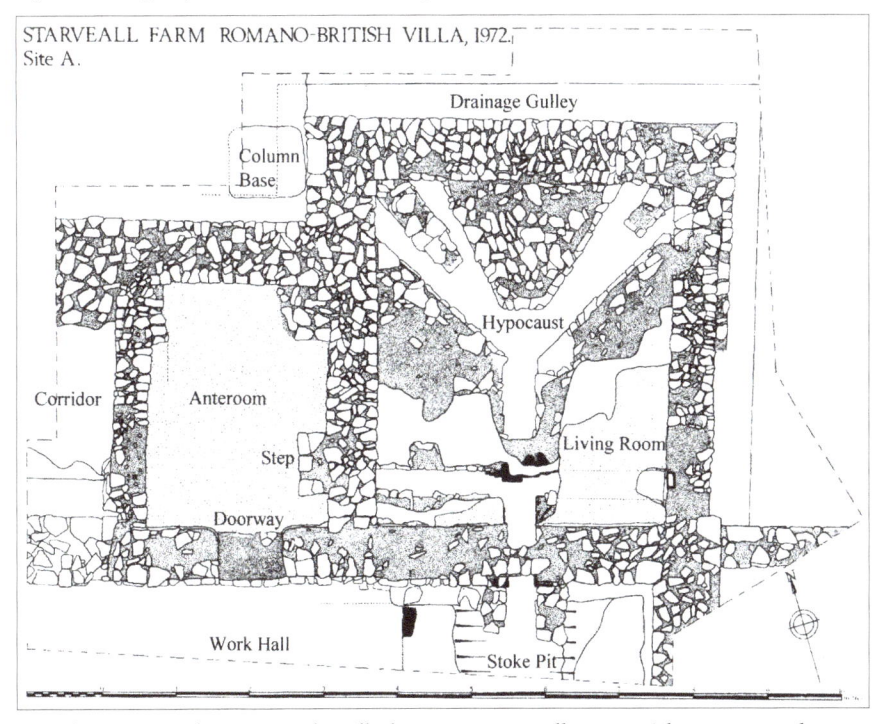

Fig. 61. Excavated rooms on the villa house at Starveall Farm Bishopstone (scale 11m)

Fig. 62. Mosaic fragment from the anteroom at Starveall Farm villa

hypocaust channels. Clearly depicted in small mosaic cubes are: parts of a red cloaked figure, a hound with open jaws and a protruding tongue, and the foliage of a stylised tree. Research points to these pieces being part of a scene depicting *Actaeon* who was trained in the art of hunting. He saw the goddess *Artemis* naked so she turned him into a stag and so he was killed by his hounds. Adjoining the room's west side a small anteroom had a suspended timber floor. Following infilling of the floor hollow with loam, the timber floor was replaced by a mosaic set on a mortar base. Of this two small areas of guilloche and part of a plain border survived. Internally the room's walls had been plastered and painted red that remained to a height of 10cm on the southern wall. At the centre of this wall a wide doorway accessed a very large chalk-floored work-hall, whilst a similarly floored corridor fronted the hall and extended westward from the anteroom. A furnace pit within the hall provided heating of the hypocaust of the main room. During the refurbishments, a columned facade which was indicated by a square foundation pad was added in front of the corridor and antechamber.

Fig. 63. Mosaic fragment depicting a hound from the Starveall Farm villa (scale 4cm)

The layout of the excavated rooms shows that the building conforms to a type known as a 'halled house'.[78] Other rooms around the central work-hall would include a bath suite, a kitchen and bedrooms.

Pottery fragments from the furnace and hypocaust channelling's ash fill that underlay the destruction debris, suggest that demolition of the house occurred in the latter part of the fourth century AD.

A small trench located northeast of the main house opened on the site of the building identified by the 1969 geophysical survey, revealed its southern exterior wall was built with mortared flints and chalk blocks. Within it, a doorway having a carved limestone step gave access onto an internal chalk rubble and mortar floor. At some stage the doorway had been deliberately blocked with mortared chalk and flint blocks. Debris overlying the floor comprised walling material e.g. oolitic limestone roofing tiles, iron nails and several fragments of painted plaster, the latter pointing to a domestic rather than agricultural or industrial function for the building. Following lifting and consolidation the mosaic fragments from the house were, along with the other finds, deposited in Swindon Museum.

During stone quarrying operations in 1897 on the south side of Swindon Hill, part of a villa house, probably of the same type as that at Starveall Farm, was uncovered adjacent to Mill Lane. Passmore investigated the remains[79] and recorded a large room 37ft (11.2m) by 64ft (20.3m) which was probably an internal hall, in part of which a channelled hypocaust had been constructed, being either under floor heating or a drier. An 11ft (3.3m) wide corridor fronted the hall and two small rooms were attached at the eastern end, both approximately 10ft (3.0m) by 15ft (4.5m) internally. Walls in part survived to a height of 4ft (1.2m) with dark red painted wall plaster adhering in one area. Fallen plaster fragments depicted a black, red and yellow panelled design, marbling and foliage. Other finds included: two inhumations, one inside the hall and the other exterior to the building; many pottery fragments; stone roof tiles; terracotta tiles; a quern stone; a coin of Constans (AD 337 to AD 350); a bronze brooch and a bone pin. Unfortunately the remains were levelled and the stone was used to pave roads.

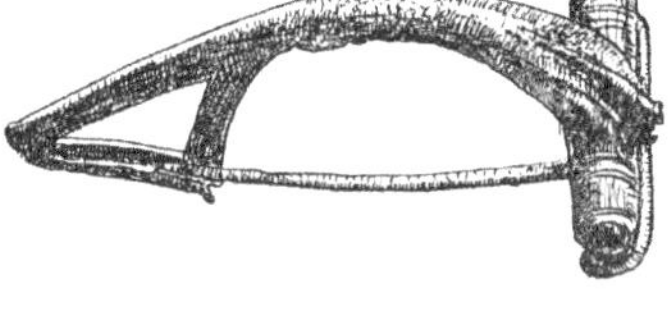

A similar fate may have occurred to another stone-walled building discovered in 1906 on the opposite side of Swindon Hill during quarrying clay for a brick works. Now this is the site of Queen's Park.[80] In addition to a few fine pottery

Fig. 64. A brooch found at Mill Lane Swindon

vessel fragments including part of a second-century AD Samian ware bowl, much coarseware pottery was found which led Passmore, who made some records of the remains, to consider the site was a potter's workshop.

Close to the River Thames at Hannington Wick, a substantial villa complex was found through surface finds, archaeological excavation and later aerial photography. During investigations in 1890 E H Goddard discovered within a stone-walled building, part of a red and white tessellated pavement, a second tessellated pavement measuring 9ft x 3ft and a concrete floor.[81] Painted plaster, bricks, flue tiles, oyster shells, Samian ware and a Constantinian coin were also found.

Southwest of Jubilee Copse in the same parish an archaeological excavation in 1934 uncovered the foundations of a coral ragstone walled building whose floor levels had been destroyed. Stone roofing tiles, nails and pottery were recovered. In 1973 fieldwalking by Swindon Archaeological Society members identified the site of a second building through the finding of building debris following ploughing.

At Westrop in Highworth construction work over many years has uncovered an extensive scatter of Romano-British pottery and coins that span the Roman period. At the centre of this scatter, stone wall foundations were seen during construction work in 1958 at Wrde Hill. Finds from here include wall plaster fragments, mosaic cubes, terracotta tiles and stone roofing tiles which clearly suggest a villa house. To the southwest a cemetery is indicated by inhumations and cremations found in the vicinity of Oak Drive and Westhill House.[82] A few years ago traces of a further building, a cremation, a large storage jar and other artefacts were found nearby.

Another villa lies within a chalk downland valley east of Russley Park in Bishopstone parish. Here ploughing exposed chalk walls, first- to fourth-century AD pottery sherds, iron nails, animal bones, also roofing and heating system tiles. This is clearly the remains of a substantial building, probably the main house. It is located a little to the west of a rectangular ditched enclosed complex, finds from which include sandstone roofing tiles, flue tiles, iron slag, a stone rubber and numerous quern stone fragments which indicate that the enclosure contained agricultural related structures. Both, as revealed by crop and plough soil marks, lie within an extensive field system defined by ploughed out banks and ditches.

Possible Villas

A Roman villa has been hinted at by discoveries made in the vicinity of Broome Manor, Swindon over the past sixty years. These include: three finely constructed stone lined wells; linear ditches; stone walling; traces of timber buildings; a sarsen stone lined dew pond and a drier which are associated with pottery and coins that range in date from the late first to early fifth century AD. One of the wells was excavated to a depth of about 2.4m by Swindon Archaeological Society members following its discovery by workmen digging a sewerage trench in 1972. From this came fragments of human skull, fourth-century AD pottery sherds, animal bone, leather sandal fragments, a faience (glazed earthenware) bead and an iron bucket handle. As yet no large villa-like building has been located although beneath the Polo Ground is a likely location.

Fig. 65. Excavating a fourth century AD well at Broome Manor

Revealed as an existing earthwork by an aerial photograph, a 45m square ditched and banked enclosure not far to the west of *Durocornovium* was briefly investigated in 1963 by John Woodward, the curator of Swindon Museum. Within it, trenching revealed a 0.6m high sarsen and sandstone wall 1.22m wide and 24m long with stone roofing tiles, much pottery and coins. Unfortunately this discovery was not followed up and complete destruction of the site occurred during the erection of a pharmaceutical company's building. Finds recovered during the construction work include tiles, pottery, tesserae and coins that point to the presence of a former small villa complex of third- to late fourth-century date.

Around Kite Hill in the village of Wanborough finds of pottery,

Fig. 66. Excavated fourth-century AD well at Broome Manor

coins and tile fragments indicate the site of a building. Close by in 2014, evidence of settlement activity was met during building work at Stanley Close. Finds here include ditches, pottery, evidence of industrial activity and a decapitated burial with its head placed beneath the knees. Such burials are rare and the reason for decapitation is uncertain. It has been suggested this was a punishment for criminals or was to prevent the spirit of the dead from haunting the living.

One site which eventually may prove to be a villa lies adjacent to Broken Street north of Great Moor Leaze in Wanborough parish. Here in 1974 a pipe trench was cut through grey and black silts extending for nearly 200 metres, central to which was an old watercourse. The silts were bounded to the south by a stone layer and on the north by a ditch and contained second to fourth century AD pottery, sandstone roofing tile fragments, terracotta flue tile fragments, part of a quern stone and a large carved sandstone block. In Blunsdon parish west of Stanton Water, the corner of a stone-walled building with pottery sherds, a coin and a tile fragment was discovered during the cutting of a pipe trench, and nearby south of Stubbs Hill, pottery and building traces were found. A substantial building is also indicated beneath the South Marston Industrial site. Here excavation in advance of development has revealed much building debris, ditches, gullies, a walled enclosure, a well and burials – all associated with first- to fourth-century pottery and animal bone.

Villa Cemeteries
A likely villa site is located south of Purton at Reid's Piece. This lies just outside the Borough and it is indicated by surface finds of terracotta tile and pottery. The status and importance of this site was revealed in 1987 when construction work at the nearby former North View Hospital unearthed a 35m square-walled cemetery. An archaeological rescue excavation uncovered some unusually rich burials including two in carved limestone coffins.[83] One contained the remains of an 18-25 year old woman enclosed in a lead coffin and accompanied by a glass perfume flask. Some finely woven cloth remained on and around the body and she had been interred wearing hobnailed sandals. Central to a circular 10m diameter stone-walled structure, a limestone cist contained a large lidded circular lead box decorated with scallop shells and St Andrew's crosses. Inside a large bulbous glass vessel held cremated bones probably the remains of a female. Amongst the ashes were burnt bird bones that included goose, seemingly being offerings cremated with her for her journey into the afterlife. Further evidencing the richness of these two burials, chemical analysis has revealed that expensive scented libations had been poured over their bodies.[84] Demonstrating that, even in death, divisions in status existed is shown by four inhumations, possibly servants, who were interred without coffins, two of whom were males aged 30+ and 50+, and two were females aged 30+ and 40+. The older woman had suffered from a lung disease which had affected her ribs. It would appear that the villa owner did not rely solely on agriculture for his income, as a short distance to the west, at Dogridge, house construction revealed a stone building and six pottery kilns. Further to the west an occupation layer exposed during the cutting of a pipe trench contained sherds, tile, tesserae and animal bones indicative of further significant buildings.

Three burials along with bones from other individuals in one of the graves encountered during the extension to a house in Whitworth Road, Swindon, point to the siting there of a sizeable burial ground.[85] Apart from a few worn Roman pottery sherds found in the grave fills and from overlying cultivated soil, no clear dating evidence was obtained. The graves were carefully cut into the natural clay and stone. Two burials lay on their backs whilst the third lay on its front with its left arm beneath the chest. Such prone burials are comparatively uncommon. Considered reasons for such interments are varied, they could be for religious purposes; to prevent the deceased from rising from the dead; or the hurried burial of an infectious body. The skeletal remains of the two burials laid on their back extended outside of the property boundary and loss due to disturbance by construction trenches meant that their remains were incomplete. Both were elderly males who had clearly suffered painful ailments in their later years, one had arthritis, an abscess in the hip and gout, whilst the other had considerable tooth loss prior to death, also caries, a tooth abscess and arthritis of the neck. Evidencing anaemia (*cribia orbitalia* – see Neolithic burials) the prone burial, a 25-35 female around 5 feet 4 inches tall also had caries in two teeth, a badly decayed molar beneath which an abscess had formed and early signs of arthritis of the lower back. The graves' non-Christian, southwest to northeast alignment and the pottery found in them point to a third- or early fourth-century, or less likely – fifth- or sixth-century Pagan Saxon date for the interments. The nearest known Romano-British occupation site lies at Rodbourne Cheney Church on

Fig. 67. Prone late Roman-British burial from Whitworth Road Rodbourne Cheney

ROMANO-BRITISH

the southern side of a shallow stream valley some 400m distant. The nature of that settlement is unknown but finds include terracotta tile, and pottery signifying a substantial building. That the graves were in a linear alignment suggests they were dug adjacent to a boundary, defined either by a fence, wall, hedge, bank or track. It is feasible that the burials lay within an enclosed burial plot such as that at Purton. Lack of grave goods and the trauma evidence could then suggest these were family retainers buried at the edge of the cemetery.

Villa or Healing Shrine

A substantial building complex was exposed during the preliminary cutting of roads for a housing estate at Groundwell Ridge in 1996. Fortunately, in this case co-operation between the builders Robert Hitchin Associates Ltd, Swindon Borough Council and archaeologists has enabled the site to be scheduled and preserved largely intact. As revealed by archaeological excavation, geophysics[86] and an earthwork survey,[87] the site consists of a group of Roman buildings overlooked by a series of artificially created, south-facing terraces and a sequence of platforms. Several springs issue forth from the upper terrace whilst the middle terrace had on it a large pool represented today by a waterlogged

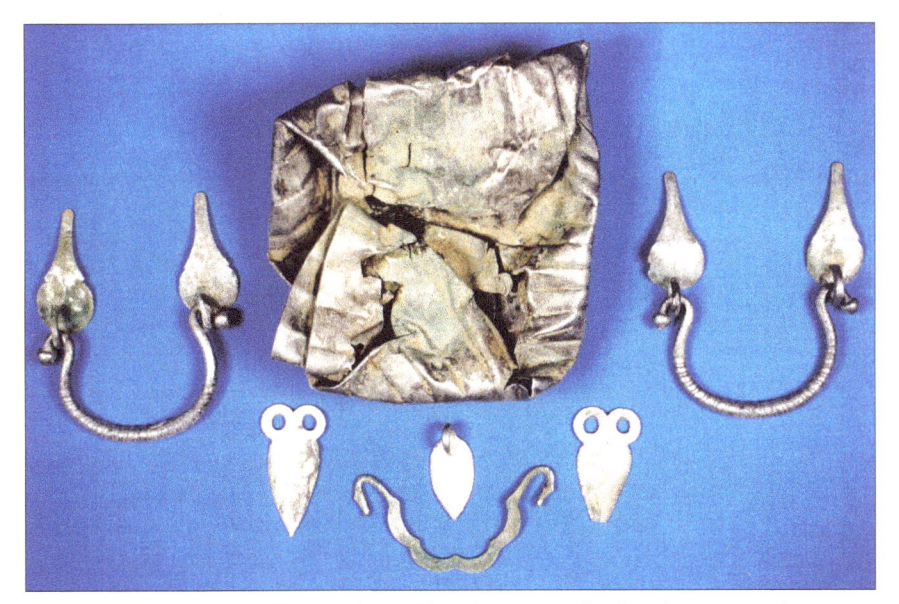

Fig. 68. Fourth century AD silver hoard found at Groundwell Ridge (Luigi Thompson)

area. The initial road cutting exposed remains of a coral-ragstone-built courtyard wall and a building that had within it traces of a heating system, also close by there was a large stone-lined water cistern built into a silted-up pond.[88]

Directed by the author and Bryn Walters, evaluation trenching was undertaken the following year to ascertain the nature of the remains. This revealed corridors and rooms of a coral-ragstone-walled aisled building separated from the 1996 structure by a paved courtyard.[89] Associated with the building remains were decorated wall plaster fragments and mosaic cubes. Some of the plaster fragments painted in grey, green, yellow, black, white, blue and red, depict parts of an architectural landscaped and figured scene. From a cutting dug into the floor of one room came a silver hoard seemingly having been tightly wrapped within a cloth or bag. It comprised a deliberately crushed 40cm diameter fluted bowl dated to the mid fourth century AD and the drop handles from two others. It could be that it represents a votive offering, the vessel being ritually 'killed' by crushing prior to its burial, or more likely hidden for later retrieval. Coins and pottery found range

Fig. 69. Carved stone water shrine at Groundwell Ridge

in date from the early second century AD till the late fourth century AD while animal bones include those of cattle, horse, pig, sheep/goat, deer, fowl and hare. On the topmost terrace the cutting of a second trench revealed a 1.2m x 1.45m carved limestone-block-lined cistern. Cut into the surface of an upper stone, two adjacent parallel overflow channels fed into a drain and inset internally at the bottom a lead pipe provided drainage of the cistern when needed. Its siting, construction and further carved stones amongst demolition debris suggest that it was part of an elaborate spring-fed water shrine (*nymphaeum*). A star-shaped slot cut centrally into the cistern's stone slab floor probably supported a metal column, on which would have stood at or above water level the figure of the shrine's deity.

Conducted by Peter Wilson of English Heritage during 2003-5, further excavations focused mainly on the building that had been damaged by road construction in 1996.[90] These showed a freestanding apsidal-ended structure which had very deep foundations, that had been replaced during the early second century AD by a building incorporating a bath-suite and a 1.7m deep timber floored cellar. White plastered walls with niches for lamps or statues were found in the latter. Water was channelled into the baths from the springs to the north and a channel to the south of the building took waste water away. The bath complex underwent many alterations and additions during its long use before abandonment in the early fifth century AD. Subsequent collapse of the building was followed by levelling and erection of a substantial timber structure which incorporated an oven.

Re-excavation of a trench dug by machine for a large drainage pipe on the middle terrace where it had cut through the waterlogged area confirmed the existence of a pool and its Roman or earlier origin. Much environmental material and fragments of a wooden writing tablet were recovered. On the same terrace the earthwork survey had indicated the presence of a cambered road approaching the site which had drainage ditches on either side. A trench excavated across it exposed a metalled surface which, although much disturbed in the medieval period had a Roman origin.

Finds from the English Heritage excavations include coins, fragments of glass vessels, window glass, glass beads, a stylus, brooches, bracelets, iron horseshoes, a lead water pipe and a life-size plaster eye.

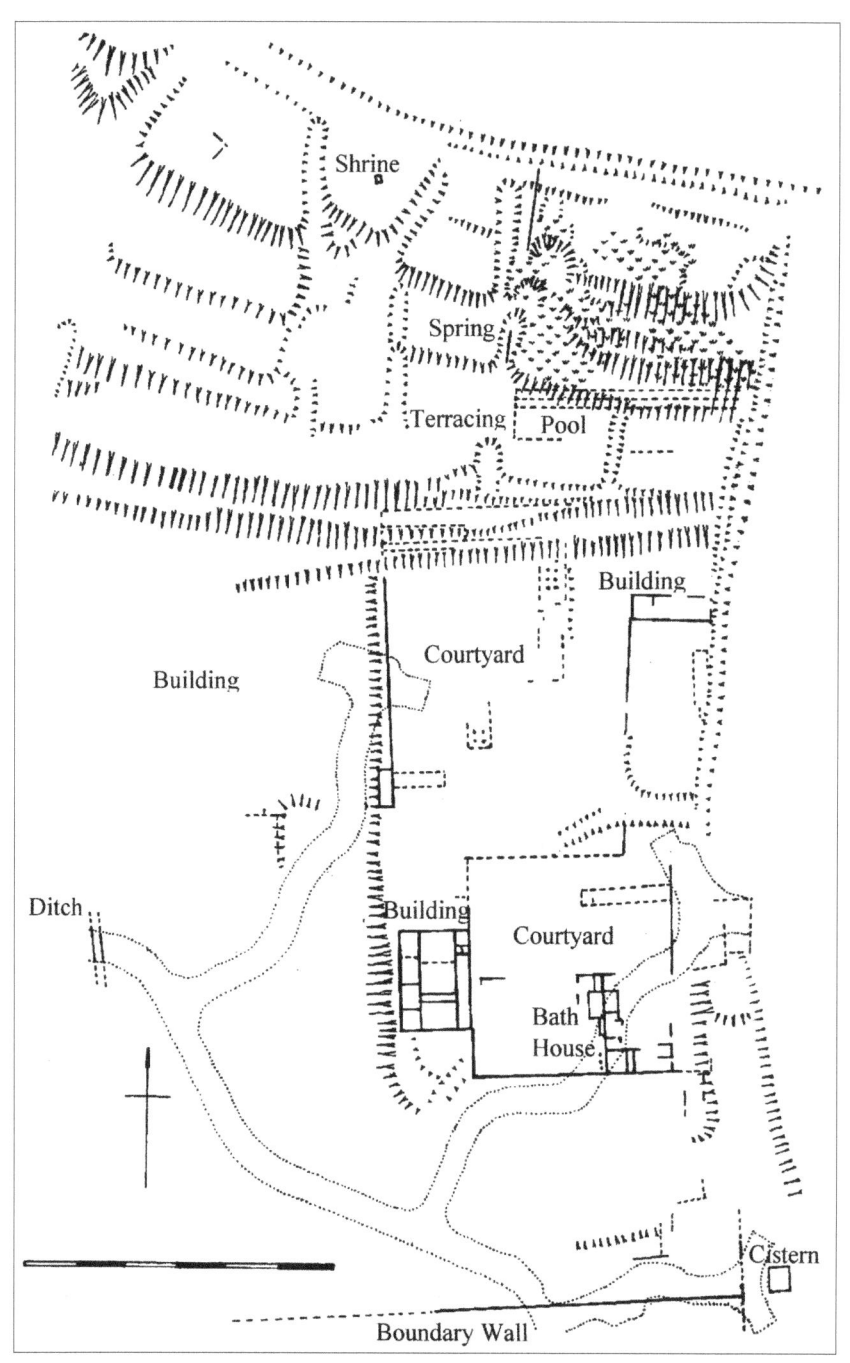

Fig. 70. Plan of the shrine/villa at Groundwell Ridge Swindon (scale 60m)

Items representing body parts were deposited on healing shrines by people who wanted that part cured. Most notable though was a small lead plaque depicting the bust of the goddess *Isis* offering her right breast. It has been suggested that the worn plaque was a model used to make open clay moulds for the casting of bronze appliqués.[91] An enamelled bronze ring also found shows a star and crescent moon design. The star Sirius was a symbol of Isis.

Evidence relating to the cult of Isis outside London is rare in Britain. An altar dating to the 250s AD found re-used in London's riverside wall is inscribed 'IN H D DM MARTIANNIVS PYLCHER V C LEG AVGG PRO PRAET TEMPLM ISIDIS C...TIS VETVSTATE COLLAPBVM RESTITVI PRACEPT' which translates as 'In tribute, a gift donated by Marcus Martiannius Pulcher, most honourable of men, pro-praetorian legate of the emperors, who restored this temple to Isis, which had collapsed through old age and lay in ruins'. From the River Thames, a first-century AD earthenware jug bears the inscription 'LONDINI AD FANVM ISIDIS' (From London at the temple of *Isis*). Other small items from the city prove the worship of the goddess. These include decorative bone hairpins, a lead weight depicting Isis and a small bronze figurine of the goddess and her son *Horus*.[92]

Fig. 71. Lead plaque depicting the goddess Isis found at Groundwell Ridge

From present knowledge, the function of the site at Groundwell Ridge is open to two interpretations – a moderately prosperous villa or a healing sanctuary. Due to only partial excavation the complete layout or function of the bath suite and aisled building remains unknown as does that of the other buildings indicated by geophysics and earthwork surveys. Consequently the case for a villa lies in the aisled ground plan of the eastern building and the fact that its rear corridor was sub-divided at a later date, a feature common on many villa sites. Confirmation of the site being a villa would be the discovery of barns, driers, and agricultural implements. These could await discovery on the level ground between the excavated buildings and the terracing behind. However, water provided by the copious springs clearly played a major part in the siting of the complex. In the Roman world sources of water were held sacred, the belief being that water rising from the earth carried life-giving properties from the gods, thus they were places of healing and fertility. On the upper terraces along with the nymphaeum, as demonstrated by the geophysical and earthwork surveys, there may have been at least two more shrines, which with the presence of ponds/pools, the early apsidal building and the other stone lined cistern may point to the presence of a water cult's healing sanctuary. Then the buildings would have provided accommodation, bathing and other facilities for visitors seeking cures. If this is a sanctuary, a candidate as the chief deity would be the Egyptian goddess Isis as hinted at by the plaque and the spring, as her sanctuaries are commonly associated with water. As a divine healer Isis shared the secrets of healing and preparation of medical potions to her priestesses. She was also worshipped as the ideal mother and wife as well as the patroness of nature and magic and she was the friend of slave, sinner, artisans and the down trodden, whilst she also listened to the prayers of the wealthy, maidens, aristocrats and rulers.[93] It is of note that the springs that issue from the hillside eventually feed via the River Ray into the Upper Thames, known to the Romans as the Isis.

Farmsteads

Buildings of a lesser status than villas, those lacking embellishment and perhaps best classed as farmsteads, have also been identified in the Borough. These were built of stone, stone and timber, or just timber.

Examples include a site destroyed by M4 construction west of Wanborough Plain Farm on the chalk downs.[94] Salvage excavation recorded ditches and the foundation trenches for a timber walled structure associated with pottery, tiles, shell and animal bone. Other finds include: single coins of the emperor Nero (AD 54 to 68) and Constantine

I (AD 306 to 337); two brooches; a small bronze mount in the form of the head of a satyr and a bronze finger ring. Another site, also on chalk and partially revealed during the M4 construction, is located south of Medbourne in Liddington parish. Here, wall foundations of large sarsen stones set in shallow trenches were encountered in association with first to second century AD pottery fragments.[95] At Cloverlands in Haydon Wick parish, Swindon Archaeological Society members led by Mike Stone excavated part of a small stone building with a cobbled floor and traces of a timber building. Second- to fourth-century AD pottery sherds, tiles and fourth-century AD coins were found. At City Corner, Little Hinton, surface finds following ploughing consisted of first- and second-century AD pottery. Within an adjacent hedgeline, numerous sarsen stones derived from field clearance probably came from building foundations. One hundred metres to the east at 'Holy Well' the cutting of a drainage trench revealed much second-century AD pottery and animal bone. A subsequent archaeological test trench showed that these came from a large silted-up, spring-fed pond. On Hinton Downs, surface finds from another likely farmstead site include pottery, quern stone fragments, brooches, an awl and first- to fourth-century coins which include a hoard of nine late Roman silver coins.

Hamlet and Village

Around the Roman town of *Durocornovium* at Lower Wanborough several sites have been identified that comprise a cluster of small domestic buildings. Hence they cannot be classed as villas or farmsteads although they may well have been linked with, but set well apart from such. These seem to have been hamlets or small villages for workers conveniently located close to their place of work whether agricultural or industrial.

Fig. 72. Excavation of a Roman burial at Saxon Court in Old Town

Fig. 73. Iron artefacts from Saxon Court in Old Town (scale 4cm)

On Swindon Hill to the east of Old Town's High Street archaeological excavations in the later 1970s undertaken by Wiltshire County Council's Archaeological Section revealed traces of four stone-walled buildings. Badly disturbed by post-Roman occupation and subsequent garden cultivation these structures at the rear of Lloyds Bank and at Saxon Court[96] date to the late third or fourth century AD. Clearly a small Romano-British cemetery existed close to the Saxon Court buildings as three burials were uncovered. One inhumation was contained within a stone slab-lined and capped grave. Adjacent, a stone-lined cist contained a lower rotary quern stone set face-up, below a stone slab on which had been placed a pottery beaker and a leg joint of lamb. Presumably this was a ritual offering to a local deity in the hope of good harvests or an offering to the ancestors. Further burials without grave goods discovered at the junction of Wood Street and Devizes Road many years ago may also be associated with this settlement. Features of an earlier date include pits and ditches, also the cutting of a very large cone-shaped shaft seemingly for the construction of a well that failed when a thick strata of stone was encountered. Subsequently it was used as a rubbish dump, many tip lines being discernible in the infill. Slight traces of an early timber building were also found at Saxon Court.

Fig. 74. Failed well pit at Lloyd's Bank in Old Town

Artefacts recovered during the excavations include an iron pruning knife and an ox goad, items suggestive of an agricultural function of the site; whilst a bronze balance arm and an iron stylus suggest trade and record keeping. Other finds comprise much pottery, an iron hammer head, a knife, a meat hook and door fittings as well as bronze brooches, bracelets, buckles and coins (Vespasian AD 81-96 to Honorius AD 393-402). A paved road at the Roman town site of *Durocornovium* heads towards Swindon Hill, implying a direct link to the settlement from the town. This road and some of the later buildings in *Durocornovium* are built in Swindon stone, signifying quarrying on the hilltop and maybe indicating that the hilltop settlement also housed quarry workers. Passmore noted traces of Roman stone quarry pits at Okus and at the 'Olde Quarre' west of Headlands School, and excavation on the former Penfolds Nursery site found stone quarrying pits and a hoard of 22 bronze coins dating from AD 259 to AD 273.

On Highworth Hill, at its eastern end, a similar settlement was observed during the 1975-85 construction of Haresfield Estate. Here the Highworth Historical and Swindon Archaeological Societies, along with Mike Collins, an amateur archaeologist, made and recorded many archaeological discoveries.[97] At Priory Green five stone-walled rectangular small buildings linked by stone-paved tracks were found. One building measuring 6m by 9.5m was divided into two rooms by a cross-wall and its long axis was aligned to a track. The outer walls were 0.75m thick and the interior roughly flagged. Adjacent and located at a point where two tracks met, a further dwelling measured 6m by 8m and this had external walls over 1m thick. Internal dividing walls created four rooms of varying size floored in clay, cobbles or flags. Cobbling and postholes defined a north facing entrance which gave access to the largest room. Around 12m north of the first building, another measuring 11.2m by 6.9m overall had roughly built walls and was divided internally into three rooms floored in an assortment of flags, cobbles and gravel.

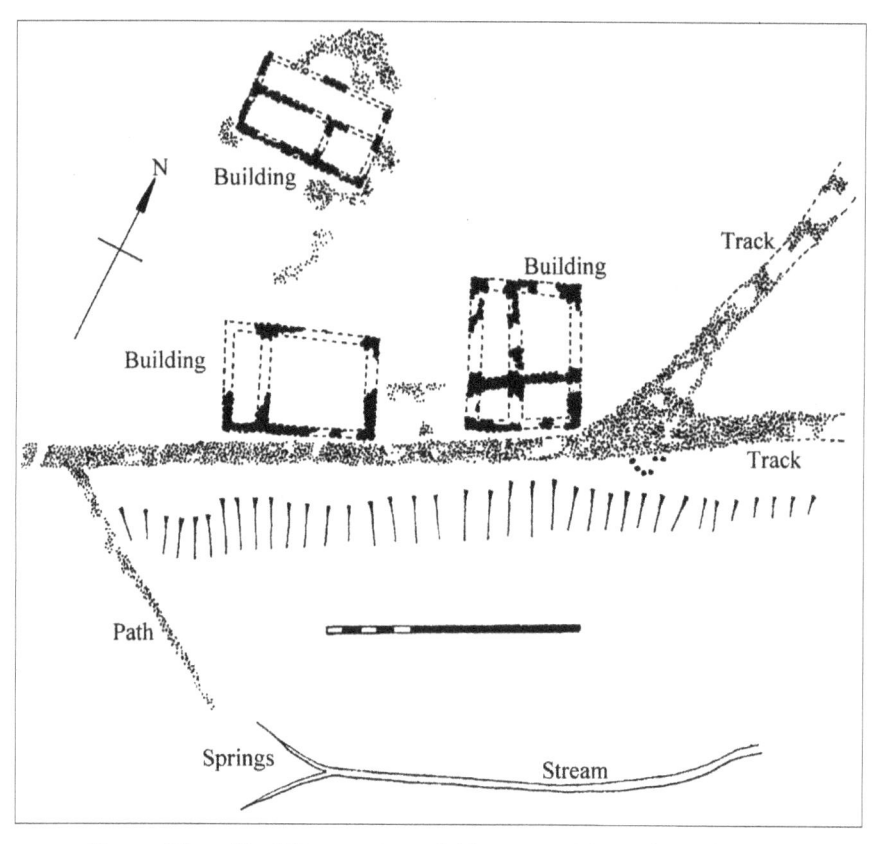

Fig. 75. Plan of buildings at Haresfield Estate Highworth (scale 30m)

Like the previous structure, it had a north-facing cobbled entrance but here it was flanked by massive stone blocks. Some distance higher up the hillside to the northwest a single-roomed building measuring 5.2m by 9m was floored with rough flagging. The entrance to this was by a wide eastern doorway, perhaps implying a non-domestic use. Overlying the floor was a distinct layer of midden-like material. The fifth construction located c.125m to the northeast of the second dwelling, had rough walling which extended outside the area being developed. As uncovered, it measured 5m by 7.2m and was floored with small pebbles and grit. It contained one partition wall which appeared to be a later addition. Pottery and coins date the settlement's occupation from the early third century AD until the end of the fourth century AD. To the north, at Knowlands, traces of a further small rectangular stone walled building floored with gravel were discovered and also close by this was an inhumation in a stone lined and capped grave. Coral ragstone used for the building's walls was much employed in the region for road and structural construction. At Highworth old quarries have been found and it maybe that similar to the settlement on Swindon Hill, these were the homes of agricultural and quarry workers.

Straddling the Ridgeway track on Burderop Down close to Barbury Castle, a fairly large settlement is shown through surface finds. Passmore noted traces of rough stone flooring, terracotta tiles, pottery, iron slag and stone roofing tile.[98] Field walking by Swindon Archaeological Society members in 1973 determined that the site extended over an area of about 2.25 hectares (5.6 acres). Finds made then included stone roofing and terracotta heating tile fragments as well as pottery fragments which dated from late first century AD to the end of the fourth century AD. Also found were a carved sandstone moulding, a late third century AD coin, a bronze bracelet, an early bronze brooch and pieces of quern stone. It is feasible that future discoveries will show this to be a villa but on present evidence a village is more likely to have existed there, catering for agricultural workers and perhaps drovers and travellers using the Ridgeway.

Pottery Kilns
Of the vast amount of pottery found on the Roman settlements in the region, some were made in kilns in France, Germany, Spain, Italy and North Africa. The majority however was made locally. The siting of potteries depended on a number of factors: a ready market, a good clay source, water, accessibility and a convenient and manageable timber supply. Such production sites would have had a major impact on the landscape with kilns, clay quarries, waste dumps, drying areas and buildings for storage, potting and domestic use.

The finding of pottery wasters and kiln debris by the author in March 1972 at Whitehill Farm led to the discovery of an extensive Romano-British pottery manufacturing industry that operated from the late first to the beginning of the fifth century AD.[99] Situated 1km to 2km west of Swindon Hill and lying on Kimmeridge Clay, nine separate kiln sites have been identified so far. They lie adjacent to or not far from three streams, western tributaries of the River Ray, which flows around the south and west side of the hill. A ridge extending southwest from Shaw

Fig. 76. Remains of a pottery kiln at Whitehill Farm West Swindon

and rising between the two northernmost streams appears to have been a focal point for the industry as on it lie at least three kiln sites: East Leaze Farm, Upper Shaw Farm, and Old's Close; as well as four settlement sites: Office Campus, Catholic Church, Greendown and Lydiard Park. The latter three include substantial stone-walled buildings. On the opposite bank of a stream at the ridge's southern foot there is a major production site at Whitehill Farm.[100] Lying 1km away to the northeast and similarly sited is a further kiln site – Westlea Down. Other kiln sites at Freshbrook and Toothill Farm are located 1km southwest and 1.2km southeast of Whitehill Farm. Undoubtedly associated with the potteries, a fifth settlement site was located at Blagrove Farm. A further settlement to the east of Toothill Farm and south of West Leaze has been recently indicated during road construction, by the finding of pits, postholes, ditches and many pottery fragments, as well as bones of horse, cattle and goat/sheep. To date a total of twenty four kilns have been uncovered at five locations: East Leaze Farm, Upper Shaw Farm, Whitehill Farm, Toothill Farm and Westlea Down through archaeological excavation, salvage excavation and observation, prior to and during development. The other kilns sites are indicated by the finding of many wasters and much kiln debris. Whitehill Farm when excavated in 1973/4, under the direction of Scott Anderson, also produced remains of a circular timber-built potter's workshop and part of a rectangular timber building, both of which were floored in clay. Pottery waster fragments lay scattered for over 100m around the kilns on the latter site and similarly at Shaw. Fairly large stone-walled rectangular buildings, these serving as workshops or for potters' accommodation, have been noted at Toothill Farm and East Leaze Farm kiln sites. Large clay quarries were recorded close to the kiln sites at Toothill, Shaw and Whitehill Farm.

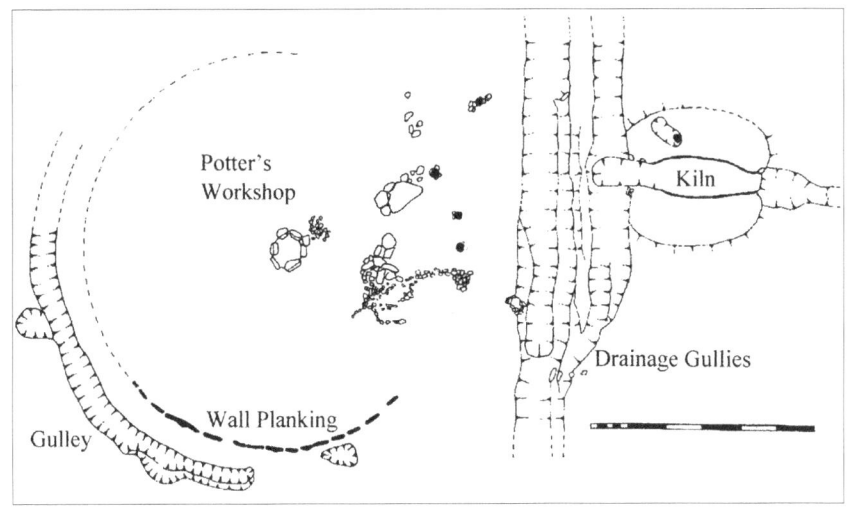

Fig. 77. Plan of a potter's workshop and kiln at Whitehill Farm West Swindon (scale 6m)

The pottery vessels (West Swindon ware) produced in the kilns, mainly kitchenware, were manufactured in grey (reduced) and orange (oxidised) fabrics. Vessel types comprised: wide- and narrow-mouthed jar; storage jar; cooking pot; lid; bowl; dish; sieve; tankard; beaker and flagon. Rarer products include: unguent jar; candlestick; lamp filler; pepper-pot; bottle; cheese press and cup. Decoration was largely confined to neck cordons, girth grooves and burnished rims and shoulders. Less common was the use of burnished line decoration, either wavy, straight or lattice and, occasionally, on drinking vessels indenting, angled, vertical or horizontal combing; random applied pinched clay lumps (rustic ware); applied slip dots in rows and rouletting.

In the second and early third century AD the potters at Shaw specialised in oxidised flagons and tankards, many of the former having

Fig. 78. Pottery vessels from Whitehill Farm West Swindon

a white coating. There is some evidence for white-coated mixing bowls (*mortaria*) being manufactured also. Some of the latter, datable to the second century AD, found at *Durocornovium* are stamped I•VO•NER•F,[101] as is a taper holder.[102] It is also likely that fine colour-coated, decorated beakers[103] were made from the early second century until the mid or late third century AD, somewhere amongst the kilns.[104]

Distribution of West Swindon wares covered a large area, being found on the town sites at Cirencester (*Corinium*), Lower Wanborough (*Durocornovium*), White Walls on the Fosse Way; and villa sites at Littlecote near Hungerford, Barnsley Park near Cirencester and Challow in Oxfordshire and on most sites in between.

All the kilns dating from the late first to the mid-third century AD have a single boat-shaped chamber which, working on the up-draught principal, served for containment of the fire and the vessels to be fired. This type of kiln is uncommon, being confined to the south and southeast of Britain, notably on the Savernake/Oare, Wiltshire and at the Farnham Hampshire pottery industries.[105] The majority are aligned in a northeast to southwest direction and vary in length from 2.6m to 4m and in width from 0.7m to 1.5m. In most cases they were formed by cutting the chamber within a 1m or higher oval mound of clay. At each end a short flue occasionally built in tiles gave access to the chamber from a stoking pit. Air-dried pottery vessels were stacked in layers within the kiln, the lowest lying directly on the chamber floor. The stack then would have been completely covered with thin fired clay plates and then turves to complete an airtight seal apart from a central hole which acted as a chimney. This would have been sealed at a late stage in the firing process if a grey colour (oxidised) was required, if not an orange colour (reduced) was obtained. Significant evidence of re-flooring and wall repair shows that kilns had a long life. Some kilns of the late third and fourth century AD date, as were found at White Hill Farm, were circular with single flues formed within clay mounds dumped on top of the discarded broken and distorted pottery waste.

The substantial buildings discovered amongst the kilns at the Catholic Church, Greendown and Lydiard Park are (based on range and quality of finds) the homes of the kiln site owners. During construction work at the Catholic Church site, salvage excavation revealed a very substantial rectangular building which had stone walls surviving up to eight courses high. Lying close to the top of Shaw Ridge it commanded an extensive view southwards to the chalk downs. Investigation of the interior proved impossible, but fortunately it would seem that the building was not entirely destroyed, so more investigations may be possible in the future. Pottery from the site, which included imported wares, shows that occupation continued throughout the third and fourth centuries AD. Only partially uncovered during the construction of a cycle track, the stone-walled structure at Greendown had traces of a tessellated floor. The presence of a building at Lydiard Park was located in 1977 when the cutting of a pipe trench revealed black earth containing pottery, building stone and tile fragments, some with mortar adhering. Excavation adjacent, by Wessex Archaeology in 2003 prior to construction of a car park,[106] uncovered stone wall foundations of a room and a large pit. The latter cutting the building's walling, contained high status material which included painted wall plaster and *opus signinum* fragments, terracotta roof and heating tile fragments, as well as local and continental made pottery.

A further pottery production site uncovered in 1963/4 during levelling of ground for a sports field on the eastern outskirts of Swindon, lies close to Covingham School only a short distance from *Durocornovium*.

A small salvage excavation exposed a single flued circular kiln and adjacent a dump of kiln debris. Pottery produced here appears to have been large storage jars datable to the second century AD.

Tileries

Terracotta tile was used in the construction of Roman buildings for roofing, heating systems, flooring, as bonding courses in walls and for the lining of windows and doorways. It was also used on most of the West Swindon potteries in kiln and building construction. Cubes formed by sawing up flat terracotta tiles were also found on several of the West Swindon kiln sites pointing to a side-line in the making of *tesserae* (cubes) for pavements. Consequently it is likely that a small tilery which supplied the kilns and the locale awaits discovery beneath West Swindon. Of note is that the Catholic Church building site produced two tile fragments bearing their makers mark IANVS, presumably an abbreviation of the tilery owner's name. Two other tile fragments bearing this mark are known, one came from a small Romano-British building site at Haydon Wick and the other from *Durocornovium*, the Roman town at Lower Wanborough. Other tiles stamped with their maker's mark found in the Borough include those of IVC.DIGNI. These may also be of local manufacture as analysis of the tiles fabric suggests that the clay used came from the Kimmeridge clay which is plentiful in the area.[107] Examples of tiles by this maker have been found on the villa at Badbury, the settlement at Burderop Down and the town site of *Durocornovium*.[108]

Two tileries, which were operating from the late first century AD, have been located a little outside the Borough at

Fig. 79. Roman tiles bearing the partial marks of IANVS and IVC.DIGNI

Oaksey[109] and Brinkworth.[110] From the former tilery came tiles stamped with the marks of their makers TPF and LHS. Tiles so stamped have been found at *Durocornovium* and on the villa at Stanton Fitzwarren.

Roads

All the sites would have been linked by a network of paved roads bounded by drainage ditches or simple dirt trackways that today are only definable by their former side ditches. Other than the major mid-first century AD roads of Ermin Street and Broken Street, and the road linking Swindon Hill and the town of *Durocornovium*, evidence of this network has only been encountered occasionally.

As can be expected, industries such as pottery manufacture and stone quarrying required well-constructed roads to enable the safe and easy transport of materials and goods. At Upper Shaw Farm amongst the West Swindon pottery production sites, a north to south aligned flint cobbled road was uncovered during development with one of its side ditches being packed with second century AD pottery wasters and kiln debris. Of later date, a connecting side road was also located heading in a southeast direction. A few years ago another potential road was located as a surviving raised, linear earthwork and by a geophysical survey west of the kiln sites in Lydiard Park.[111] South of Swindon Hill during the construction of the M4 in 1969-70 the re-cutting of a stream bed to provide better drainage revealed a sandstone and flint constructed road which led towards Nightingale Farm. There during the M4 motorway construction, further stone paving was exposed along with pits containing second century AD pottery, mainly West Swindon products.[112]

In 1997 adjacent to a probable Roman stone quarry at Groundwell Farm, an evaluation revealed a stone paved 5.8m wide and 0.32m thick road.[113] Deep ruts on the left side and lighter ones on the right, suggest that the rules of the road were the same as we have today. Carts leaving the quarry laden with stone used the left side whilst returning empty carts used the right side. Three years later, also on Groundwell Ridge not far from the sanctuary/villa site, an evaluation by Cotswold Archaeology exposed a 2.5m wide trackway. Aligned northeast to southwest this was constructed of well compacted, small sub-rounded limestone fragments. Observed by Foundations Archaeology staff immediately west of the villa at Stanton Fitzwarren, a cambered metalled road with side ditches was revealed in a pipe trench. These three roads extend towards and, presumably linked with, Ermin Street. To the north of the Stanton Fitzwarren villa a further road partly surviving as a modern farm track, was sectioned by a pipe trench cutting at Stanton Water. From its alignment it connected the villa to another track which extends from Ermin Street at Seven Bridges to Highworth. Archaeological cuttings across the latter revealed a slightly cambered coral-ragstone-constructed surface edged with kerbstones.

10
Late/Post Roman

Late Defence

The period between the end of Roman rule and the emergence of Saxon kingdoms was a time of conflict and great turmoil. Many regular troops had been withdrawn from Britain to protect Rome's heartland during the latter years of the fourth century AD and in the early years of the fifth century AD. Various usurpers had also been declared Emperor in Britain by the military so this meant that troops accompanied the usurpers to the continent whilst they sought advancement in territory and power in Gaul and beyond. Amongst these usurpers were Magnus Maximus (AD 383-8), Marcus (AD 406-7), Gratian (AD 407) and Constantine III (AD 407-11). Few if any of these troops returned. Consequently the country's defences were much weakened at a time when the regular and militia armed forces were trying to repel raids by Germanic warriors on the southeast coast, Pictish warriors to the north and to the west Celtic warriors from Ireland.

Objects of Germanic origin, notably military belt fittings found within cemeteries,[114] suggest that leaders of towns in eastern Britain began to hire foreign mercenaries to aid their defence. Most of these people would have brought their families with them and were provided with land to settle on.

Like other towns and many villas in the *Britannia Prima* province, late coinage at *Durocornovium* is present in large numbers in direct contrast to elsewhere in the country.[115] This may well signify the presence in this provincial border town of a military force, since coinage normally

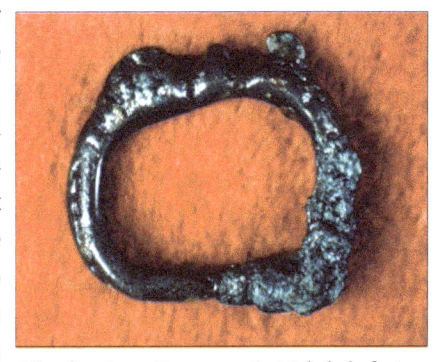

Fig. 80. Late Romano-British belt fitting from Old Town depicting horse heads (width 2.2cm)

entered general circulation from soldiers pay. Another indication of such a force are distinctive brooches and belt fittings found within the province.[116] Many of the latter depict stylised animals. Locally they include part of an ornate belt fitting from the villa at South Farm near Chiseldon, a buckle from Old Town in Swindon and a buckle tongue from *Durocornovium*. The latter two were decorated with horse heads so may imply the existence of mounted militia.

The End of Roman Britain
Britain had stopped minting its own coinage in AD 326 and so relied thereafter on Gaulish mints for supply. The issue of bronze coins to Britain ceased in AD 402 and silver and gold coins in AD 406. Consequently coinage in circulation dwindled and this resulted in the breakdown of a functioning monetary system that had been relied on to pay for goods, services and taxes. People now had to rely on self-subsistence, barter or bullion to survive. Therefore mass production industries such as pottery manufacture ceased to operate. Skilled workers such as masons, carpenters, mosaicists and metal workers could not be paid, which resulted in the structural decay and eventual collapse of buildings, particularly those built of stone. Undoubtedly a breakdown in Government control and social order quickly followed.

Further deterioration within the settlements and on the villas occurred due to the raiding war-bands, brigand activity and periods of plague. Added to this unstable situation, foreign mercenaries hired by leaders of towns in eastern Britain rebelled against their employers. Thus further destabilised, Britain's defences were unable to repel Germanic tribes (Saxons, Jutes and Angles) who seeking fertile land on which to settle joined with the rebels. The numbers of these incomers is debatable, but they were sufficiently large to introduce a new language the basis of which we speak today (Hill 2003). Clearly land was taken and the former owners were either slaughtered, enslaved or driven out while lesser folk such as the tenants of the former landowners may have submitted to the newcomers' rule, simply swapping one property-owner for another. Gildas, a British cleric, penned a sermon '*De Excidio et Conquestu Britanniae*'. Although written over a hundred years after the events, the sermon definitely records some grains of truth regarding the happenings of that traumatic period. He notes

All the major towns were laid low by the repeated battering of enemy rams and laid low too all the inhabitants – church leaders, priests and people alike as the swords glinted all around and the flames crackled.

Self-subsistence for the remaining Romano-British people was easier to achieve in the countryside where arable land was available, so partial or total abandonment of large settlements took place. Notably some hillforts such as Liddington Castle and Barbury Castle, appear to have been refortified at this time suggesting that some of the local population had retired to them as places of safety. Gildas records

…the cities of our land are not populated even now as they once were; right up to the present they are deserted in ruins and unkempt.

II
Anglo-Saxon (AD 450 – AD 850)

Mount Badon

Many battles followed as the British in the west fought back. Eventually the Saxon advance was halted after defeat by the legendary Arthur and his troops, during the three-day siege and battle of *Mons Badonicus* (Mount Badon) in *c.*517 AD. Nennius, a Welsh monk, in his writing *Historia Brittonum*, *c.*800 AD, tells us that the mythical Arthur's twelfth

Fig. 81. Liddington Castle. Site of the Battle of Monte Badonis?

battle was on Badon Hill and in it 960 Saxons fell in one day from a single charge by Arthur. A very likely contender for this battle site is Liddington Castle, which dominates the area between two major Roman roads and overlooks the Ridgeway. Early maps refer to the hill on which the fort stands as Badbury Hill. Nearby is the village of Badbury which

ANGLO-SAXON

is recorded in a Saxon charter of AD 955 as *Baddeburri* (Badda's burh).[117] This name may relate to the fortification that dominates the skyline immediately to the southeast of the village.

Such a major defeat of the Thames Valley Saxons may have prompted an emblematic record to have been created. Carved into the

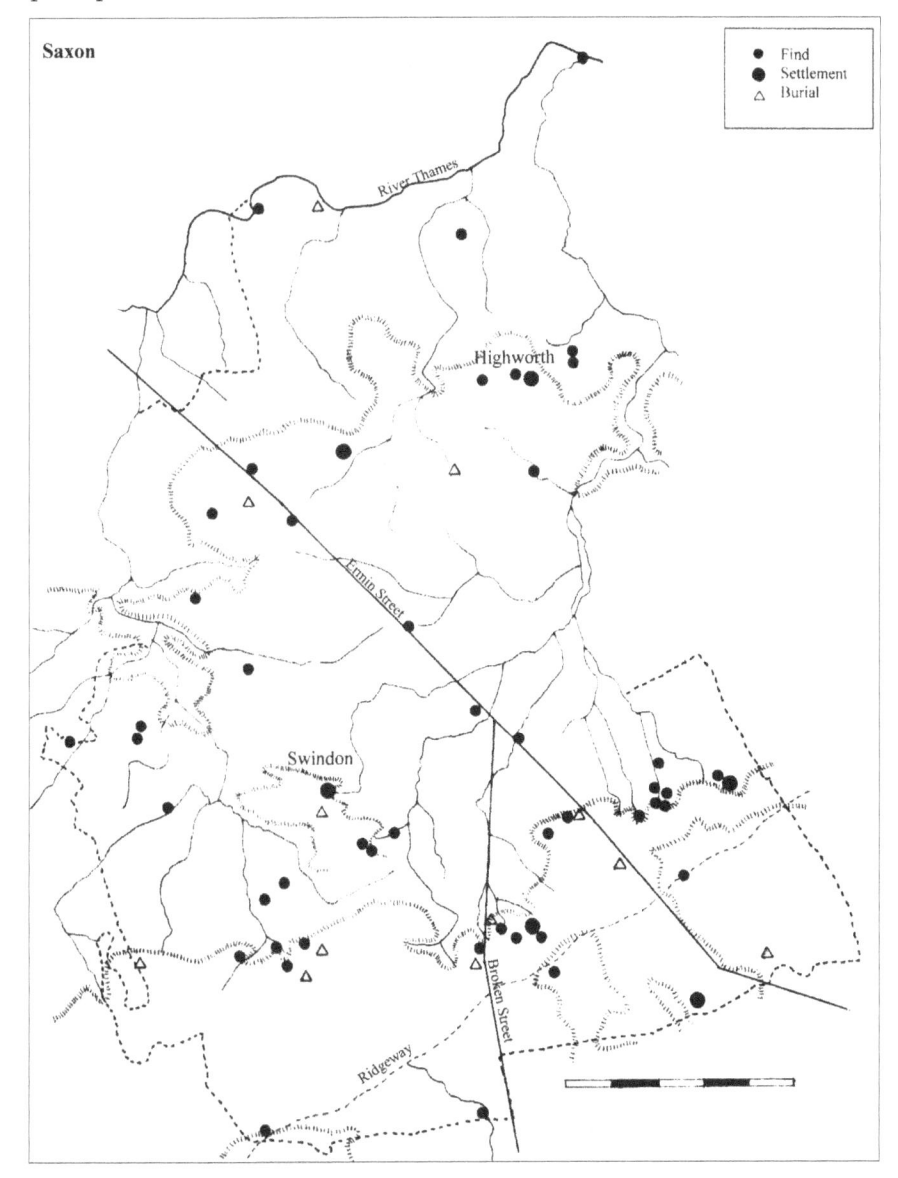

Fig. 82. Distribution map of Saxon sites and artefacts (scale 5km)

chalk hillside at Foxhill south of Wanborough, where it would have been clearly seen from Liddington Hill, a giant south facing figure has been identified. This is visible as an indistinct parch mark on an aerial photograph which was taken by a Swindon College tutor Gerald Woollard and initially noted by Bryn Walters. The figure stands legs spread out on a curved feature, which may represent the prow of a ship. His left arm is stretched forward whilst his right arm is thrown back and holds a spear. However later geophysical investigations failed to fully confirm the figure's existence. Bryn considers the figure to be much older dating to the late Neolithic or Early Bronze Age.[118]

The fall of Britannia Prima

During this lull in the fighting the Saxons consolidated their realm in the east before again invading mid and western Britain. The Roman western province of *Britannia Prima*, which archaeological and documentary evidence demonstrates withstood the Saxon advance for a long period of time, finally began to crumble. The *Annales Cambriae* record that Arthur was killed in AD 537 at the Battle of *Camlann* (possibly in Somerset). The British were defeated in AD 556 at the battle of *Beranburh* (Barbury Castle)[119] by the forces of Cynric and Ceawlin. Following defeat at the Battle of *Deorham* (Dyrham in South Gloucestershire) in AD 577, the

Fig. 83. Saxon chaff tempered pottery sherds from Old Town

cities of Cirencester, Gloucester and Bath were taken, signalling the end of *Britannia Prima*. By the seventh century AD, five large Saxon kingdoms had emerged, namely Wessex, Kent, East Anglia, Mercia and Northumbria. The eighth century AD saw the dominance of the Midlands kingdom of Mercia under King Offa.

Saxon Rule

To achieve effective rule Saxon kingship entailed regular visitation to all parts of the kingdom, which resulted in the establishment of many royal villas (*Villa Regia*). Wessex comprised four shires: Wiltshire; Hampshire; Somerset; and Dorset; each named after a settlement that surrounded a royal villa: Wilton; Hampton; Somerton and Dorchester. Many other royal villas existed within each shire, often attached to a royal estate. Each of these provided the centre for a settlement which took on local administration and served as a market for locally produced and imported goods. They also served as a focus for religious events and military organisation.

Saxon Settlement

Evidence for a very early Saxon occupation in the area is difficult to establish as pottery, the commonest dating material, changed little in form or fabric between the mid fifth and the late eighth century AD. This mainly undecorated pottery, was hand-made and mostly tempered with organic material. However some fragments found within Saxon buildings at Old Town in Swindon[120] and Medbourne below Liddington Hill[121] appear to copy late Roman pottery in shape and surface treatment so may date to the mid or late fifth century AD. By the mid sixth century AD, Anglo-Saxon occupation is clearly shown through the datable items of weaponry and jewellery found on a number of sites in the Borough.

Town life was virtually unknown to early Saxons as their settlements largely comprised a cluster of small buildings arranged around a large hall, or occurred as isolated farmsteads. These buildings were traditionally built in timber since the Saxons were highly skilled in the use of this. They had little if any knowledge of construction in stone, so buildings urban and rural which were deserted by the Romano-British fell into decay. An example of this is the bath building at Groundwell Ridge, Swindon. Having been abandoned probably in the early fifth century AD, subsequent collapse was followed by the levelling of the remains and then erection of a substantial timber posthole structure which incorporated an oven.[122] Unfortunately no pottery was found in association there to assist in dating this event.

Saxon Highworth

One of the small Roman buildings uncovered at Priory Green, Highworth, had cut into one corner of its ruins a hollow which measured 4.5m x 4m, around which was an arc of angled postholes. Clearly these had contained timbers which leant against the former building's remaining stone walling, so forming the supports for the structure's wall and roof.[123] Within the hollow a ring of burnt stones showed the location of a hearth. From the hollow's subsequent infill came pottery fragments, part of a clay loom-weight and a decorated bronze clasp. A short distance away a flat-bottomed 7m square and 0.5m deep hollow is typical of a Saxon sunken floored hut (*grubenhaus*). This hollow had, on two opposing sides, posts holes which had been centrally cut so they would have supported the roof's central truss beam. In one corner an entrance was indicated by a cobbled ramp. Small stake holes for the wattle walling were located around the hollow's exterior. Pottery sherds and a bronze garter hook came from its eventual infilling.

Fig. 84. Saxon gold stud from Old Town (diameter 10mm)

Saxon Swindon

In Old Town at the east end of Swindon Hill, ten sunken floored huts have been recorded through archaeological excavations and construction work. Such structures are considered, based on the finds found within them, to have been sheds used for the manufacture of woollen cloth or storage. They range in size from 3.08m x 2.4m with a hollow of 0.22m depth to 9.74m x 5.7m with a hollow of 0.44m depth. Eight of the huts were discovered in 1975 to 1977 prior to, or during the construction of Saxon Court in the garden of the demolished Swindon House which fronted the east side of the Market Square.[124] Two of these had been

ANGLO-SAXON

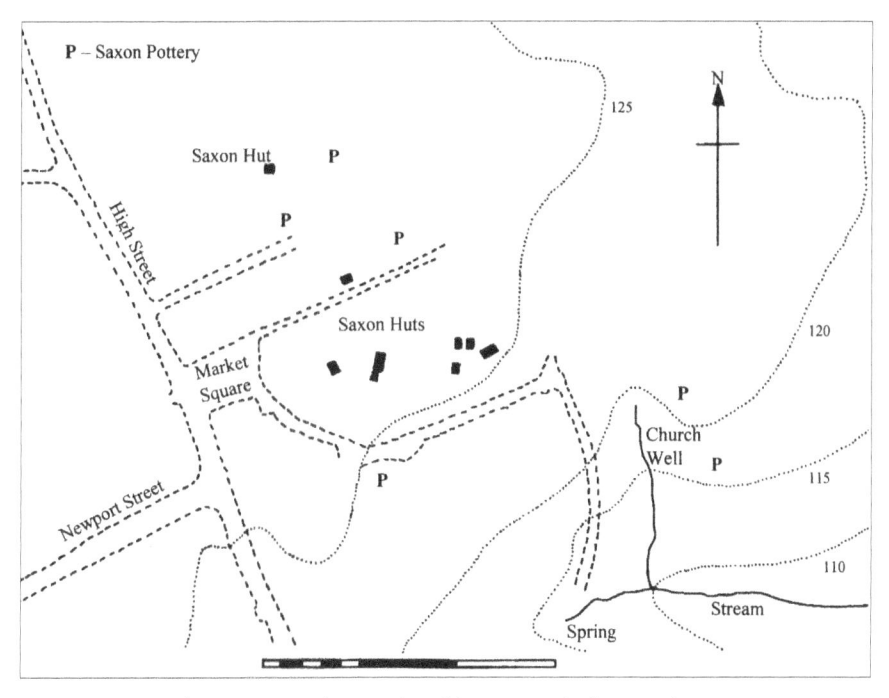

Fig. 85. Saxon settlement in Old Town Swindon (scale 150m)

cut through very late Roman occupation layers and building demolition debris. Another hut was found in 1977 at the rear of High Street's Lloyds Bank[125] and one of the others was found prior to the building of the Hermitage Surgery in Dammas Lane in 1993.[126] Many more and perhaps a timber hall undoubtedly await discovery, as the settlement clearly extends into The Lawns, where further Saxon pottery sherds have been found and where a copious spring known as 'Church Well' would have served the site. Controversy exists regarding whether the hut hollows were boarded over or if the base of the hollow formed the floor. Certainly the larger huts at

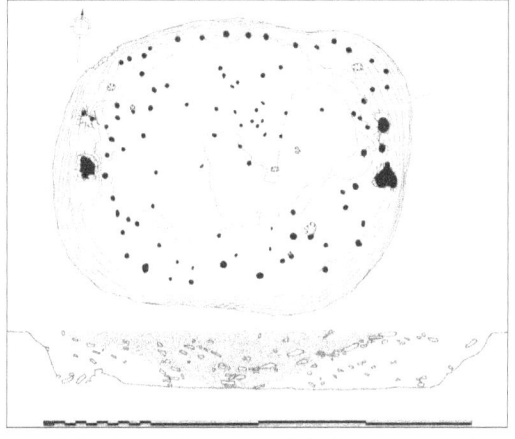

Fig. 86. Plan and section of the hut excavated at Lloyd's Bank in Old Town (scale 4m)

Fig. 87. Excavating a sunken floored hut at Lloyd's Bank in Old Town

Old Town were of the latter type, one having a clay layer formed from broken and discarded loom weights trampled into the ground, evidently in front of looms. Another had a scatter of small objects which had been dropped on its sandy base, notably items relating to cloth making.

Aligned east to west the hut excavated on the Lloyds Bank site measured 4.24m x 3.35m and 0.54m deep and had single substantial post holes central to each end which would have held posts to support the main roof beam. Just inside the hollow around its edge, numerous stake holes define the wattle and daub walls' location. Following the building's demolition, soil that had seemingly been banked against its walls externally, and which probably originated from the digging of the hut's hollow, was pushed back in. To complete the infilling of the hollow, soil containing domestic refuse had been used. From this came: two double-sided bone weaving combs, one excessively worn; an iron knife

Fig. 88. Walling plaster from Old Town Swindon showing wattle impressions

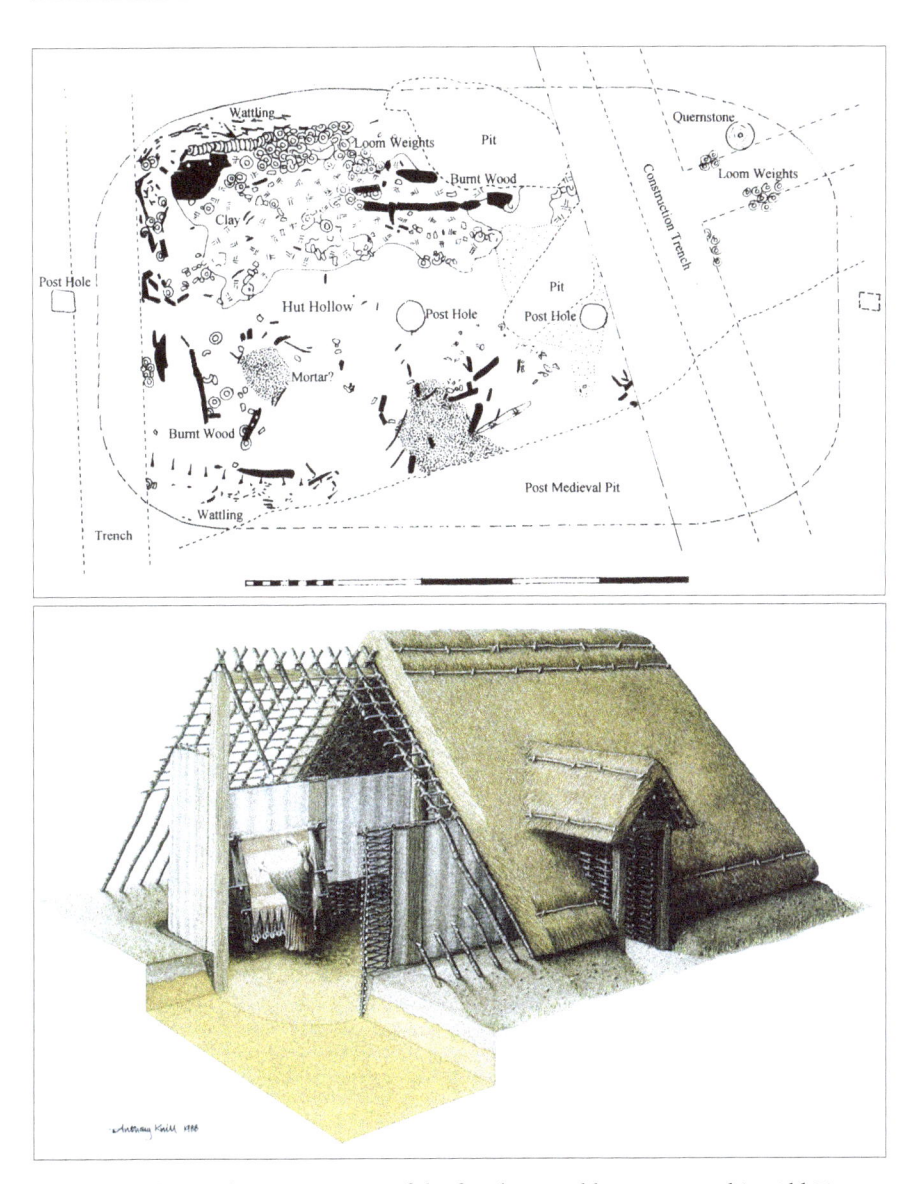

Fig. 89. Plan and reconstruction of the fire-destroyed hut excavated in Old Town (scale 5m)

blade; an antler knife handle; an iron trowel blade; a bone spindle whorl and a bone pin beater.

At Saxon Court, similarly constructed but much larger, a hut measuring 8.4m x 4.8m and aligned north to south had four central ridge post holes, two equally spaced within the building and one at each end. The wattle and plaster walling, following the hut's destruction by fire, was pushed into the hut's hollow. Due to the fire, much plaster blackened by the fire's heat and weighing over a ton survived. It bore impressions of the wattles and cut timbers which had formed the hut's framework. Beneath the plaster, charred wood consisted of wattles of chestnut, a few structural timbers and possibly part of a weaving loom. The loom's location was indicated by a long row of loom-weights that fell from it during the fire. Over 150 loom-weights were found within the hut. Further items relating to cloth manufacture were discovered including bone pins, a bone weaving comb, a bone pin beater and a bone weaving sword, a whetstone, iron shears, and an iron knife. Fragments of glass, pottery and charred wooden vessels were also found, as well as

Fig. 90. Loom weights in the burnt hut, Old Town

a lower quern stone placed in the hut's northwest corner. The hollow of this seventh or eighth century AD hut had been dug into the infilled hollow of a larger building measuring 9.74m x 5.70m (31.8 feet x 18.7 feet). This had substantial close-set post and stake holes located just inside its hollow, showing that the walling comprised numerous large upright timbers fronted by wattling. Within it revealed by a line of stake

ANGLO-SAXON

Fig. 91. Finds from a hut destroyed by fire in Old Town (comb 17.7cm long)

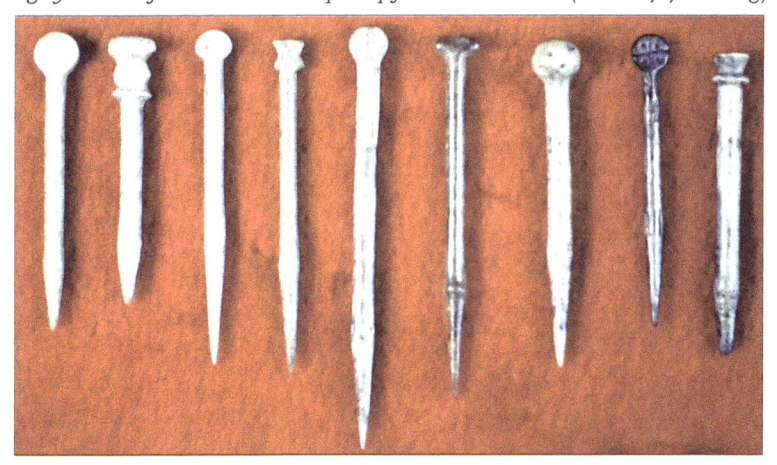

Fig. 92. Decorated bone pins from the Swindon House excavation in Old Town (longest 4.2cm)

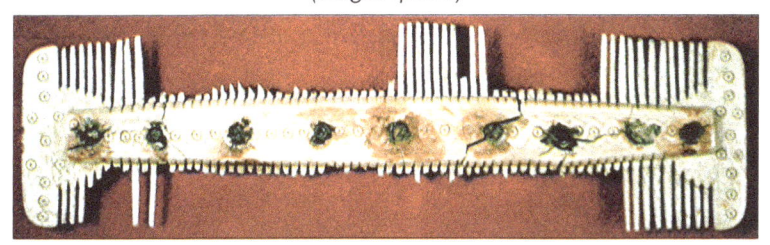

Fig. 93. Decorated bone comb from the Lloyd's Bank excavation in Old Town (length 16.6cm)

holes cut into the floor, a wattle screen divided the building into two rooms of equal size. Clearly the building had a long existence as it had some timber posts which had been replaced and a western entrance had been blocked and then later re-opened. From on the floor came: small decorated bone pins; a bone weaving comb; a bone pin beater; spindle whorls of bone, stone, pottery and shale; clay loom weight fragments; three Roman coins (two pierced for suspension); a Roman bronze brooch; a whetstone and a beaded gold stud with a central gold foil backed garnet – a setting from an ornate brooch. Although the finds show that weaving and spinning took place here it is likely, based on the type of construction, that it also served as a dwelling, since its size is comparable to the Saxon halls found on other sites.

Animal bones recovered from the building's infills show that the commonest animals present were sheep/goat, followed by cattle then pig.[127] Sheep besides providing mutton were important as they would have supplied the wool for cloth manufacture, whilst cattle provided milk, beef and leather. Also present in much smaller numbers were poultry, horse, dog and deer.

Other Saxon Settlement Sites
Sunken floored huts have been discovered elsewhere within the Borough. Examples include one discovered at Medbourne during the M4 motorway construction,[128] another at Upper Bury Town Farm near Blunsdon and four at Harlstone House in Bishopstone. Undoubtedly further investigations on these sites will unearth other associated buildings.

At Popplechurch to the south of Wanborough and near the Half Moon Plantation, aerial photography has shown two hall-type buildings, seemingly a farmstead. Ensuing field walking of the site following ploughing, recovered Saxon pottery sherds. In 2010 an archaeological evaluation at Rickfield House, Liddington revealed two ditches associated with Saxon pottery. At least fourteen other farm or settlement sites spread across the Borough have been revealed by pottery finds. They include locations in: Little Hinton, Upper Wanborough, Stratton St Margaret, Blunsdon St Andrew, Shaw, Haydon Wick, Wroughton and in the Marlborough Road area of Swindon.

Saxon Burials

A number of Saxon burial grounds have been identified within the Borough. Found during landscaping in 1822 and dating to the sixth century AD, the first of these was located in the grounds of Bassett Down House in Lydiard Tregoze parish.[129] Skeletons uncovered include two young adult males lying side by side equipped with spears, shields and knives; whilst paired brooches, pins and beads provide evidence of female burials. Just outside the Borough, at The Fox, Purton, ten or eleven male and female inhumations with grave goods were excavated by M E Cunnington and E H Goddard in 1912[130] and C H Gore in 1925. Finds include glass beads, iron swords, iron knives, iron spearheads and a bone pin. Also of sixth-century AD date, a further six or eight inhumations were excavated in 1941 at Foxhill Stud south of Wanborough.[131] All these were apparently adult males. Associated finds comprise a globular pot, a bronze belt buckle, an iron knife, an iron sword, an iron shield boss and an iron spearhead. They may have been warriors killed in battle, as may be a young male discovered in 1927, who had been buried nearby at the top of Callas Hill with a socketed iron spearhead and an iron knife.[132] Also an inhumation accompanied with a tanged knife was found east of Stanton Fitzwarren in 1906 and another on Hinton Down; this body was interred within a Bronze Age burial mound and was equipped with an iron spearhead. Many years ago, at Evelyn Street in Swindon, a male skeleton was discovered interred with a spearhead and knife. Here in 1978, archaeological excavation revealed a crouched burial overlying a small pit containing sherds of Saxon pottery. North of Forty Acre Barn near Castle Eaton, ploughing disturbed a female burial with grave goods consisting of three pierced Roman coins, three glass beads, a melon bead and part of a bronze buckle. In 2000 two late sixth-century AD burials were excavated by the author following the discovery of human bone and metalwork by Peter Hyams at Brimble Hill, Wroughton. One grave contained the remains of a female child whose grave was cut into the infill of the grave of an adult male. Associated with the child was

Fig. 94. Saucer Brooch from Foxhill Bishopstone (diameter 4cm)

Fig. 95. Sixth-century warrior burial at Brimble Hill Wroughton

a pair of large gilded bronze saucer brooches and two beads, one of amber and the other of glass. The adult was accompanied by a sword, two spearheads, a shield boss, decorative studs and a small strap buckle all made of iron. The pattern-welded sword found cradled in his right arm measured 89.8cms long and had been buried in its leather and wood sheath, traces of which remained. One spearhead measured 45.1cms in length; the other 24.3cms. Two weapons defined the Anglo-Saxon social order – the spear and the sword. Ownership of a spear defined a man as free and a warrior of Germanic society, whilst a sword marked a man of rank. Found nearby, a fifth-century AD bronze annular brooch was decorated with incised dots and circles. It appears that the burials had been positioned at a corner of the bounds of *Ellandune* (part of Wroughton parish), as defined in a tenth century AD charter.[133] Perhaps there the burial mound served as a spiritual boundary marker. In 2007 an excavation revealed two late seventh-century AD burials at Abbeymeads, Blunsdon St Andrew.[134] One, which was a 36-45+ age female, was accompanied by a silvered copper pin mounted with a gold foil-backed silver-framed garnet. It lay on the burial's chest, whilst a long cylindrical glass bead had been placed by the skull along with an iron-bound wooden bucket. The other, a male aged at least 26, lay in a crouched position and was associated with a copper alloy buckle and an iron knife. Near Fresden a decorated glass bead found in ploughsoil may indicate a further burial site, as could a gilded bronze saucer brooch found near to Charlbury Hill in Bishopstone parish. The latter had cloth traces in the corrosive products on its rear. A female burial was excavated at Harlstone House in Bishopstone in the area of the excavated Saxon buildings. An iron *scramasax* (single edged sword), iron knives and an iron spear have been unearthed at Barbury Castle which may hint at another burial site.[135]

It was north of Barbury Castle in AD 825 that the battle of Ellandune[136] was fought between the Mercians, led by King Beornwulf (ruled AD 823-825), and Wessex under King Egbert (ruled AD 802-839). The resulting victory for Egbert makes this one of the most decisive battles of Anglo-Saxon history as it effectively ended Mercian supremacy over the southern kingdoms of Anglo-Saxon England and established West Saxon dominance in southern England.[137] Shortly after this Egbert sent a large army under the command of his son Athelwolf, ealdorman Wulfheard and Ealhstan the Bishop of Sherborne into Kent. They drove out the local king Baldred and the territory was annexed.

Fig. 96. *Silver penny of King Baldred*

12
Late Anglo-Saxon/Early Medieval (AD 850-1066)

Mid ninth-century AD England comprised four independent Kingdoms: Mercia, Northumbria, East Anglia and Wessex. Norse incursions into northern and western Britain commenced at the end of the eighth century AD. These led to settlement in AD 865 following invasion of Northumbria and capture of York by a great Norse army led jointly by Guthrum, Ivar the Boneless, his brother Halfdan and Ubbe Ragnarsson. A few years later two Norse armies, one led by Bagsecg and the other by Halfdan, invaded central and southern England. A planned assault on Wessex in AD 871 was defeated at the battle of *Ashdown* by the forces of King Alfred who ruled from AD 871 to AD 899. This battle site is thought to lie on the Ridgeway near Wantage, Oxfordshire. Bagsecg was killed and the routed army retired to northern England. Attacks continued and by AD 876 only Wessex remained whole. But the Danish leader Guthrum continued to attack Wessex and eventually, on Epiphany 6 January AD 878 he launched a surprise night-time attack on Alfred and his court at the fortified town of Chippenham, Wiltshire. Utterly defeated, Alfred and his surviving troops fled from the battle to take refuge in the Somerset Marshes. There he built-up and armed a new army. Alfred subsequently defeated a great army led by Guthrum in May AD 878 at the battle of *Ethandun*, thought to be at Edington in North Wiltshire. Guthrum and the remains of his army retreated to Chippenham. Here he was besieged by Alfred and after two weeks Guthrum on the verge of starvation, sued for peace.

Saxon Towns
Part of Alfred's successful defence of Wessex had been achieved through the placing throughout Wessex of fortified towns (*Burhs*) defended by 27,000 warriors. This enabled the rural populace to retire to them for safety during Norse raids.

Swindon and Highworth are located in what was the northernmost part of Wessex, the River Thames being the border between Wessex and Mercia. No fortified towns existed in Swindon Borough, the nearest was that of Cricklade set on the southern bank of the River Thames. Others nearby include the Wiltshire town of Malmesbury and Wallingford in Oxfordshire.

The towns brought about major changes. Scattered farming communities saw in their midst the creation of an urban-based society not known since the end of Roman rule over four hundred years earlier. Inhabitants of burhs constituted an increasingly important class, who exercised rights of justice and land-lordship. These townsfolk, having strong royal military and ecclesiastical interests, represented an elitist element which supplied the market with a widening range of goods and helped create the demand for items produced both locally and further afield. Now people who had gained varied skills rather than continuing to make a living from agricultural activity, found they could set up in specific trades like metal, wood, leather, bone and horn working; textile manufacture; as shop and inn keepers; potters or even as moneyers. Evidence that demand encouraged new industries are the locally produced handmade pottery vessels found in quantity in the towns of Malmesbury and Cricklade and the surrounding area. These vessels in a coarse limestone-tempered fabric comprised cooking pots, pitchers, dishes and bowls.

Increasing Wessex Power
Offensives by an army from Wessex, aided by Mercian forces and increasing raids from Denmark, ultimately weakened Norse military power in the north. This led to their submission to Edward the Elder who was born *c*. AD 874-7 and died in AD 924, in return for protection, resulting in the north becoming part of Edward's England.

Danish Supremacy
King Aethelred (born *c*. AD 968, died 1016), feared a resurgence of Norse and Danish power in England, so in the year 1000 he plundered the Isle of Man and parts of the Anglo-Scandinavian north to try to crush the independently-minded Scandinavians living there. His continuing fear finally led to him ordering the massacre of all Danish men living in

England. In revenge Svein Forkbeard from Denmark brought an army to England and raided south and east England throughout 1003/4, although a famine in England forced Svein to take his army back to Denmark in 1005. He continued raiding until 1013 when he returned with his son Canute intending to conquer England. This he achieved, so Aethelred fled to Normandy. The following year Svein died and Aethelred returned and expelled the Danes who were now under Canute's leadership. In August 1015 Canute returned and in the following year, at the Battle of *Assandun* (Ashingdon or Ashdon in Essex) he defeated Edmund II (born AD 989, died 1016), Aethelred's third son and successor. A treaty was drawn up in which Canute took control of northern England whilst Edmund controlled the south. Canute soon became the first Danish king of all England as Edmund died shortly after signing the treaty. Canute proved to be a good king ruling justly, building churches and, whilst he also ruled the Danish homelands, he was able to protect England against attacks. He died in 1035 and was buried at Winchester. Harold I then became King and reigned for five years. He was followed by Hardecanute his son and then Edward the Confessor in 1042.

Late Saxon Settlement

Some original documents and later copies survive from this period which along with archaeological discoveries, enable a much clearer picture of settlements and people's lives to be envisaged.

Within the Borough, settlements recorded on ninth and tenth century AD boundary charters are: *Wenbeorgan* (Wanborough) AD 854; *Cyseldene* (Chiseldon) AD 880; *Ellendun* (Wroughton) c. AD 890; *Mehandun* (Mannington) AD 900; *Lidgerd* (Lydiard) AD 901; *Snodeshelle* (Snodd's Hill now beneath Liden); *Lidentune* (Liddington), *Medeburne* (Medbourne) AD 940 and *Mordun* (Moredon) AD 943; *Inggenshamme* (Inglesham) c. AD 950; *Baddeburri* (Badbury) AD 958 and *Grundewylle* (Groundwell House) AD 963. Many other settlements went unrecorded, their presence only being indicated by artefactual finds.

Late eighth- to eleventh-century pottery found at Penfold Nurseries[138] and Swindon House[139] during archaeological excavations in the latter part of the 1970s, besides local products include a few fragments from kilns at Oxford and Michelmersh in Hampshire. At Earlscourt, near Wanborough, tenth- or eleventh-century pottery fragments were found during archaeological evaluations in 1999 and 2000/1 and at Stratton St. Margaret during construction work. Dredging of the River Thames between Castle Eaton, Wiltshire and Kempsford, Gloucestershire has produced many artefacts covering a long time span indicating the presence of an ancient river crossing. Amongst the finds are a tenth-century AD iron spearhead, iron axe and adze heads and an iron stirrup with silver inlay.

Late Saxon Activity at Lower Wanborough

Around 1902 on the Roman town site at Lower Wanborough a farm worker found a gold ring within the field in which the Roman *mansio* and bath house were located. Hidden beneath stone flagging, the ninth century AD ring may well have been from one of those buildings that may still have been standing and in use. It is inscribed 'BUREDRUD' followed by alpha and omega symbols and Celtic crosses.[140] Such a ring is an Episcopal ornament which is conferred during the rite of consecration and is commonly regarded as a symbol of the betrothal of a bishop to his church. A mid eleventh-century spurious charter that records the bounds of Wanborough and Little Hinton parishes notes boundary markers on the eastern edge of the Roman town: *Ham Dic* (farm boundary ditch); *Heafod Stoccas* (head stakes); *Dorca* (River Dorcan); *Ealdanig Dic* (the old island meadow boundary ditch) and *Smita* (River Cole).[141] Head stakes, as the name implies, were markers on which heads of criminals were displayed following execution.

Fig. 97. Inscription on an Episcopal ring from Lower Wanborough

Late Saxon/Early Medieval Churches

Some of the old parish churches in the Borough existed in some form prior to the end of this period, but rebuilds and alterations have largely concealed or destroyed the evidence. Amongst these, Inglesham Church dedicated to St John the Baptist, has a late Saxon core which was added to around 1205. Set into the south chapel's internal south wall but originally located outside, is a late Saxon Madonna and child relief with

Fig. 98. Carving of Madonna and child, Inglesham

a later sun dial carved on it. At St Swithun's Church, Little Hinton, the tower and nave architecturally may be of late Saxon or early Norman date, as is likely the font which had been carved in several phases. Depicted are columns, interwoven ribbons, birds, fish, a curled serpent and a wolf from whose mouth coiling foliage sprouts. A carved stone incorporated into Rodbourne Cheney Church tower's external north wall has a ninth- or tenth-century AD window-head, whilst inset into the north nave's west wall a cross shaft is believed to be from a late Saxon or early medieval preaching cross. Chiseldon Church was granted, in a charter to the New Minster at Winchester in AD 903. Incorporated in the south aisle's outer wall internally are several Anglo-Saxon carved stone fragments and in a nave column the top of a window. The presence of a church at Wroughton is demonstrated by the mention of a church wall in the bounds of Ellendune appended to a charter of AD 956.[142]

Fig. 99. Detail from the font at Little Hinton

13
Medieval (AD 1066-1485)

Norman Conquest
William Duke of Normandy (born c.1028, died 1087) in 1066 laid claim to the English crown following the death of Edward the Confessor. However Harold Godwinson (born c.1022 died 1066) had been crowned first. William gathered an army and set sail, landing on the south coast. Harold had just defeated his brother Tostig, another claimant to the throne, and his supporter the Norwegian King Haradrada and his army at Stamford Bridge, when he heard of William's invasion. Harold and his men hurried to confront the threat and in the ensuing battle at Hastings Harold was killed and the English army was beaten. William was crowned on Christmas Day 1066 at Westminster Abbey despite continued resistance mostly in the north. This led in the winter of 1069-70 to the '*Harrowing of the North*' when William's army burnt whole villages, slaughtered the inhabitants, destroyed livestock and food stores, and salted the land. Of the people who escaped the carnage it is said that 100,000 later died of hunger and some even resulted to cannibalism.

Medieval Social Order
William, as king, headed a social pyramid with un-free peasants at the bottom. Noblemen received from the king gifts of land in return for military support (*knight's fee*). The aristocracy in turn had ordinary freemen bonded to them by similar ties. This was the system known as *feudalism*, essential to which was the concept of the manor, which released knights from work on their farms to fight for the king. Work was carried out on the manor, usually containing a single village, by the tenants who held lands from the lord and who were given protection in return for service on his or her land. *Villeins* (villagers) made up the main element of a settlement's population. They swore fealty to their lord but enjoyed no rights under common law. The lord could evict

MEDIEVAL   141

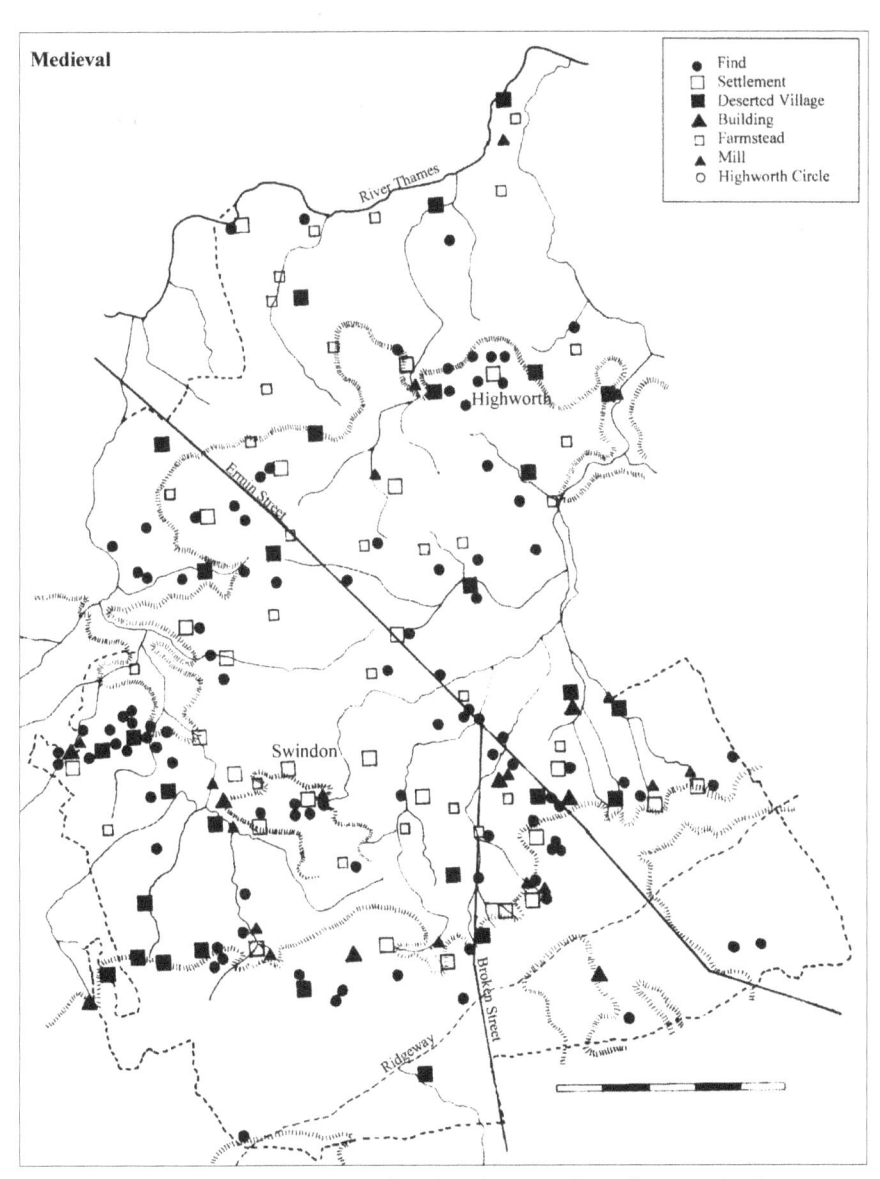

Fig. 100. Distribution map of medieval sites and artefacts (scale 5km)

them from their fields, increase rents or impose *tallage* (tax) on them as he saw fit. Despite this, they could become successful farmers in their own right, holding between ten and forty acres. Below *villeins* were *cottars* (cottagers), who had no more than five acres and whose dues to the lord were different. A *cottar* might work as a ploughman

Fig. 101. 'Ridge and Furrow' in pasture at Liddington

for his lord in return for the right to use his lord's plough and team. *Bordars* (smallholders), middle class peasants, usually had more land than a cottager but less than a *villein*. Superior to *villeins* were freemen, but legal free status did not necessarily mean superior wealth, as a rich *villein* could employ a poor freeman. Their dues to the lord tended to be of a more administrative order. The lowest was a slave who owed personal service to another and could not move home, work, change allegiance, or buy or sell without permission.

Swindon Borough at the Domesday

A picture of the existing settlement is presented by the *Domesday Book* of 1086, a pattern that is still identifiable today. Commissioned by King William this survey of all the land and resources in his realm, was to know what financial and military resources could be drawn on.

Varying greatly in size, late eleventh-century English manorial estates followed an ancient pattern of isolated farms, hamlets and tiny villages scattered over most of the cultivatable land. The old patchwork pattern of small rectangular fields established in the Bronze Age gave way to an open field system. In this system large unenclosed fields were divided into furlongs of around 200m wide and 220m long, which were further subdivided into long narrow strips called selions or ridges that consisted of about 0.2 hectares (0.5 acre).

Within the Borough of Swindon twenty-four manors existed in 1086 lying within seven *Hundreds* (large administrative subdivisions of land).[143] They were populated by 246 villagers, 34 cottagers, 191 smallholders and 1 Frenchman. Also there were 22 mills with presumably 22 millers, which made a total of 483 heads of households. To this can be added 73 slaves. Allowing for resident landowners, wives, children and elderly folk as well as nuns, monks and priests, and seemingly a few hamlets that were missed out, it is probable that the Borough had a population of around 2,500. The largest settlement was Wroughton with around 304 people, followed by Chiseldon with approximately 260 then Liddington, having roughly 192. Swindon came eighth with an estimated population of 92 and Highworth twenty-first which had about 24 people.

Medieval Castles

Most of the estate owners built manorial buildings to live in. A few with the king's consent, built castles with which to protect their possessions. During this period just after the conquest, castles comprised earthworks and wooden buildings protected by timber palisades. The commonest

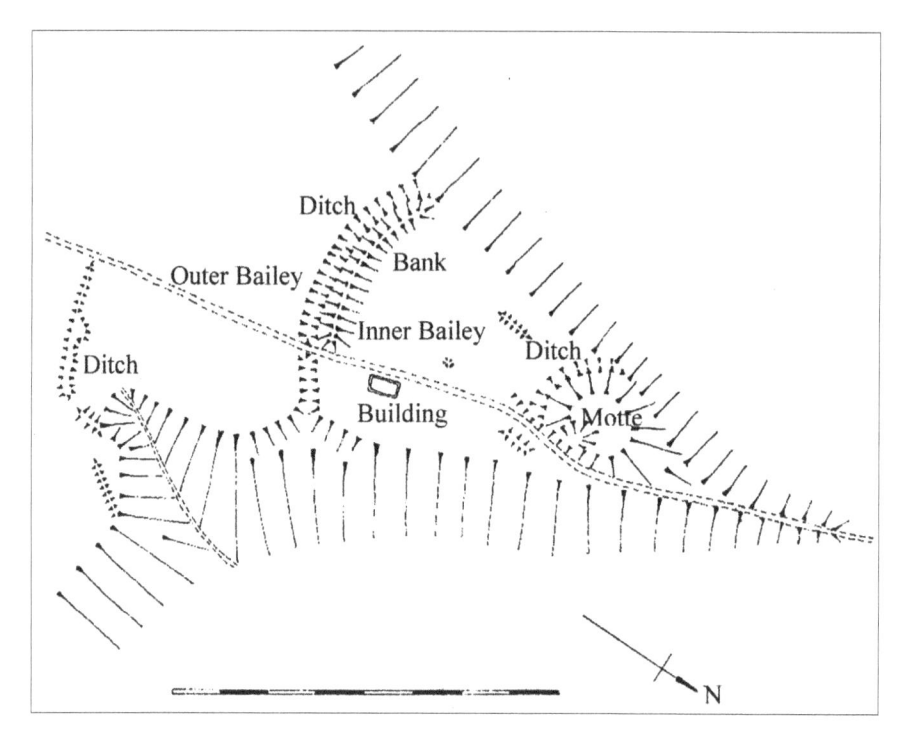

Fig. 102. Plan of the motte and bailey castle at Bincknoll (scale 80m)

form is a conical earthen mound surmounted by a tower (*motte*) with an attached fortified enclosure (*bailey*) containing ancillary buildings.

Only one possible castle is evidenced within Swindon Borough, at Stanton Fitzwarren, with a few others being located nearby: Lewisham Castle on Aldbourne Chase; Norwood Castle at Oaksey and the nearest is Bincknoll Castle in Broad Hinton parish on the Borough's western boundary.[144] At Stanton a small earthen mound, known as a *motte*, can be seen surrounded by watercourses just off Mill Lane. Bordering the River Thames, Castle Eaton's name implies the former existence there of such a fortress, but remains and documentation are lacking.

Possibly partly of Iron Age origin, the scheduled earthworks at Bincknoll take advantage of a narrow spur of land which sticks out from the chalk escarpment. The 3.2m high and 52m diameter flat-topped *motte* is somewhat damaged by chalk quarrying and is bordered to the south by a deep ditch. It is positioned at the tip of a triangular enclosure, known as a *bailey*, whose outer south-facing defensive ditch and bank, the latter partly quarried away, crosses the steep sided promontory. Within

MEDIEVAL

the *bailey* the grass-covered walls of two undated rectangular buildings are discernible as are other features. The bank of an outer *bailey* is just discernible further to the south. This bank has been largely quarried for its chalk make-up but appears to have originally been quite substantial like the inner *bailey* bank which is about 1.5m high. Finds from the site include medieval pottery fragments and a gilt bronze casket mount strip. This castle was built for Gilbert of Breteuil, a Norman knight and companion of and possibly a cousin of the king. It lay at the centre of five neighbouring estates which belonged to him in Bincknoll, Clyffe Pypard and the Broad Hinton parishes.[145]

Fig. 103. Bincknoll Castle motte and ditch

Medieval Churches

By the time of the *Domesday* many of the settlements which were referred to would have had a church. Unfortunately these buildings were seldom included in the survey and within the Borough only that at Highworth is. Besides those previously referenced above late Saxon, early medieval or Norman features such as door and chancel arches, fonts, columns and window surrounds are evident in the parish churches of South Marston, Blunsdon Saint Andrew, Bishopstone, Wroughton, Castle Eaton, Hannington, Stanton Fitzwarren and Liddington.[146] Of particular note within Highworth Church, a fine eleventh-century *tympanum* (a semi-circular or triangular carving placed over an entrance) exists which depicts Samson fighting a lion. The churches of Wanborough, Swindon and Lydiard Tregoze are referred to in eleventh- or twelfth-century documents. A church at Draycot Foliate mentioned in a document c.1210 was demolished in 1572[147] and the stone was used in building work on Chiseldon Church. The parish churches of Broad Blunsdon and Stratton Saint Margaret exhibit thirteenth-century features but in all probability have earlier origins.

Fig. 104. Norman Tympanum in Highworth Church

Due to their listed status, and the sanctity of their graveyards, little excavation has been carried out in or around these churches. Only rarely when essential building work is undertaken the opportunity arises to discover more about their origins and history through archaeology. In 2006 it became expedient to cut a drainage channel to alleviate damp

MEDIEVAL

Fig. 105. Holy Rood Church, The Lawns Swindon

Fig. 106. Excavation at Holy Rood Church in The Lawns Swindon

on the north wall of the chancel of Holy Rood Church which stands in The Lawns, Swindon.[148] Excavated by the author and Mogs Boon, this hand-cut channel revealed a lime plaster on the chancel wall, a former vestry wall foundation and demolition debris. Finds included medieval stone roof and fired clay ridge tiles; fragments of architectural stone; eighteenth- and nineteenth-century iron coffin fittings; as well as Roman, Saxon and medieval pottery. The fabric of the clay ridge tiles and medieval pottery show that they were made on the known kiln sites of Minety[149] and Nash Hill,[150] both in North Wiltshire. A document of 1154 recording the giving of the church by the Lord of the Manor Robert Pont de l'Arche to the Southwick Augustinian priory in Hampshire, is the first reference to its existence.[151] At its most extensive this comprised a chancel, a side chapel, a nave, side aisles, porches to the north and south, a tower and a vestry. After the building of Christ Church on the northern edge of Old Town in 1851-2, which was needed due to an increasing congregation, Holy Rood was abandoned and largely demolished.

Fig. 107. St Swithun's Church Little Hinton

Inglesham Church is of particular importance due to the survival of medieval paintings on many of its internal walls. An archaeological evaluation in 2007 within the nave uncovered stone paved floors relating to construction in the twelfth or thirteenth century. Fragments found of *encaustic* glazed floor tiles, which have an impressed design filled with slip before glazing and firing, include two made on the Naish Hill tile kilns at Lacock, Wiltshire in the late thirteenth or early fourteenth century.[152]

Recent archaeological test pits cut by the author and Mogs and Jonathon Boon around the tower of Little Hinton Church revealed a sandstone chamfered plinth overlying massive sarsen foundations. Finds here include: Roman, Saxon and medieval pottery, as well as a charnel pit. A survey of the interior showed that within the south aisle at its eastern end many late thirteenth-century decorated floor tiles had been laid. Their jumbled pattern and worn state show that they had been originally laid elsewhere, perhaps in the chancel or nave. Combined, some tiles formed circular patterns depicting floral motifs, hybrids (half-man, half-bird), winged wyverns and crosses; whilst others standing alone depict shields, multiple triangles, fleurs-de-lis and the 'Green Man'. They are attributable to a group of tile makers given the name 'Wessex School' who, based on finds distribution, had kilns in the Salisbury area.[153] It is considered that in medieval art the 'Green Man', depicted partly concealed by foliage, is meant as a warning about the devil's entrapment of the unwary.[154] His portrayal is fairly common within the Borough and examples include two nineteenth-century stone carvings on Chiseldon Church exterior, a timber roof carving in the interior and Victorian tiles in Bishopstone Church. The latter is a copy of the medieval Wessex School 'Green Man' tile.

Fig. 108. The 'Green Man' carving on a roof beam in Chiseldon Church

Other Medieval Religious Establishments

No medieval monasteries existed within Swindon Borough but a few monastic properties did. Run by lay-brothers at Burderop near Chiseldon, a grange (an agricultural estate centred about a manor house) belonged to Hyde Abbey. The lay-brothers took vows of obedience to the abbot and were chiefly responsible for managing the land and animals to supply the abbey with food, clothing, utensils and building materials. In 1995 archaeological excavation in front of Burderop House revealed sarsen stone foundations assumed to be part of the grange.[155] It is said that a monastic grange existed within the King's Manor at *Margrete Stratton* (Stratton St Margaret) and that an Alien Cell of Benedictine Monks existed there,[156] but these await confirmation. Cells were a residence of several monks not lay brothers, as on a grange, although they too exploited an estate for the benefit of its distant mother house. The 'Highworth Rolls' record that in the latter half of the thirteenth century the Augustinian Priory of Bradenstoke and the Hospitallers' preceptory of Quenington held lands in Stratton.[157] It is also recorded that the monks of Farleigh had an estate at South Marston.[158]

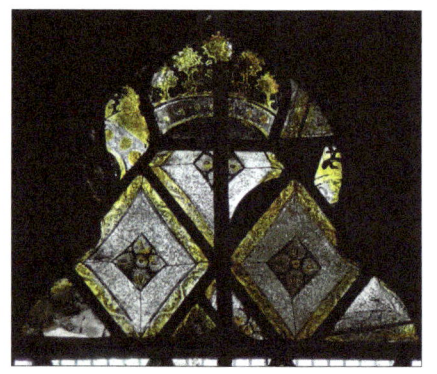

Fig. 109. Medieval window glass in Chiseldon Church

Medieval Moated Houses

Within Wanborough parish lay three moated sites: Hall Place; Cold Court and Earlscourt. Hall Place, the scheduled site of a large mansion, is located on the eastern edge of Wanborough village just below the chalk escarpment.[159] Here are earthworks of three large platforms, the lowest of which is bordered by two large ponds separated by a causeway. Also a possible moat and walling of a 20m by 10m building are discernible. Adjacent in 1987, a little to the west, cutting of a pipe trench for a gas main revealed a sarsen walled building and medieval pottery. It is said that in the field known as 'Ambrose' where the medieval house site lies,

MEDIEVAL   151

Fig. 110. Thomas and Edith Polton brass, dated 1418, Wanborough Church

a chapel dedicated to that saint existed. Ambrose born at Trier in about AD 337, was the son of Ambrosius Aurelius praetorian prefect of Gaul. He became Bishop of Milan in AD 374 and died in AD 397. Hall Place was the home of the Polton family. Thomas Polton's and his wife Edith's burials in 1418 are recorded on a brass on the floor of St Andrew's Church, Wanborough.

In Wanborough Marsh, Cold Court was the home of Maurice FitzMaurice, Lord of the Manor, and his wife Emily Longespée.[160] A broad deep moat enclosed an area 41m (135ft) by 30m (100ft). Contemporary documents provide evidence of buildings which lay within it. Besides the manor house there were a granary, a chapel, and a chamber and a wardrobe for the priests and the chapel ornaments. Dedicated to St Katherine, the large chapel had a chancel and more than one altar. It was founded by Emily in 1270 following the death of her husband. Demolition occurred about 1540 and its carved stone door arch was moved to Wanborough Church. Stone robbing at Cold Court in 1903 uncovered a large collection of fourteenth-century patterned tiles and a lead coffin. St Katherine was one of the most influential saints

Fig. 111. St Katherine's chapel door arch in Wanborough Church

of the late middle ages. She was born in Alexandria to a pagan family but converted to Christianity in her late teens. The Roman emperor Maxentius (AD 306-12) had her beheaded for attempting to convince him of his moral error in persecuting Christians. Emily endowed St Katherine's Chapel with 60 acres of land which lay to the south of Cold Court, thus creating the Manor of Warneage.[161] Other lands added included in 1329 Wanborough mill which stood next to Cold Court. The Warneage Manor buildings were demolished in 1926. Passmore wrote in his notebook ...'taking up the foundations of the old house, about 45 yards long from W to E much Swindon stone, sarsen and chalk, no brick worth mentioning. Some old bottles with seals....'

A forged charter claiming to be by Ethelwulf, King of Wessex (ruled AD 839 to AD 856) dated AD 854, granted an estate later called Earlscourt[162] to the Church of St Peter and Paul at Winchester. In 1423 buildings here comprised a hall, two chambers, barn, a stable and a sheepfold. Excavations and a watching brief were carried out here by Foundations Archaeology in advance of and during building work in 1999 and 2001/2. Containing Saxo-Norman pottery, a 2.5m wide and at least 0.70m linear deep ditch uncovered may represent a moat or enclosure boundary. Further discoveries include traces of stone flagging, postholes and other ditches. To the north of the existing buildings two trenches were cut as part of an archaeological evaluation by the author, prior to tree planting. These and subsequent field-walking produced numerous thirteenth- to fifteenth-century pottery fragments over a fairly extensive area, indicating a former village site associated with the manor.[163]

Within Wroughton a square moat is visible at the junction of Priors Hill and the High Street. Little is known about it, but in 1993 when the ditch was cleaned out and enlarged medieval pottery was found. It is likely that a manor house of early medieval date enclosed by the moat was demolished in the late medieval period. In 1488 a substantial manor house is recorded as having had a great gate, giving entrance to a courtyard and a large barn. It stood adjacent to the moat's eastern side.[164] In 1649 this manor house is noted as having had a hall, a parlour, seven chambers, various smaller rooms and many outhouses as well as a dovecot, a fishpond and a large moat.[165] It was demolished in 1961 following a terrible fire.

MEDIEVAL   153

Fig. 112. Numbers 1 and 2 High Street Highworth (the old manor house)

Medieval Manorial Buildings

No observable standing medieval manorial buildings are evident within the Borough. However some fairly ancient structures do exist, so perhaps a detailed architectural survey would identify medieval buildings incorporated within the existing houses, cottages and barns. Most notable are numbers 1 and 2 in the High Street, Highworth (the Old Manor House) although dated 1656 could be a recasting of a much older structure incorporating a fifteenth-century hall. Other buildings which may encapsulate earlier remains include: the Manor Farmhouse at Hannington Wick which appears to date to the later seventeenth century; a small manor house at Liddington of mid seventeenth-century date largely restored in the nineteenth century; and Broad Blunsdon manor house in the High Street which is thought to date to the early seventeenth century with late seventeenth-century additions.[166]

Near Wroughton at Quidhampton Wood is the site of the medieval village of *Quidhampton* and this was first recorded in 1249. Its name translates as 'dung house' perhaps meaning a farm with good manuring.[167] Referred to in later deeds as a manor one document of 1324 mentions a hall, ox-house, dovecote and court. Village traces and the manor house were largely buried in a great landslide following a violent storm in 1825.[168]

A manorial building which grew to become a substantial mansion is Lydiard House in West Swindon.[169] The present house when viewed from the front appears to be a rather grand structure of the eighteenth century. An inscription in the attic records that it was rebuilt in 1743 by John Viscount St. John (died 1748) who had married Anne Furnese a wealthy heiress. In fact the house was only partly remodelled. A map circa 1700 and an examination of the existing building showed that it had developed from a late medieval halled-house with solar and kitchen wings. In 1086 the estate was held by Alfred of Marlborough but soon passed to Harold, son of Ralph, Earl of Hereford, who gave Lydiard Church to Gloucester Abbey in 1100. In 1256 the existence of a hunting park at Lydiard Tregoze is indicated as the King gave the owner of the manor Robert Tregoze, Sheriff of Wiltshire, some deer from Braydon Forest to restock it.

Fig. 113. Lydiard Tregoze House

Fig. 114. Overshot mill depicted in the Luttrell Psalter c. 1320–1340

Mills

Of the 22 mills recorded within the Borough in the Domesday Book and undoubtedly more that were built later on, few remain in evidence today, the last ceasing production in the early twentieth century. Single mills existed in 1086 as listed in the Domesday Book on the manors of: Castle Eaton; Lus Hill; Blunsdon; Stratton St Margaret; Westlecott; Chiseldon; Badbury; Wanborough and Widhill. Additionally Swindon, Hannington and Liddington had two mills and Wroughton had a remarkable seven mills, all apparently located on the same stream.[170]

There are three main types of mill so named according to where the water struck the vertical millwheel – undershot, breastshot and the more efficient overshot. A rare fourth type had a horizontal wheel.

Slightly north of Little Hinton an earthwork known as 'Millbank' bordered on the east side by the *Smita* stream, has remains of a substantial sarsen stone dam in its bed and banks.[171] In 2003, adjacent to the dam, an exploratory trench was cut within a deep and extensive hollow which had clearly been cut into the earthwork. Revealed were the base of a stone wall and a chalk floor separated by a gulley, which contained late sixteenth- or early seventeenth-century pottery. Only an extensive excavation will confirm the use, size and layout of this building, but from its location next to the dam and standing on the hollow's base it is likely that it was a mill constructed to allow water to flow onto the millwheel top – an overshot mill. To the south of the hollow a second trench cut into the earthwork revealed a few late medieval pottery fragments associated with patches of chalk flooring, in all probability these were traces of an undershot mill that the other mill had replaced. Within the hollow, the building was demolished and the hollow partially infilled in the late seventeenth century. The fill contained clay pipe and pottery fragments, animal bone and surprisingly much iron slag. Notably some mills were adapted or constructed to work forging hammers.

Further down the *Smita* a little south of Hinton Marsh Farm, a mill is indicated on an Ordnance Survey map of 1829 and by remnants there of a demolished nineteenth-century, brick-built structure and channelling.[172] Andrew and Dury's map of 1773 however, positions a mill north of the lane adjacent to the farm, presumably a predecessor of the mill to the south. Indeed it is recorded that Hinton Marsh Farm and perhaps thus the adjacent mill, suffered a disastrous fire at the beginning of the nineteenth century. The earliest record of a mill in Hinton

Fig. 115. Overgrown brick channelling of the later mill at Hinton Marsh Farm

Fig. 116. Traces of a stone dam on the Smita stream Little Hinton

parish is in 1248 when it formed part of the manorial estate. Later fifteenth- to nineteenth-century documents refer to two mills, 'Berry Mill' and 'Cuttle Mill'.[173]

A vital aspect of medieval life, mills and millers are well documented but were not always for the milling of grain. Upper Mill near Liddington Manor gained some notoriety as Thomas Chauler was torn to pieces by its mill wheel in about 1248.[174] A verdict of misadventure was declared. The mill wheel as the instrument causing the death, was valued by the coroner's court at three shillings. The mill owner was expected to pay this amount by law as a forfeit (*deodand*), if he could not his township was held responsible. D*eodands* were paid to the crown and were supposed to be put to some pious use. The mill remained in use until the early twentieth century, as did a second mill known as Lower Mill a little to the north on the same stream. An incident in 1275 shows that a mill existed at Lydiard Tregoze, as Robert the village miller had fifteen of his sheep held in a pen.[175] Without his knowledge two perpetrators, Maud Sproet of *Haydon Wyke* and John de Babbe Cary, skinned them and carried of their fells (skins). This Robert is further recorded at Lydiard in 1287.[176] John the miller of Stanton Fitzwarren and his wife Isabel la Berde in 1303, accused William Whitheved of North Widhill and Bartholomew le Mariner of stealing goods to the value of 22 pence. A jury found them not guilty so John and Isabel were taken and fined 20 pence.[177]

The 'Highworth Hundred Rolls' record a number of millers who include: Robert the miller from Stratton in 1280 and 1284; Walter the South Marston miller from 1275 to 1285, William the Hampton miller in 1279; Roger the miller from Widhill in 1283 and Robert the miller at Highworth in 1280.[178]

Documented Swindon mills include two in Even Swindon recorded in a settlement manuscript made by Robert Avenel and Christine his wife in 1313.[179] In 1339 a mill, dwelling house, other buildings and land at Eastcott and Nethercott were conveyed to William Godhyne and Margery his wife by Robert de Colcote and his wife Maud.[180] The location of another mill valued at four shillings belonging to Odin the Chamberlain mentioned in the Domesday Book, is uncertain but may have been where William Kemble a Swindon baker erected an overshot mill in 1755/6.[181] This lay west of the Holy Rood Church in The Lawns

Fig. 117. Nineteenth-century painting of Swindon Mill, The Lawns Old Town

and was supplied with water from a pond fed by the spring called 'Church Well'. Kemble's mill was demolished in 1852.

Other recorded mills in the Borough in 1263 include one at Fresden near Highworth which was owned by Baldwin de Isle. It was rented by Sampson Foliate and valued at 20 shillings a year, which was payable to the priory of Garinges.[182] A document relating to Adam de Stratton shows that he owned two mills at Sevenhampton in 1271. One was rented by William Aylmer along with a house and 30 acres of land and was valued at 20 shillings annually, whilst the other rented by Robert the Miller with similar property was valued at 12 shillings a year.[183] On the death of Henry de Cerne in 1296 a document showed that he owned a mill valued at 13 shillings 4 pence annually at Draycot Foliate.[184] It is described as a winter mill, so presumably only sufficient water was present in the stream for winter operation. A document called a 'Feet of Fines' of Edward I records a dispute over a mill and land at Chiseldon, between Richard de Chuseldun and Philip atte Mulle in 1305.[185] Another document from the same source shows that a mill disputed by William Fiz Waryn and John Bernard and Joan his wife existed at *Brodebluntesdon* (Broad Blunsdon) in 1324.[186] A mill either in *Bluntesdon Gay* (Blunsdon

MEDIEVAL

Gay) or *Westwydyhull* (West Widhill) is also referred to in the 'Feet of Fines' and concerns an Adam de Bromesdon and Agnes his wife in 1305 and 1308.[187]

Once fed by a tributary of the River Ray at West Leaze on the edge of Swindon's Wichelstowe development, is the likely site of Westlecott Mill defined today by two adjacent irregular shaped mounds north of Mill Lane.[188] It was first recorded in 1086 and was valued at 5 shillings in 1262. A mill was leased here in 1687 by Thomas Goddard esquire of Swindon to George Thorne a Swindon baker for four years, with toll of grinding corn and with meadow adjoining.[189] Almost certainly this was a later mill building that was shown on the Goddard Estate map of 1763 south of the lane and was demolished in the early twentieth century. The sites of the seven mills recorded in AD 1086 at Wroughton are unknown. However two mill buildings now converted to homes exist – Mill House in Perry's Lane and Old Mill in Baker's Road. Both are of relatively recent date but in all probability they stand on the site of earlier mill buildings.[190] Mill House was recorded as the home of Nicholas De Moledino and Richard Atte Mulle in 1412.

Windmills

Windmills made an appearance in England *c.*1180, the earliest type being the post mill. This was so named due to the large upright post on which the mill's body containing the milling machinery was balanced. By mounting it this way the mill could be turned by hand to face the prevailing wind. First, the large post was sunk into the ground and then an earthen mound built around it for added support. Finally the timber superstructure and workings were constructed around the post.

The 'Court Rolls' of Adam de Stratton mentions a windmill at Highworth in 1275.[191] It is also recorded in 1279 when the parson of Highworth complained that Walter le Wayte had ploughed or dug up the highway above the windmill.[192] A windmill was still standing at Highworth in 1740 when a great storm of wind almost demolished it.[193] 'Wiltshire Inquisitions Post Mortems' refer to a windmill on Almer de Valance's Swindon estate in 1324.[194] In 1287 a windmill worth 6 shillings 8 pence stood on the holding of John de Mohun at Elcombe. This was noted again in 1348.[195] Roger le Writel had, in Broad Blunsdon and Chelworth one windmill, one dwelling and land.

It is not clear though whether the mill stood in Chelworth or Blunsdon. Also recorded is a windmill on the Wanborough estate of Amauri de St. Amand in 1310.[196] Apart from the Swindon medieval mill, which is considered to have stood in Wood Street at the rear of the King's Arms Hotel, none of these windmill sites have been located.

Fig. 118. Windmill depicted in the Luttrell Psalter c. 1320–1340

Peasant Houses

Peasants lived in small timber framed cottages usually with a garden for growing vegetables such as cabbage, peas and leeks; or herbs or on larger plots in longhouses. Constructed in either stone, timber, wattle and daub, clay or a combination of these they were usually roofed in thatch, shingles, or rarely in stone tiles. In a longhouse, draught animals occupied one end and humans the other, separated by a cross passage. Outside there may have been a barn, vegetable garden, animal pens and orchard. No such structures have yet been identified with certainty in the Borough. However at Rushey Platt a rectangular building having stone walls 0.6m thick, may have been a longhouse. This was cut through in 1907 during construction of a brickyard. Passmore found in association with this some twelfth- to fourteenth-century pottery sherds and a bronze annular brooch.

Villages

Many medieval settlements now underlie their present-day equivalent, their presence only discernible by finds from gardens, during construction work, or through archaeological excavation. At Castle Eaton (*Ettone* 1086), thirteenth- to fourteenth-century sherds were found in the garden of the Red Lion Inn and in gardens to the east of Saint Mary's Church. Dredged from the river nearby came a bronze twelfth-century seal, a bronze bell and a silver penny, as well as decorated floor tiles and thirteenth- to fourteenth-century pottery. Devizes Museum Day Book records iron objects, pottery and bone fragments, two coins and an iron ring from Hannington. On the northern edge of Swindon, an archaeological evaluation and a subsequent watching brief in 2004 by the author took place at 'The Grange', Blunsdon St Andrew (*Bluntesdon Seynt Andreu* 1281).[197] It revealed several ditches and fence postholes which probably represented property boundaries; much pottery; an early fifteenth-century iron spur; and also the bones of horse, sheep/goat, cattle, dog, bird and fowl. Pits containing twelfth- to thirteenth-century pottery and an occupation layer of similar date were discovered during building alterations at Broad Blunsdon (*Brade Bluntesdon* 1234). A householder digging a pit in a garden near to the Calley Arms in Wanborough (*Wenbeorgan* AD 854) also discovered numerous medieval pottery sherds there.

A large medieval village identified by contemporary documentary evidence existed at Lydiard Tregoze, but there were few indications as to its location. Feasibly it is in the vicinity of the existing church and mansion. A few medieval pottery sherds have been found in the churchyard and in the area just to the east. Also following the planting of a hedge north of the present drive, several pottery sherds were discovered and the backfill of a lighting cable trench in front of the church produced two cooking pot rim fragments, one of eleventh- or twelfth-century date and the other of fourteenth- or fifteenth-century date. Perhaps the old driveway a little south of the present drive was a former village street? An archaeological investigation by Wessex Archaeology in 2004 near the lake recorded late medieval activity through finds of: animal bone, shell, nails and pottery fragments.[198] Alternatively, the village street extended southwards from the former manor house, passing through an area where a spread of pottery fragments has been found. The cutting of a path through this area in 2008 revealed a fairly extensive area of small stones. On its surface and embedded into it there were sherds of medieval pottery, animal bone and oyster shells.[199] An excavation undertaken by the author in 2001 within the walled garden to the northwest of the house, also produced many thirteenth- to fifteenth-century pottery sherds and also bones of pig, sheep, dog, horse and cattle. Also revealed was a late medieval drainage or boundary ditch.[200]

Swindon

Many former medieval villages recorded in ancient documents have been swallowed up by the modern town of Swindon (*Swindone* in 1086). They include: Mannington (*Mehandun* AD 900), Eastcott (*Estcote* 1276), Westcott (*Westcot* 1289), Nethercott (*Neyerkote* 1252), Even Swindon (*Theveneswyndon* 1237), Rodbourne Cheney (*Redborne* 1086), Shaw (*Shaghe* 1332), Moredon (*Mordun* AD 943), Walcot (*Walecote* 1086), Groundwell (*Grundewylle* AD 962), Upper Stratton (*Netherestratton* 1281), Stratton St Margaret (*Muchelesratton* 1281), Broome Manor (*Brome* 1242), Snodshill (*Snodeshelle* AD 940), Haydon Wick (*Heydonwyk* 1249), Haydon (*Haydone*) 1242) and Liddington Wick (*Ludeemewyke* 1232). Some evidence of these settlements has been forthcoming largely through archaeological excavation in advance of construction, salvage and watching briefs during building work and documentary research.

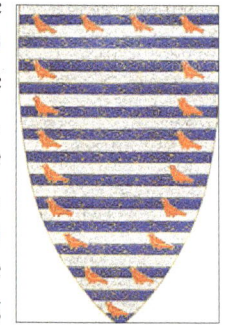

Fig. 119. William de Valance's shield

Old Swindon grew from a small hamlet which extended from Holy Rood Church in the Lawns to the Market Square into a small market town under the powerful de Valence family.[201] William de Valence

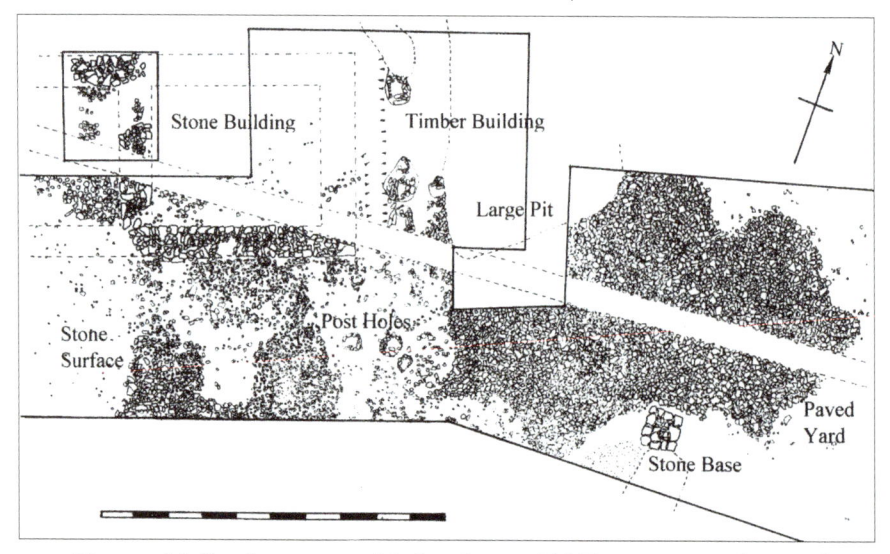

Fig. 120. Medieval structures, Market Square Old Town, excavated 1975/6 (scale 10m)

(c.1228–1296), 1st Earl of Pembroke, was a French nobleman and halfbrother of King Henry III. The 'Blakengrove Hundred Rolls' record that he had 'right of gallows and assize of bread and beer in High Swindon by grant from the crown: and has set up a new market in the vill but by what warrant they know not'. Additionally 'Close Rolls' for 1249-51 show that a deer park existed at Swindon for the lord's hunting.[202] William died at Bayonne in south-western France then ruled by England and he is buried in Westminster Abbey. Aymer his son (c. 1275-1324) who was primarily active in England, had strong connections with the French royal house and was one of the wealthiest and most powerful men of his age.[203] He died suddenly in Picardy without legal issue and Swindon, along with his many other estates, passed to his second wife Marie de St Pol who died in 1377. At that time Swindon's population had increased to 248 recorded poll tax payers[204] (those over 14 but with some exemptions), from a total population based on the 1086 Domesday survey of around 73. Archaeological, cartographical and documentary evidence demonstrates that the medieval town now occupied the High Street, Market Square, Newport Street and Wood Street. Linear burgage plots, long narrow strips of land which tenants held, are evident in property boundaries behind High, Wood and Newport Streets. These though are gradually being destroyed by modern infilling and boundary changes.

Archaeological excavations to the east of the High Street undertaken in advance of construction revealed traces of the medieval town. The earliest, in 1975-6, exposed to the rear of the Market Square, part of two adjoining thirteenth/fourteenth-century buildings – one comprising at least two rooms with walls built in stone and the other in timber.[205] The latter was defined by large stone-packed post pits. Associated with these structures a stone-paved yard had within it a small rectangular stone-built platform, perhaps being the base for a market cross. Related artefacts found included oolitic limestone and earthenware roofing tiles, and twelfth- to fifteenth-century pottery sherds. Remains of further stone and timber structures were evidenced on the Penfolds Nursery site in 1977-8[206] and earthen floors and a stone wall at the Planks and pits south of the Locarno in 2007. More pottery of mid thirteenth- to fifteenth-century date was recovered at Lloyds Bank in 1977[207] and the Hermitage in 1993.[208] Also from the latter came a fragment of late

Fig. 121. Pottery, slag, whetstone and spindle whorl from Stratton St Margaret

medieval window glass painted with a white flower having four petals surrounded by a double-lined border. A similarly painted window glass was found at a medieval hunting lodge at Ludgershall, Wiltshire.[209] Earlier discoveries include two twelfth-century pottery bowls from Wood Street (Ashmolean Museum, Oxford), a thirteenth-century cooking pot and part of another at the Goddard Arms and a handled circular bronze seal inscribed 'FLI STEFFANI'.

Evidence of the medieval settlements beneath Swindon's urban sprawl includes two adjacent sites that had survived as earthworks but these were largely destroyed by recent development: Haydon (*Haydo*ne 1242) and Haydon Wick (*Heydonwyk* 1249). Haydon was the village, whilst Haydon Wick served as its dairy farm. Archaeological trial trenching in 2003 produced evidence of drainage ditches, ponds, and a series of rubble and cobbled surfaces associated with significant quantities of mainly twelfth- and thirteenth-century pottery. Nearby traces of the medieval village of Moredon (*Mordun* AD 943) were found during an archaeological evaluation excavation on the Akers Garage site in 2000. There linear features, pits, fragments of medieval pottery and animal bone were discovered. Also at Park Farm, Moredon thirteenth-

MEDIEVAL   165

to fifteenth-century pottery sherds came from a clay and stone building platform encountered during road construction. Directly to the south of Groundwell House (*Grundewylle* AD962) evaluation trenching in 1998,[210] 1999 and 2004 revealed walls, yard surfaces and ditches associated with thirteenth- to fifteenth-century pottery fragments and animal bone. Building construction and archaeological evaluation trenching has discovered to the south of the parish church at Stratton St Margaret (*Stratone* 1086) an enclosure ditch, property boundary ditches and a low clay bank all associated with twelfth- to fifteenth-century pottery fragments. Construction of a house close by in Church Street revealed: a wide flat bottomed cutting, a packed stone layer and many fourteenth- to eighteenth-century pottery sherds. Whilst west of Ermin Street at the edge of a recreation ground the building of a boundary wall produced numerous medieval pottery sherds as did the construction of a shop and a care home in Rainer Close, west of the church. Beneath West Swindon at Wick Farm (*La Wik* in 1235) a hollow-way and house platforms were evidenced on which excavations in 1998/9 produced thirteenth- to fifteenth-century pottery sherds and an iron spearhead.

Fig. 122. Excavating a medieval building wall near the Market Square Old Town

One of the most tragic losses was the small medieval village of Mannington (*Mehandun* AD 900). Its remains survived in open pasture as house platforms and hollow-ways around Toothill Farm and extended towards Mannington House. Limited excavation took place in 1974/5 prior to its total destruction for housing. Structures revealed by excavation

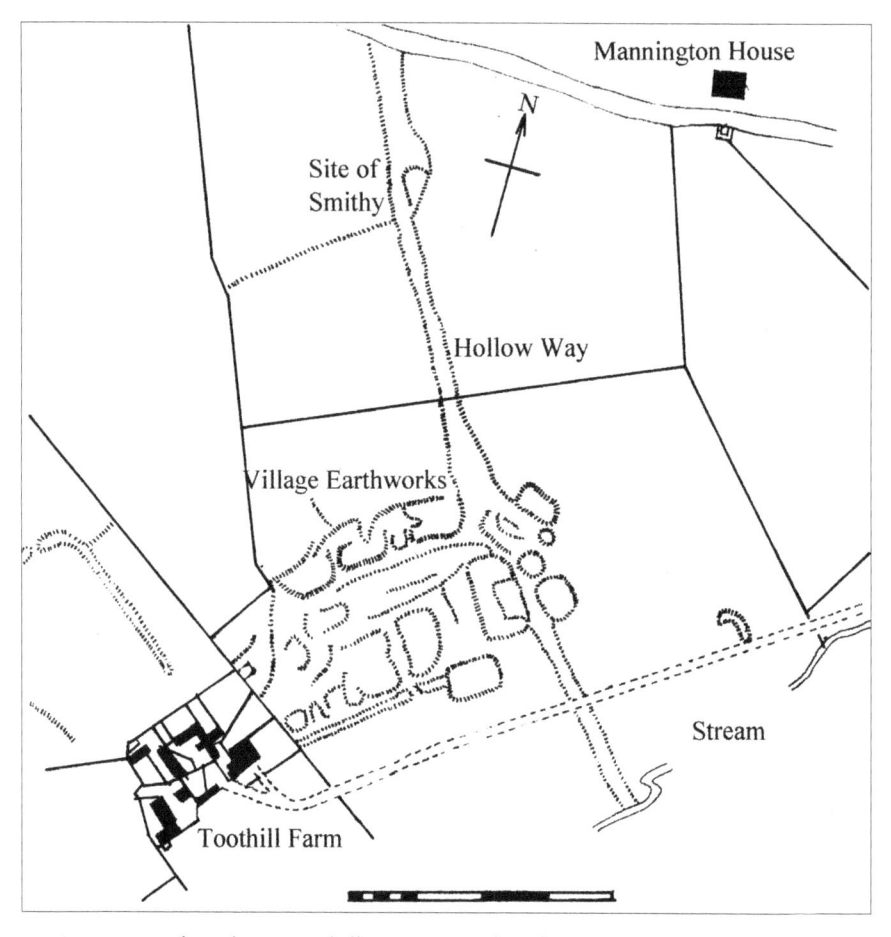

Fig. 123. Earthworks at Toothill Farm, site of medieval Mehandun (scale 100m)

were a stone lined well; the substantial stone footings of a fifteenth-century building; also traces of stone walling and flooring of a second house associated with twelfth- to fifteenth-century pottery fragments. From this building came a 6.5cm diameter early twelfth-century bronze door knocker in the shape of a human head with lentoid eyes and a late twelfth- or thirteenth-century 5cm diameter lead seal. Depicting centrally, a duck below a crescent moon the seal bears an inscription around its edge that reads 'GI?LAMTOMCTIΓHR?DA?HI???' (the T inverted). Perhaps this belonged to the Lord of the manor at that time or his bailiff. Unfortunately the manor's lordship prior to the overlordship of Baldwin, Earl of Devon (d. 1245) is unknown.[211] Various lordships and overlordships followed but none bear an appropriate name. Observation during subsequent building work revealed on the east side of a sunken way leading from Toothill Farm to Mannington House ditches, stone platforms and walling associated with pottery fragments and much iron slag, and it was thus clearly the site of a smithy.

Fig. 124. Lead seal from Toothill Farm (5cm diameter)

Fig. 125. Bronze door knocker from Toothill Farm (6.5cm diameter)

Highworth

Highworth (*Wrde* 1086) grew to include the former hamlet of Westrop (*Westrop* 1249), which lay to the south. The town's growth from a small rural community probably began under the lordship of Warin Fitzgerald the younger, hereditary chamberlain to both King Richard and King John. At the time he was granted the right to hold a weekly market on Wednesdays and an annual fair on the feast of St Michael (29th September) by King John in 1206.[212] With the marriage of Margaret, Warin Fitzgerald's only child in 1200 to Baldwin de Redvers 6th Earl of Devon, the manor together with the *hundred* (a division of a County) following Fitzgerald's death in 1216 passed into the lordship of the de Redvers family. In 1257 a further grant was made by King Henry II to Baldwin de Redvers 7th Earl of Devon (1236-62) permitting him to hold an annual fair on the feast of St Peter ad Vincula (1st August).[213] Baldwin was succeeded by his sister Isabel following his death during an expedition to France with Henry III. Highworth is recorded as being a borough having 50 tenants holding

Fig. 126. Highworth church, the west porch

whole or part burgages in 1262.[214] Medieval linear burgage plots can still be traced between the High Street, and Brewery Street and Sheep Street to Cherry Orchard. The properties that back onto the churchyard are most likely late medieval or early post-medieval infills.

Construction at the east end of Highworth Hill revealed traces of a walled enclosure with an external ditch.[215] On its cobbled paving a distinct occupation layer had accumulated. Crude stone-filled drains had served to clear the enclosed space of liquid waste and rainwater. From the lower fill of the outer ditch came fragments of cooking pots, pipkins, jugs, flagons and pans datable to fourteenth and fifteenth centuries. Close to the enclosure's southeast corner a dagger's bronze chape and a group of whetstones were found. It is feasible that the enclosure was used to pen animals prior to slaughter and perhaps during sheep shearing. To the northwest at The Cullems, construction revealed a wide scatter of twelfth- to thirteenth-century pottery sherds. Whilst in 1972 at Grove Hill in Westrop, excavation revealed pits, gullies, stone walls and a large quantity of eleventh- to twelfth-century potsherds; also animal bones and iron artefacts. In the vicinity at Coffin Close a short curving ditch, an extensive pit, and a linear feature were uncovered associated with twelfth- to fourteenth-century sherds.

Markets, Fairs and Courts
Markets and fairs could only be granted by the Crown. Their presence added much to a settlement's importance and growth. Within the Borough besides Swindon and Highworth, weekly markets and annual fairs were granted by Henry III to the manors of Hannington in 1239 and Stratton St Margaret in 1257, whilst Wanborough had an annual fair granted in 1252.[216] At Wanborough the fair sanctioned to Stephen Longespée was to be held at the manor on Whitsunday. The market and fair at Hannington allowed to Henry Trublevill and Hawyse his wife had to be held at the manor on the feast of Mary Magdalene (22 July). Granted to Baldwin de Insula, the fair at Stratton was to be held on the feast of Saint Margaret (20th July). This and the market were to take place at the manor.

Markets and fairs were events at which the manor's inhabitants could take their produce to sell and buy goods which they needed. The settlement's shopkeepers had to shut their premises and, like the other vendors, sell from stalls. The range of goods available was much larger at fairs and included goods from far and wide, as well as a variety of food and refreshments. They were usually tied to a special Christian religious occasion, usually being the feast day of the settlement's patron saint, but they could last for many days. Although the main objectives of the fairs were trade and commerce they contained some element of entertainment such as singers, musicians, acrobats, stilt walker, fools and mystery play actors. Also included were various contests such as quarter staff, wrestling and archery tournaments. Another form of amusement would have been ridiculing and mocking sentenced criminals who were placed in the stocks or pillory (whipping post). Occasionally hangings took place. Records show that an un-named thief was hung at Stratton fair in 1277 and Thomas Balle at Highworth fair.[217]

Held at various times of the year a manorial court, which all villagers had to attend or pay a fine, dealt with all but the most serious crimes. No police force existed so men were placed in groups of ten called a *tithing*. Its members had to guarantee that none of their group broke the law. If they did the group had to ensure that the alleged criminal went to the Lord's Stewards Court. In the early medieval period the accused had to face 'Trial by Ordeal'. The ordeal could be by walking over red-hot ploughshares, holding a red-hot iron or removing a stone from a pot of boiling water. Innocence was proven by a lack of injury or more commonly, the bandaged wound would be examined three days later by a priest who would pronounce that God had intervened to heal it, or that it was festering and thus the suspect was guilty thereby resulting in his/her exile or execution. After 1215 this was replaced by 'Trial by Jury'. The jury consisted of twelve male villagers who collected the evidence and decided on the accused's guilt. If guilty, they then decided on the punishment which was either a fine, placing in the stocks or pillory, mutilation or death. Very serious crimes were heard by the King's Court at intervals of several years. In Wiltshire this was held at Wilton, usually during a reigning monarch's countrywide visitation. Whilst awaiting trial the suspect was usually kept in prison.

Deserted or Shrunken Villages
Some villages have completely disappeared from the landscape and are only identifiable as distinctive mounds and hollows in pasture, or cropmarks in ploughed fields and occasionally in association with a farmhouse or two. These have been given the title 'deserted medieval villages' or if more than three inhabited buildings exist amongst the remnants 'shrunken medieval villages'.

MEDIEVAL

Research has shown that abandonment of villages occurred mainly in the fifteenth century. At this time fields cultivated for cereals and vegetables by villagers were being turned by the landowners into sheep pasture to supply the very profitable wool trade. Consequently only a few shepherds were needed to care for the animals. It was also becoming the fashion for the wealthy landowners to turn their properties into grand landscaped country mansions surrounded by hunting parks. This meant the demise of any existing village on the designated land with the villagers being evicted or resettled elsewhere. Other contributory factors that led to abandonment were soil exhaustion and disease, notably plague.

The 'Black Death',[218] one of the most devastating pandemics in human history, is widely considered to have been an outbreak of bubonic plague caused by the bacterium *Yersinia pestis* and to have started in China. Carried along the 'Silk Road' by infected travellers it reached the Crimea by 1346 and was then carried by fleas residing on black rats so it spread throughout the Mediterranean region and Europe. During the

Fig. 127. Late 13th/14th century building and infant burial at Bishopstone

summer months of 1348 the first outbreak swept across the south of England in bubonic form, before mutating into the even more terrifying pneumonic form with the commencement of winter. It is estimated to have killed around 10-15% of the population. By the end of 1350 it had subsided but never fully died out. Outbreaks continued throughout the remainder of the fourteenth century and much of the fifteenth century. In 1471 it again killed around 10-15% of the population while the plague death rate of 1479 and 1480 may have been as high as 20%.

Many 'deserted medieval villages' are present in the Borough. One of the best preserved lies at the southern foot of Swindon Hill at its western end. This site at West Leaze was recorded as *Wichelestote* in 1086.[219] A scheduled monument, it is bounded to the north by the River Ray and to the south, east and west by a boundary ditch. The main village street is defined by a deeply worn hollow-way on the long axis of the settlement. On either side are raised platforms representing house and outbuilding locations. Between the raised platforms are traces of former garden plots. The settlement is surrounded on the east, west and south sides by extensive areas of preserved medieval strip fields.

Adjacent to Fresden Manor near Highworth and also preserved under pasture is the scheduled 'deserted medieval village' of *Fersedon* first recorded in the 'Inquisition Post Mortem' of Baldwin de Insula in 1263.[220] Clearly defined by a hollow-way the settlement's main street is initially aligned east–west before turning sharply south. Flanking the northern and eastern sides are raised platforms up to 1m high which vary in size from 48m long and 30m wide to 20m long and 12m wide. These define the sites of houses and their outbuildings. Also traceable here is a mill site with its leat and millrace which is recorded in the inquisition.

A 'deserted medieval village' was found to the south of Hinton Marsh Farm, near to a later mill site. It was initially revealed on old aerial photographs as linear earthworks in a grassed field, but was subsequently ploughed. Recent fieldwalking evidenced many thirteenth- and fourteenth-century pottery sherds, animal bone and much building stone. Not far away at Foxbridge near Wanborough, the site of a small hamlet has been identified by the discovery of thirteenth- to fifteenth-century medieval sherds in plough soil and in an adjacent grassed paddock several platforms and hollows.

'Shrunken medieval villages' have been identified by the author and Mogs Boon through existing earthworks and excavation north of Bishopstone and nearby at Little Hinton. At the latter, a trench cut through the earthworks revealed stone footings of two buildings. Also found were numerous animal bones, thirteenth- to fourteenth-century pottery fragments and whetstones. The presence of sheep and cattle bones fit in well with the historical documentary evidence. For example in 1210 when over 200 sheep of various types and ten cows, as well as numerous calves were accounted for on the *demesne* (land owned and used by the manor). The finding of chiefly mature animal bones indicate that the animals were not raised solely for meat but mainly for long-term products such as wool from sheep and milk from cows. Demonstrating the latter is the recording in 1273 that on the *demesne*, 38 winter and 173 summer cheeses were produced. Many bones were gnawed by dogs suggesting that they were common on the site probably being used as watch dogs, for hunting game and rounding up of stock.[221] Similar evidence was obtained in a trial excavation at Bishopstone. Here, amongst earthworks and adjacent to the *Lenta* stream, a late thirteenth- to late fourteenth-century semi-sunken stone walled building was partly excavated. In its southwest corner an infant burial was found. Adjacent to the building a hearth, slag and furnace walling indicate that iron smelting and smithing had taken place. Nearby in Bishopstone village excavation prior to development, has revealed three eleventh- to thirteenth-century ditched enclosures and a well.[222]

The scheduled earthworks of Inglesham (*Inggeneshamme* in a *c*. AD 950 charter)[223] comprise a central curving hollow-way which branches west towards the church and north towards a tributary of the Thames. Running parallel is another hollow-way with a third occupying the lane from the main road to the existing hamlet. Irregular house platforms survive to a height of 0.75m to the south of the central hollow-way. Traces exist on the surface and on aerial photographs that the village continued south of the lane but there it was levelled by cultivation. Finds include worked stone, pottery, querns, ironwork and animal bone.

Development threatens the small 'shrunken medieval village' of Badbury Wick (*Baddenham Wyke* in 1425) which as shown by a ground survey in 2004 comprises earthwork platforms, hollow-ways, ditches and substantial steep slopes. The northernmost earthworks appear to represent a regular planned layout of properties composed of ten platforms served by a hollow-way. Present day buildings including Badbury Wick House, lie at the centre of the settlement. Adjacent to the main drive near to a pond steep slopes seem to define three sides of a rectangular moat-like enclosure. A series of well-defined platforms to the south include two of substantial proportions and a substantial ditch which marks the limit of the settlement and also served as a hollow-way for three additional platforms.

Further shrunken or deserted medieval settlement sites visible include Salthrop House (*Salteharpe* in 1086) with at least 60 building platforms and the well preserved scheduled site at Overtown (*Wervetone* in 1086) both in Wroughton parish, and also at Burytown Farm (*Buribluntesdon* in 1279) near Broad Blunsdon and Hampton (*Hantone* in 1086) in the parish of Highworth. At Sevenhampton (*Suvenhamtone* in 1211) earthworks are mainly discernible around the Parish Church. Medieval documents refer to a mill, great barns and manorial buildings.[224] In 1987 at Elcomb near Wroughton, earthworks were traced by Wroughton Historical Society members who also gathered a large quantity of pottery. Here a deer park and a chantry dedicated to St. Mary are recorded. Not far away at Costow Farm, an archaeological evaluation produced twelfth- to fourteenth-century pottery and uncovered floor surfaces amongst earthworks which comprised platforms; hollow-ways and paddocks. Near Highworth at Eastrop (*Estrop* in 1286) scheduled earthworks extend for 700m. Finds include potsherds, hones and worked stone. Around Widhill and Chapel farms below Blunsdon Ridge (*Widehille* in 1086) there are further extensive village earthworks.

Circular and Linear Earthworks
Within the Borough many circular or sub-circular banked enclosures with an internal ditch have been identified, chiefly through aerial photography undertaken by Major G.W.G. Allen during the years 1930-1939.[225] They vary from 42m to 106m (140 feet to 350 feet) in diameter and have no obvious entrance. Most are in groups: five at Common Farm; five at Little Crouch Hill; four at Pickett's Copse; ten at North Lease Farm in Highworth parish ; eight at Ashmead Brake; six at Water Eaton Copse in Blunsdon St Andrew parish ; eight at Lawn Lane in Hannington parish and four at Shepherd's Rest in Wanborough parish.

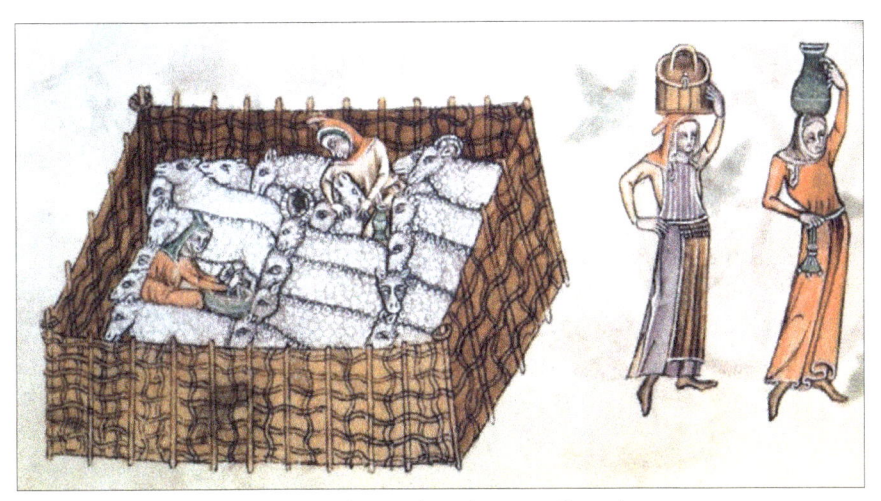

Fig. 128. Penned sheep depicted on the Luttrell Psalter c. 1320–1340

Most lie in the former 'Highworth Hundred' so it is very likely that they originated there, either from local custom or agricultural practice. The excavation of an enclosure at Stratton Park by Chris Gingell in 1975/6 prior to its destruction by road construction, showed it to have a very narrow south facing entrance and to be of late medieval date.[226] Animal bones recovered were chiefly of sheep, but also include horse, dog and cattle. Based on entries in the medieval 'Highworth Hundred' documents Gingell suggests that they were used for the impounding of animals that had strayed or had been found grazing illegally. However their size and the total recorded (around sixty) seems too much for that sole purpose. It is clear that these earthworks having an inner ditch and outer bank, were constructed as pens for temporarily holding animals with the bank presumably being topped with a wattle fence or hedge. They would have been chiefly useful at sheep shearing time, lambing or gathering in of the animals prior to driving them to market.

Many medieval documents refer to sheep, shepherds, sheep pens and sheep commons,[227] showing that their rearing for the wool trade had become important within the area predominantly in the later medieval period. Sheep stealing, taking of their skins or stealing wool appear to have been often recurring crimes. One document records that Simon Rufus and Henry Cole of Broome stole twenty-seven sheep.[228] Simon was hung at Lambourn and Henry fled eventually being declared 'driven out and outlawed'. Thomas Tutty was arrested at Nethercott because he entered Maud de Nethercott's fold by night to steal sheep there. However the jury found him not guilty.²²⁹ In Hannington town four sheep valued at four shillings were stolen by Richard Emelote, William the son of Walter Rycher and William son of Geoffrey atte Eleye.²³⁰

Another type of medieval earthwork of which few have been tentatively identified within the Borough, are so called 'pillow mounds'. Two exist on Sugar Hill in Wanborough parish and another southeast of Liddington Castle. These low elongated mounds surrounded by a ditch were used as artificial rabbit warrens. Thought to have been introduced by the Normans rabbits were considered a delicacy, whilst their skins made fine leather providing a warm lining for winter clothes. The mounds are sometimes found with an adjacent house platform where the *warrener* (rabbit keeper) lived. At Woodland Farm, Lydiard Tregoze a likely warrener's house site is evidenced within Webb's Wood as a 0.4m high rectangular platform associated with two 0.4m high pillow mounds.

Fig. 129. Medieval silver pennies and a halfpenny

Fish also provide a further source of food particularly for the wealthy. Surviving traces of a fish pond can be seen in Lydiard Park to the south of the main lake. Others existed in Lower Wanborough at Hall Place and Cold Court. The latter external to the moat was fed by Wanborough mill's pool and was referred to in documents as 'the great fishpond'.²³¹ In 1305 a recorded dispute between Hugh le Fishere and John Maryz refers to a 'fishery in the water of the Thames' at *Hanindone* (Hannington).²³²

Other Discoveries
In 2007 at Great Moore Leaze, Liddington following the re-cutting of a drainage ditch stone surfaces were exposed associated with many

thirteenth- to fifteenth-century pottery sherds. Moore Leaze is recorded as the home of William de la More in 1233.

Continued activity was shown on the Roman town site at Lower Wanborough by the finding of medieval coins, including a penny of Henry III embedded into the stone surface of Ermin Street, as well as a club-shaped terracotta floor tile in the River Dorcan. Settlement here seemingly had shrunk to three farms – Nythe first recorded as *Niweam* in 1232, Covingham which may relate to the farm (*Ham* in *Ham Dic*) as indicated in a mid eleventh-century charter and Lotmead first noted in court rolls of 1649.[233]

Near Chiseldon a late fifteenth-century silver coin hoard found by Ray Stone comprised 26 silver groats and 29 silver pennies from the reigns of Henry III, V and VI, and Edward I and IV.[234]

Interred in a fourteenth-century iron-hinged chest, an east to west aligned inhumation was excavated at Coombe House in Liddington following its discovery during garden alterations. Another burial was previously found here when the dwelling was built around 1967. Perhaps a small chapel had existed in the vicinity associated with the nearby manor house.

A farmstead site was located by aerial photography northeast of Liddington Warren Farm. When visited by Swindon Archaeological Society members in 1974, found in the plough soil were: glazed earthenware ridge and Cotswold stone roofing tiles, fourteenth- to eighteenth-century pottery sherds, and seventeenth/eighteenth-century clay pipe and glass wine bottle fragments.

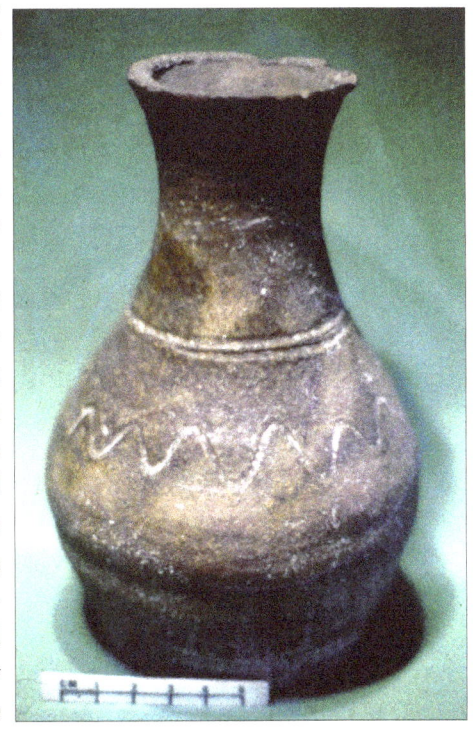

Fig. 130. Fourteenth century flask found in Mill Lane Swindon (scale 5cm)

Medieval Industry

Apart from agriculture little additional industry was evident in the Borough.

Near Blunsdon Abbey Stadium, an archaeological evaluation in 2000 evidenced a small settlement, conceivably connected with stone quarrying activities. Besides large quarrying pits, other features included smaller pits, post holes, scoops and ditches along with twelfth- to fifteenth-century pot sherds and animal bones. Large quarries found close to Groundwell Farm which originated in Roman times most likely continued to be sourced for building stone. Records also show continued quarrying on Swindon Hill as stone extracted from there was used to make tiles for the roofing of two barns at Sevenhampton in 1301.[235] Master carpenters and masons would have been employed to oversee the construction of churches and manor houses using local labour. Lesser buildings would have been constructed entirely by the villagers themselves.

A smithy where agricultural equipment could be manufactured and repaired, horses shod, and weapons, nails, household items and building fittings forged, would have existed at most of the villages. Slag (unwanted minerals run-off during iron smelting) indicating such activity, has been found associated with medieval pottery at Great Moore Leaze near Liddington, Stratton St Margaret, Mannington and Bishopstone. A smithy would have contained a smithing hearth, bellows, a water tank, an anvil and areas for fuel and raw material storage. Close to these would normally have been a charcoal-fuelled furnace in which iron ore could be smelted to produce a bloom (a mixture of iron and slag). Hammering of the hot bloom removed remaining slag and formed an iron billet from which items could be made. Smiths are recorded in the 'Court Rolls' of Adam de

Fig. 131. Iron working depicted in a medieval manuscript

MEDIEVAL

Stratton[236] and these include Robert of Stanton in 1277 and Henry of Hannington in 1281. The 'Highworth Hundred Rolls' of 1275-1287 record further smiths and so presumably the location of smithies in some of the Borough's villages: Hannington Wick; South Marston; Blunsdon; Lydiard; Highworth; Stanton and Stratton.[237] In 1249, Geoffrey a smith at Chiseldon quarrelled with Walter of Highworth and killed him, he fled and in his absence he was found guilty and outlawed.[238] Outlaws in medieval England were criminals who were declared to be living outside the protection of the law. Anyone could steal from, assault or even kill an outlaw and not face criminal justice themselves, as the outlaw was beyond the protection of the law.

Pottery

No pottery or tile kiln sites are known within the Borough. The population was being supplied during the early medieval period by potters who worked in the vicinity of Cricklade and Oxford. During the eleventh- to

Fig. 132. Pottery sherds from the a kiln site at Minety

twelfth-century changes are detectable in pottery manufacture with new forms, increase in vessel size and the application of lead glazes, and also the increased use of decoration. Throughout this period and into the thirteenth-century vessels made on kilns in the Kennet Valley dominated the region.[239] Others came from kilns at Minety and Selsley Common in the thirteenth to early sixteenth century[240] and Naish Hill in the late thirteenth and fourteenth century.[241] Glazed pottery, mostly jugs, came in small quantities from more distant sources: Brill/Boarstall (thirteenth to sixteenth century);[242] 'Coarse Border' ware from the Surrey/Hampshire border (late fourteenth to early sixteenth century)[243] and Ham Green, Somerset (thirteenth century).[244] Kilns belonging to Johannes Liftlot are recorded at Highworth in 1276 and 1284 as causing a nuisance.[245] Sadly the nature of the kilns is not noted and therefore they may have been malting or lime kilns rather than those for the manufacture of pottery.

A Notable Local Medieval Character
Adam de Stratton, the son of 'Thomas de Argoges, or Arwillis' was born in Stratton St Margaret and in 1256 he become a Royal Clerk at the Exchequer.[246] His rise through the ranks was rapid and in 1263 he became master of the King's Works at Westminster and then the Chamberlain of the Exchequer in 1276. Most of his vast wealth however came from moneylending, primarily by acquiring debts from Jewish moneylenders. Acting as Isabella Countess of Devon's steward he apparently committed various grievous offences. By the late 1280s complaints of corruption in the Royal administration reached the ears of King Edward I who commenced a purge. Stratton was relieved of his office and his worldly goods in 1290. On his arrest £12,888 17s 7d was found in his house, a vast sum at that time equivalent to twelve million pounds in present day money. Friends procured a pardon for 500 marks and so in the following year Stratton was released. A subsequent conviction of forging a grant caused him to be imprisoned in the Tower of London. By August 1294 he was dead, although it is not clear whether he was executed or died of natural causes.

14
Post-Medieval (AD1485-1850)

The medieval period is considered to have ended with the defeat, by Henry VII, of Richard III at the Battle of Bosworth Field in 1485. Henry made England a prosperous country and when he died in 1509 his son's (Henry VIII) succession was not challenged so the Tudor dynasty was established. Throughout this period and into the Industrial Revolution little changed within the Borough. Both Swindon and Highworth remained small rival market towns relying on surrounding farms and villages for their prosperity.

Swindon

In 1563 a legal contract showed that the manor of Over Swindon and Nether Swindon (alias East and West Swindon) comprised 60 messuages; 40 cottages; 2 water mills; 1 dovecote; 100 gardens; 100 orchards; 600 acres of land; 200 acres of meadow; 120 acres of pasture; 30 acres of wood and 1000 acres of heath.[247] Clearly the extent of the town was then much the same as in the fourteenth century and would continue so for another 270 years. As shown on Andrews and Dury's map in 1773 it comprised the Market Square, High Street, Newport Street, Wood Street, Old Mill Lane, the Planks and Dammas Lane.

Apart from the ruins of Holy Rood Church in The Lawns, no structures remain above ground which stood in the medieval or early post-medieval period. The earliest survivors are a few buildings that date to the seventeenth century. Little structural evidence of post-medieval Old Town has been revealed through archaeological excavation, mainly due to investigation having taken place in the gardens away from the plot frontage where most buildings still stand or stood.

An exception occurred in 1993 prior to the construction of the Hermitage Surgery in Dammas Lane. Here a medieval *burgage* plot extending west to east appears to have been divided up into small sections each accessed from the lane on its south side. Two sandstone-walled

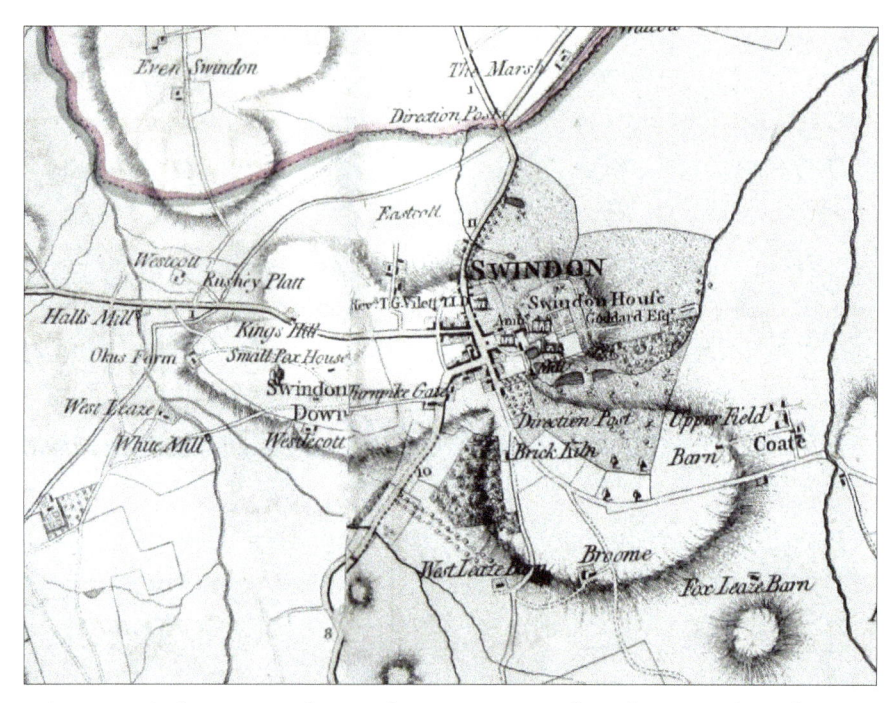

Fig. 133. Swindon 1773 Andrew and Dury map (Local Studies, Swindon Libraries)

buildings were found along with a stone lined well during the excavation by Chris Chandler.[248] In about the mid eighteenth century one building, an apparent two-storey L-shaped cottage, was erected facing west with its south end abutting onto Dammas Lane. Three rooms existed on the ground floor, the northernmost being the kitchen as it had a fireplace and a well just outside its front door. Beneath the central room a cellar was reached by a flight of stone steps and was floored with stone slabs. An extension on the building's east side which was only partially excavated may have been a washroom or brew-house, as a hearth and a drain lay within its southwest corner. Partly uncovered, the second building also abutted Dammas Lane and is of a similar age. At its rear a large rubbish pit contained much pottery dating to the early Victorian period. Both buildings were deliberately levelled in the mid nineteenth century and the site was turned into a formal garden attached to Redlands House. The buildings' demolition may have been partly due to a damning report written in 1851 regarding sanitation within the properties fronting onto the lane. It states 'In Dammas Lane, the cottages have narrow back premises with cesspools. The house refuse is cast into a drain which

Fig. 134. Reconstruction of a cottage excavated in Dammas Lane (Luigi Thompson)

discharges into the fields.' Relating to the cottages occupation artefacts recovered include coins of George II, George III and Victoria, two pistol flints, a lead pistol ball, a cast iron cauldron, late seventeenth- to mid-nineteenth-century pottery sherds, clay pipe fragments and sheep, cattle and pig bones.

In Britannia Place which previously extended off Devizes Road, an excavation in 1976 prior to development exposed a terrace of early nineteenth-century cottages, each with a well in their front garden.[249] Finds here included coins from George II to George V, potsherds, clay pipe fragments, clay and glass marbles, a doll's leg, a GWR button, bone and pearl buttons, numerous bronze dress making pins, a bronze thimble, glass beads and a bone toothbrush. All these objects reveal some of the everyday activities of the adults and children that lived in the terrace.

From the 1975-8 excavations at the rear of Lloyds Bank, Horders, Penfold Nurseries, and Swindon House,[250] the pottery found spans the period from the sixteenth century to mid-twentieth century. Other finds include numerous clay pipe fragments, two bronze Nuremberg gaming *jettons* (tokens) of Hans Schultes (1550-1574) and a glass wine bottle fragment bearing a seal marked W Williams 1790.

Other Sites
Archaeological excavation and observation of construction in Highworth has produced little evidence of post-medieval activity. Of note however is evidence of seventeenth-century brick manufacture at Cherry Orchard Court, Glebe Place northwest of the Methodist Church (see industry below).

In 1971 at Rotton Row, Wanborough, a pipe trench cut through the sarsen wall foundations and chalk floors of two structures. In association with these was a thick black occupation layer which extended up the hillside for 60m, and contained seventeenth- to eighteenth-century pottery sherds and clay pipe fragments.

Farm Sites
Several former farm sites have been revealed by archaeological investigations prior to and during construction work within Swindon's boundaries.

At Moredon, building of an access road for new school buildings and a large pond revealed part of a farmyard complex.[251] Andrews and Dury's map of 1773 does not show any buildings here, although the 1829 Ordnance Survey map reveals an extensive complex that comprised a house and outbuildings called North Leaze. Salvage excavation recorded rough coral ragstone surfaces and a yard at least 21m long and 3.8m wide, composed of rectangular sandstone cobbles. On its north side a long 3.2m wide clay floored brick and stone structure was recognisable as animal stalling by an internal drain for waste. It ran the building's entire length before exiting via the eastern wall. Two cast iron tanks set into the southern edge of the cobbling were connected to iron piping. Similar piping leading from a coral ragstone lined well exposed to the south, suggested that

Fig. 135. Silver coin of Louis XIV of France, found at Liddington Wick

the tanks and pipes were part of a system to provide animals with water and for general cleaning. Pottery demonstrates activity on the site from the late eighteenth to mid twentieth century. The 'Swindon and District Directories' for 1876 and 1878 show that North Leaze Farm was occupied by John Whitting, a dairyman, whilst the 1929 edition identifies the occupier as Rose Hendy. The buildings were not shown on the Ordnance Survey map of 1961 proving that they had been torn down prior to that date.

Adjacent to the demolished seventeenth-century Park Farm site at Haydon Wick, evaluation trenches exposed linear features and limestone-filled gullies and a compressed limestone and rubble path. Whilst close to Liddington Wick Farm a possible yard surface was found during an excavation by Swindon Archaeological Society in 1969. Associated were: building debris; a silver coin of James I (1603-1625) and another of Louis XIV of France dated 1705, seventeenth- and eighteenth-century pottery and bronze and iron artefacts.

Lydiard House
The grounds of Lydiard Tregoze House were landscaped in the early years of the seventeenth century. Formal gardens now lay in front of the house and to the southwest of the house three avenues of trees. Further alterations occurred to the house and gardens over the subsequent centuries, including damming a stream east of the house to form a lake in the mid eighteenth century. A pond further to the south clearly predates the lake as it is recorded on the 1766 map as the 'Old Pond', whilst the lake is referred to as the 'New Pond or Canal'. Fairly recently a number of archaeological investigations in the grounds have taken place as Swindon Borough Council sought to restore much of the park for the benefit of locals and visitors. The earliest archaeological investigation occurred in 1972 when Swindon Archaeological Society assisted by RAF divers examined stone walling and flooring discovered at the edge of the lake. From overlying debris came seventeenth- and eighteenth-century pottery; leather shoes, wine bottles; window glass, wooden artefacts (including a seventeenth-century bowling ball), metal work and a carved stone hand from a statue. It is unclear whether the structural remains identify it as a boathouse or part of the former walled garden of which traces can be seen as low grassed mounds in front

Fig. 136. A brick plinth and garden wall revealed at Lydiard House

of the house. Excavation in 1980 directed by Julian Heath at the north end of the lake adjacent to the dam which created the lake, revealed oyster and fish breeding tanks. Close by, Wessex Archaeology in 2004, exposed at the northwest corner of the lake a brick and stone structure with steps leading down to a flagged floor. Rendering on the walls internally suggests that it was a plunge pool or a holding tank for fish.[252] Archaeological trial trenching, to the west of the house in the existing walled garden, was undertaken by the author in 2001 to determine whether traces of its original mid eighteenth-century layout survived.[253] Revealed were former pathways lined with deep planting beds and subsequent alterations which included tree planting pits and clay pads – seemingly foundations for garden ornaments. Later investigation by Wessex Archaeology located a well and an adjacent stone trough base in the centre of the walled garden.[254] In 2007 alongside the mansion's rear wall the author and Mogs Boon recorded the cutting of a channel for a land drain.[255] Exposed were a narrow brick plinth of eighteenth-century date, a demolished porch foundation, two arched brick culverts and the base of a former garden wall.

Civil War

Archaeological evidence relating to the English Civil War (1642–1651) is slight within the Borough.

Dredging of the River Thames in Castle Eaton parish north of Blackford Lane, produced eleven human skulls and weapons of the period. Further along the river west of Kempsford House, silver coins of Elizabeth I and Charles I were recovered following dredging. A coin hoard consisting of 219 silver coins and remains of their pottery container were found at Waterfall Cottage in Wroughton during the laying of a patio in 1998.[256] These coins date to the reigns of Edward VI, Mary, Mary and Philip; Elizabeth I, James I and Charles I pointing to burial during the early years of the Civil War.

Fig. 137. Hoard of Civil War period coins from Waterfall Cottage, Wroughton (Swindon Museum)

More information is forthcoming from documents which show that by 1643 traders heading for Highworth's cattle market were experiencing great difficulties due to Royalists quartered in the area. Soldiers would simply take what they wanted in the way of corn and livestock. Oxen and horses had also become very scarce as they were needed as draught animals for pulling supply carts and cannon,

Fig. 138. Highworth Church, Civil War cannonball shot-hole

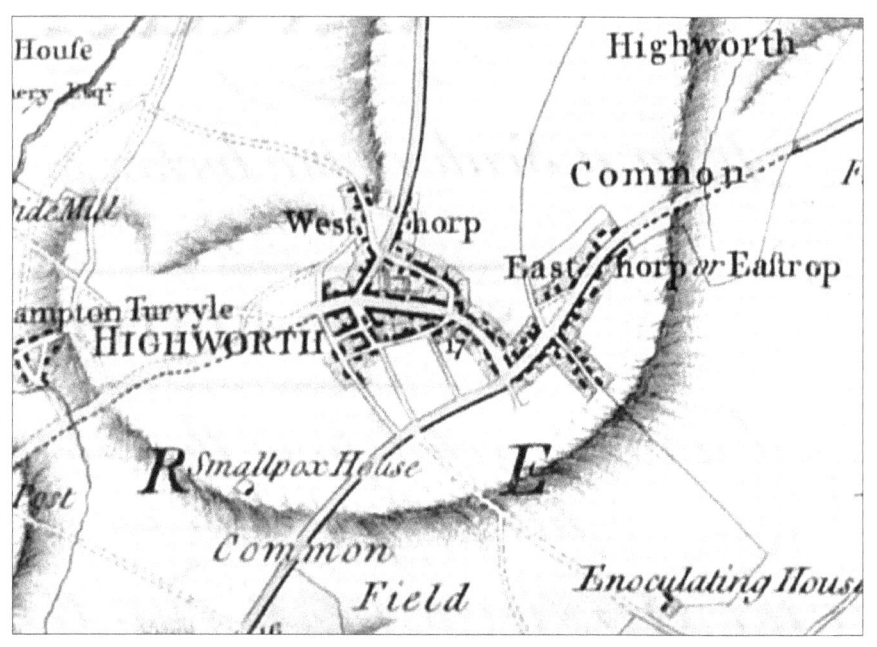

Fig. 139. Highworth 1773 Andrews and Dury map (Local Studies, Swindon Libraries)

or for the latter as mounts for the cavalry. In September of that year Prince Rupert besieged and captured the stronghold of Cirencester held by Parliamentarians. Highworth and other towns in the area were put under pressure to accommodate some of the resulting sick and wounded soldiers. In the April of the following year the Royalists fortified Highworth making Saint Michael and All Angels Parish Church its strong point.[257] A ditch and bank with an arrow-shaped projection to enable flanking fire, formed an outer defence work. Road works in 1980 to the northwest of the church possibly uncovered part of these defences, a 2m wide ditch that contained seventeenth-century pottery. Major Henry Henne, appointed by King Charles as governor of Highworth, had command of 200 soldiers. On June 27th 1645 a Parliamentarian army led by Thomas Fairfax laid siege to the garrison. Fortunately for the town the defenders quickly surrendered.[258] A Parliamentarian force then took command until an order was passed in the House of Commons on 14th August 1646 'that the garrison of Highworth was to be slighted and dismantled'.[259] This took place in October of that year. The burials of seven soldiers are recorded in the Highworth Parish Register for the period 1643-1645.

The presence of troops at Highworth and an outbreak of plague there in 1646 benefited Swindon as – greatly discouraged from attending its market – dealers, graziers and other traders moved to a more peaceful and safer place. John Aubrey wrote

> At Highworth was the greatest market on Wednesdays for fatt cattle in our county, which was furnished by the rich vale and the Oxford butchers furnished cattle themselves here. In the late civill warres it being made a garrison for the King the graziers to avoid the rudeness of the souldiers quitted that market and went to Swindon four miles distant where the market on Munday continues still which before was a petty inconsiderable one. Also the plague was at Highworth before the late warres, which was very prejudicial to the market there, by reason whereof all the countrey sent their cattle to Swindown market as they did before to Highworth.

Later of Swindon he records

> Here is on Munday every weeke a gallant market for cattle which increased to its greatness upon the plague at Highworth about twenty years since.

Swindon did not fully escape the attention of the warring armies, as injured and sick soldiers were clearly housed in the town, the parish registers recording the burial of eight soldiers between 1643 and 1645. They also note that in 1643 Robert Devereux, Earl of Essex passed through the town with his Parliamentarian army on the way to the first Battle of Newbury. Undoubtedly the town also suffered as much as the surrounding villages and farms from requisition and looting of food supplies, livestock and equipment, and the loss of manpower as labourers and others joined the various armies.

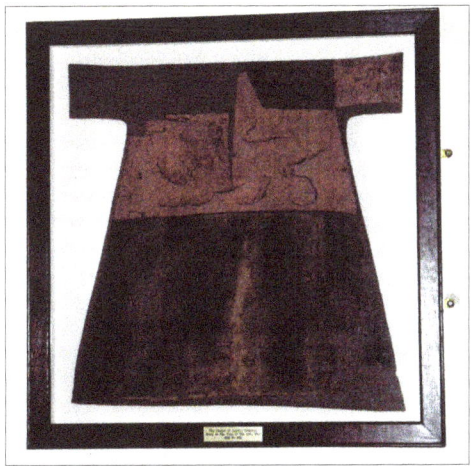

Fig. 140. Tabard worn during the Civil War (Highworth Church)

Industry

Throughout much of this period industry within the Borough, whether in the villages or towns, was almost entirely agricultural or small scale manufacture based on or aimed at local needs. For the latter trades evidence by various documents comprise coopers, wheelwrights, horners, glovers, cloth and silk weavers, tailors, fullers, blacksmiths, saddlers; and also comb, rope, shoe, yarn, quilt and felt makers. Less common trades are clockmakers at Swindon, The Marsh in Wanborough and Highworth; gun makers at Highworth and Swindon; a silversmith at Highworth; and a fisherman at Inglesham.

Heavier industry is provided by continued stone quarrying on Swindon Hill. Quarries being worked included Windmill, Olde Quarre, Westcott and Flaxlands.[260] During the Civil War Richard Goddard, the 'Lord of the Manor of Swindon', had sided with the King and at the end of hostilities he was fined 400 pounds, equivalent to £30,000 in today's money. To avoid bankruptcy he formed a company to start quarrying operations in West Swindon Field, now the site of the Town Gardens.

Fig. 141. River Thames at Inglesham, site of a fishery

Here fine Purbeck limestone deposits had been discovered. John Aubrey notes in his 'Wiltshire Recollections' of 1672

> At Swindon is a quarrie of stones, excellent for paveing halls, staire-cases &c: it being pretty white and smooth, and of such a testure as not to be moist or wett in damp weather. It is used at London in Motagu-house and in Barkeley-house. This stone is not inferior to Pubac grubbes, but whiter. It takes a little polish, and is a dry stone. It was discovered about 1640 yet it lies not above four or five foot deep. It is neare the towne and not above (ten) miles from the river of Thames at Lechlade.

The earliest recorded quarrying in the field was a half-acre site for which Guy Hopkins purchased the lease in 1669.[261] Other quarrying families were: Farmer, Archer, Ewen, Humphries, Bury, Cox, Jones and Simmons. Quarries were worked as small enterprises and much of the stone was sent to help in the rebuilding of London following the 'Great Fire' in 1666. With the opening of the Wilts and Berks canal in 1810 it became easier for Swindon stone to be transported so this, along with the construction of Swindon New Town and its railway workshops in the 1840s, created much work for the quarriers.

One product of the quarries were plank stones – long narrow slabs of stone used for paving and fencing such as found flooring the cellar of the house excavated in Dammas Lane in 1993. The use of these stones probably gave the lane 'The Planks' its name. In 1808 the 'Court Book' records that 'the plank stones in the front of the dwelling house of Richard Horne to be out of repair and dangerous'. It further states that 'he do repair the same within one month under the penalty of ten shillings'.

Digging out of stone within the West Swindon quarry continued into the early 1880s, whilst disused parts served other functions including the storage of gunpowder, lime burning and a slaughterhouse. Exhausted of good stone the quarry was purchase by Swindon Council and in 1894 gardens were opened to the public within its precincts. Quarrying continued on the hill with new quarries being opened alongside Okus Road on the hill's northern side.

Brick manufacture seems to have been introduced into the Borough in the seventeenth century. Fairly recent archaeological work was carried out in Highworth by the Avon Archaeological Unit prior

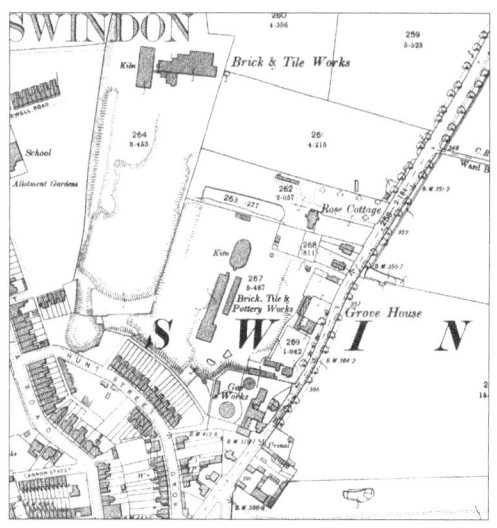

Fig. 142. Turner's brickworks in Drove Road Swindon

to construction at Cherry Orchard Court, Glebe Place. Clay quarry pits were found there which were full of: sixteenth- to eighteenth-century potsherds, animal bone and clay tobacco pipe fragment. Also found was a brick kiln of seventeenth-century date.[262] John Ralph brick maker, is recorded at Highworth on a 1737 marriage bond. A nineteenth- to early twentieth-century brickworks was also located in Swindon Road.

On Andrews and Dury's map of 1773 a brick kiln is shown south of Swindon near Piper's Corner. The town's rapid growth in the nineteenth century encouraged the setting up of further brickworks. A brick, tile and pottery manufacturing yard off Drove Road began operations in the late eighteenth century. This came into the hands of Thomas Turner in about 1870. Thomas also owned four more brickworks in Stratton at Kingsdown, Stratton Park Cross, Gorse Hill and Stratton Green. Examples of his more artistic products can be seen in Drove Road, Turner Street, Hunt Street, Bellevue Terrace and Westcott Place. The Drove Road site closed in 1901 and the site became derelict. Eventually the water filled clay quarry and the surrounding land was transformed into Queen's Park, a tranquil green oasis near the town centre. In the nineteenth century at the bottom of Kingshill were the Bath Road brickworks and the Great Western Railway had a brickworks within its factory complex to supply the builders of the railway works and New Town. Their bricks were marked 'GWR'. A further late nineteenth-century maker is evidenced by bricks bearing the name 'F J WILLIAMS/SWINDON'.

Brick makers are also known at Wroughton.[263] It is said that bricks from here were used to build a barn at Burderop in 1717. These may have come from brickworks which lay north of Burderop Park at Nightingale

POST-MEDIEVAL 193

Farm and which are referred to in the estate's clay works book of 1736. A nearby brick yard operating in 1857 at Badbury Wick was taken over by Hills in 1903. In Wroughton Thomas Buckland, proprietor, owned a piece of land known as 'Bendry's Allotment' in Perry's Lane which had on it a brick kiln and cottage in 1845. It was sold in 1861 and ceased manufacture around 1906. A John Spackman in 1864 had his works at the Black Horse on the Wroughton Road and another was called North Wroughton Park Brickworks.

Fig. 143. Turner's show houses in Drove Road Swindon

Pottery
Pottery vessels such as plates, bowls, dishes, jugs and chamber pots used during the first two centuries of the post medieval period were chiefly made in lead glazed redware. Potters recorded in the Ashton Keynes Parish Records seem to have been the main producer of redware for the region. Clearly they were continuing the very long tradition of pottery manufacture in North Wiltshire. Seventeenth- or eighteenth-

Fig. 144. Pottery sherds, including wasters, from a Ashton Keynes kiln site

century kiln remains and discarded misfired pottery reject fragments have been discovered within a ploughed field on the edge of the village. Production at Ashton Keynes continued till the late eighteenth or early nineteenth century. In addition, early post medieval pottery found in the Borough included in relatively small quantities Surrey green-glazed whiteware, Cistercian ware, and from Raeran in Germany salt glazed wares. The Hermitage Surgery excavation finds included that of a seventeenth-century lustre ware dish made in Catalonia, Spain, which depicts internally a female bust. It must have been a heirloom as it came from a much later context.

Pottery from excavations in Swindon saw the arrival in the seventeenth century of brown glazed wares from the Verwood potters of East Dorset; West Country sgraffito decorated red wares; delftware from London and Bristol; lustre stoneware from Nottingham; and a variety of German stonewares.

Feathered slip ware appeared early in the eighteenth century at a time which also saw major changes in pottery glazes and designs. White salt glazed ware developed by Staffordshire potters in 1720 brought about the demise of delftware and was itself replaced by creamware produced by Josiah Wedgwood in 1760. In 1779 Wedgwood also invented pearlware that soon ousted creamware. Production of English porcelain commenced in the mid eighteenth century with factories at Worcester, Bow, Liverpool, Caughly and later at Plymouth and Bristol. The following century saw pottery mainly composed of plain, transfer printed or hand painted pearlware. Glazed redware vessels were produced at Thomas Turner's kiln site in Drove Road, Swindon, in the nineteenth century as a sideline to brick manufacture. Sherds of these various wares found during the excavations in Old Town include plates, saucers, tea bowls, coffee cans, teapots, coffee pots, jugs, bowls, chamber pots, tankards and ornaments.

Clay Pipes

Numerous clay pipe fragments were found during excavations and through construction work. Many bear their maker's name or mark. These fragments reflect the trends in pipe smoking and the local changes in pipe style during more than three hundred years. Tobacco smoking was introduced into Britain during the 1560s but it remained very much a luxury until the turn of the century. Then it rapidly gained popularity despite the efforts of James I to tax it out of existence. In 1637 in order to achieve more control on tobacco importation and gain more revenue Charles I appointed Lord George Goring and his son George, Sir Drew Deane and Sir John Latch to act as King's agents for the selling of tobacco

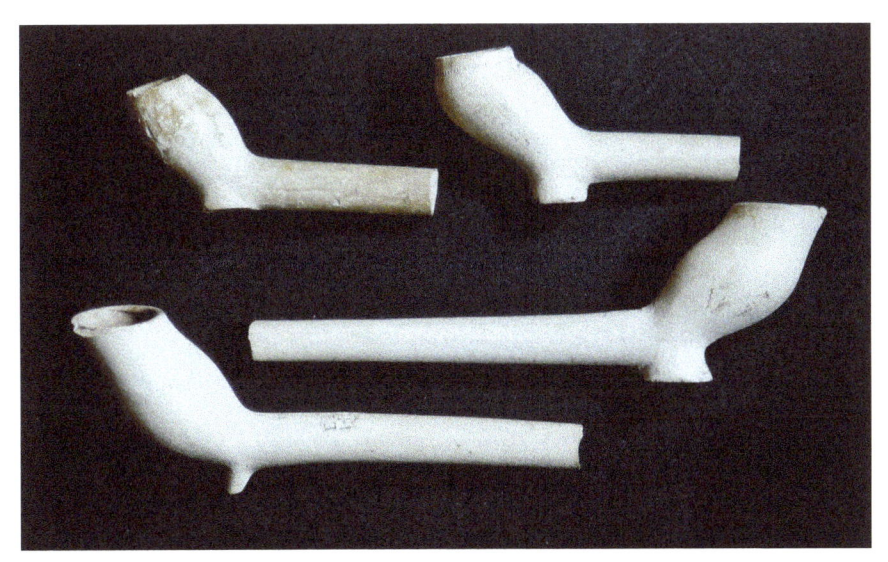

Fig. 145. Mid-seventeenth to early eighteenth century clay pipe bowls

licences. Leonard Hammel, an official dealer, paid £5-0s-0d for the licence to supply Swindon and Ludgershall. Two Swindon tobacconists and tobacco cutters were Henery Restall and William Webb. They issued farthing and halfpenny tokens – the former in 1656 and 1664, and the latter in 1669. Tokens were issued by tradesmen due to the lack of official small change in circulation and usually they could only be used at the place of issue. By the turn of the century the cost of tobacco was significantly reduced, enhancing its popularity and encouraging makers to produce pipes with larger bowls.

Pipes first entered the region, in small quantities from the early pipe making centres of London, Bristol, Salisbury and Amesbury. Pipe makers began manufacturing in Marlborough around the middle of the seventeenth century. Most notable and prolific of these were Thomas Hunt (working c.1660-1691) and his son also Thomas (working c.1690-c.1730). Other pipes from Marlborough found commonly in the Borough were made by John Greenland, working c.1690 to 1737, also William Fery who worked from 1695 to 1712 and John Clefard who made pipes from 1696 to 1749. Strong competition occurred at the end of the century from makers who had begun pipe production at East Woodhay in Hampshire, chiefly Richard

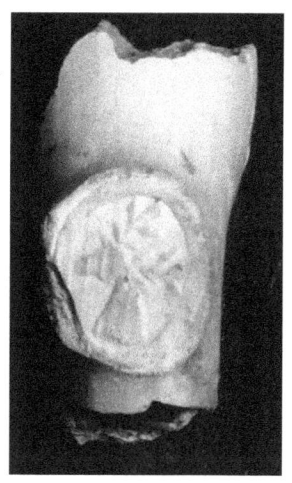

Fig. 146. Heeled clay pipe bowl fragment, c. 1650, from Old Town

Cvtts (working c.1690-1731), and to a lesser degree by pipemakers from Ashton Keynes, Malmesbury, Cirencester and Devizes. At Ashton Keynes, Giles Chaperlin (working 1677-1714) was a major pipe seller to Highworth but oddly his wares seem to have never been sold in Swindon. Pipe makers largely confined their sales to a twenty- or thirty-mile radius from their workshops, the distance convenient for distribution by horseback or cart. It is likely that makers sold their produce chiefly through tobacconists, inns or alehouse, while some may have been sold in the markets or hawked from door to door. Decline in the popularity of tobacco smoking, as snuff taking found favour in the third quarter of the eighteenth century, saw the demise of the Marlborough, Malmesbury and Ashton Keynes pipe making industries. At East Woodhay production continued into the nineteenth century. Later, pipes largely came from makers in Bristol, Broseley in Shropshire, Basingstoke and Salisbury.

Barges and Trains

Although the opening of the Wilts and Berks canal in 1810 had a slight effect on the growth of Swindon which was mainly due to an increase in quarrying activity, rural life for the inhabitants soon underwent a dramatic change. The cause of this was the establishment of the railway works in 1841 by Brunel and the building of New Swindon on the clay lands north of Swindon Hill.[264] Within fifty years from 1831 when the population of Swindon was 1,742 it had climbed to 11,720 and by 1911 it had reached 50,751.

Swindon continues to grow, and in its path many archaeological remains and artefacts await discovery. What happens today will be history tomorrow so the Borough's archaeology will never be an ending story.

Fig. 147. Brunel statue in Havelock Square Swindon

Swindon Museum and Art Gallery

Swindon Museum and Art Gallery is located in Bath Road, Swindon, SN1 4BA, Tel. 01793 466556. It is open Tuesday to Saturday from 11.00am to 4.30pm.

Besides the Borough of Swindon'jgs Archaeology, the Museum houses local history and geology displays. The Art Gallery exhibits some of the remarkable Swindon collection which includes works by Ben Nicholson, Henry Moore, Graham Sutherland, L. S. Lowry and Paul Nash. There is also a significant collection of studio pottery with works by David Leach, Lucie Rie and Hans Coper amongst others.

At present, Swindon Museum and Art Gallery is hoping to move from its current location to a new purpose built or adapted facility in the town. Such a move will enable the Museum and Art Gallery to promote, exhibit and teach the story of Swindon and its people that can be traced back many thousands of years ago. It will also be able to display more of its impressive collection of 20th century British art and host touring exhibitions.

Many of the artefacts recorded in this book can be seen in the Museum's Archaeological Gallery. They include:-

Neolithic
Arrowheads and axes from Stratton and Swindon

Bronze Age
Looped axe (palstave) from East Swindon
Spearhead from Coate Water
Dagger and wrist guard from the Masonic Hall, Old Town
Pottery urn from Bouverie Avenue

Iron Age
Reconstruction of Groundwell Farm hut and various artefacts found on the site

Chalk loom weights from Okus
Gold coins from Chiseldon
Bone weaving combs from Swindon Hill and Russley Down

Roman
Bronze wine strainer from Lower Wanborough
Stone statue of *Mercury* from Lower Wanborough
Brooches, glass beads, and pins from Lower Wanborough
Pewter bowls from Lower Wanborough
Lead curse from Lower Wanborough
Glass vessel and lead container from a burial at Purton
Silver bowl and vessel handles from Groundwell Ridge
Wallplaster from Badbury villa
Very large Savernake ware pot from Highworth
Cremation vessels from Lower Wanborough
Pottery lamps from Lower Wanborough

Saxon
Bone weaving combs from Saxon Court in Old Town
Sword, and spears from the Brimble Hill, Wroughton warrior grave

Medieval
Lead seal from Toothill
Bronze door knocker from Toothill

Post Medieval
Civil war period silver coin hoard from Wroughton
17th/18th century wine bottles from Lydiard House
Iron objects from Wick Lane

Bibliography

Allen, G. W. G. and Passmore, A. D., 1937: 'Earthen circles near Highworth', *Wiltshire Archaeological and Natural History Magazine,* volume 47, pp 114-22

Anderson, A.S., 1978: Wiltshire Fine Wares in Arthur P. and Marsh, G., *Early Finewares in Roman Britain*, British Archaeological Reports, British Series 57, pp 373-392.

Anderson, A. S., 1979: *The Roman Pottery Industry in North Wiltshire,* Swindon Archaeological Report No. 2

Anderson, A. S., 1980: 'Romano-British Pottery Kilns at Purton' *Wiltshire Archaeological and Natural History Magazine* volume 72/73, pp 51-58

Anderson, A. S., Wacher, J. S. and Fitzpatrick, A. P., 2001: *The Romano-British 'Small Town' at Wanborough, Wiltshire,* Britannia Monograph Series 19

Archer, P. J., 1973: Highworth and Round About, private printing, pp 62

Arkell, N. T and W. J., 1944: 'New Bronze Age site found at Highworth', *Wiltshire Archaeological and Natural History Magazine,* volume 50, pp 373

Arkell, W. J, 1945: 'Swindon Geology', *Wiltshire Archaeological and Natural History Magazine,* volume 52

Askew, P., et al, 2014: Excavations at South Marston Industrial Park, (Plots D, E, F), Swindon, Wiltshire, *Wiltshire Archaeological and Natural History Magazine,* volume 107, pp 50-65

Aubrey, J., 1982: *Monumenta Britannica, Part III,* (ed. R. Legg), Sherborne

Bailey, D. M., 2001:' Lamps', in Anderson, A. S., Wacher, J. S. and Fitzpatrick, A. P., *The Romano-British 'Small Town' at Wanborough, Wiltshire,* Britannia Monograph Series 19, pp 177-178

Barton, K. J., 1963: 'A Medieval Pottery Kiln at Ham Green', *Bristol and Gloucestershire Archaeological Journal,* volume 82, pp 95-126

Bishop, S., 2004: *Magnetometery Survey at Blunsdon,* Oxford University

Blackford, B., 1988: 'Brick Making' in *Wroughton History, Part 4,* Wroughton History Group

Boon, R., 1999: *Bury Mill, Hinton Parva,* GCE 'A' level thesis

Brett, M., 1999: Commonhead Roundabout Site, Liddington, Swindon, Wiltshire, Cotswold Archaeological Trust, client report

Brickstock, R., et al 2006: *Groundwell Ridge Roman Villa, Swindon, Wiltshire – Excavations 2003-2005,* English Heritage Research Department Report Series no. 77/2006

British Listed Buildings -online – britishlistedbuildings.co.uk

British Museum Blog – online
British Museum collection
British Museum research – online
Browning, E: Excavation notes, Swindon Archaeological Society
Burchard, A., 1970: 'The Sword', *Wiltshire Archaeological and Natural History Magazine*, volume 65, pp 193-195
Burl, A., 2004: 'A. D. Passmore and the Stone Circles of North Wiltshire', *Wiltshire Archaeological and Natural History Magazine*, volume 97, pp 197-210
Burne, A., 1949/50: Ancient Wiltshire Battlefields, *Wiltshire Archaeological Natural History Magazine*, volume 53, pp. 397-412
Butler, C., 2005: *Prehistoric Flintwork*, Tempus
Cameron, A., Bayley, J. and Keepax, C., 2001: 'The Bones' in Anderson A S, Wacher J S and Fitzpatrick A P, *The Romano-British 'Small Town' at Wanborough, Wiltshire*, Britannia Monograph Series 19, pp 342-344
Canham, R. and Phillips B., unpublished: *Excavations in Old Town, Swindon, 1975-77*, records Wiltshire County Council Archaeological Section, Chippenham
Chadwick Hawkes, S., 1961: 'Soldiers and Settlers in Britain', Fourth to Fifth Century, *Medieval Archaeology*, volume 9, pp 1-70
Chandler, C. and Phillips, B., 1993: '*The Hermitage, Old Town, Swindon*', Fresden Archaeological Services client report
Close Records, 1249-51, entry 249 and 509
Coles, S., 2011: 'Medieval enclosures at Cue's Lane, Bishopstone', Wiltshire, *Wiltshire Archaeological and Natural History Magazine*, volume 104, pp 151-165
Collins, M. D. H., 1986: *Haresfield Estate Highworth, Archaeological Report 1975-1981*, private publication
Collins, M. D. H., 1992: 'Highworth during the Roman Period', in *A History of Highworth Part 3*, Highworth Historical Society, pp 325-342
Corney, M. J., 1997: *Earthwork Survey at Blunsdon Ridge, Swindon, Wiltshire*
Cox, Rev. T., 1720-31: *Magna Britannia et Hibernia, Antique et Nova*, London, 6 vols. 4to
Creighton, O. H., 2000: 'Early Castles in the Landscape of Medieval Wiltshire', *Wiltshire Archaeological and Natural History Magazine*, volume 93, pp 105-119
Crittall, E., 1959: 'Poll Tax Payers of 1377' *Victoria County History of the Counties of England, A History of Wiltshire* vol. 4, pp 304-313, The University of London Institute of Historical Research, Oxford University Press
Crittall, E. and Pugh, R. B., 1955: Anglo-Saxon Wiltshire, Anglo-Saxon Art, Domesday. *Victoria County History of the Counties of England, A History of Wiltshire* vol. ii, The University of London Institute of Historical Research, Oxford University Press

Crittall, E. and Rogers, K. H. 1970: *Victoria County History of the Counties of England, A History of Wiltshire* vol. 9, The University of London Institute of Historical Research, Oxford University Press

Crowley, D. A. (editor), 1980: 'Wroughton' *Victoria County History of the Counties of England, A History of Wiltshire* vol. 11, The University of London Institute of Historical Research, Oxford University Press, pp. 235-252

Cunnington, M. E, and Goddard, E. H., 1912: 'A Saxon Cemetery at 'The Fox', Purton', Wiltshire *Archaeological and Natural History Magazine*, volume 37, pp 606-608

Cunnington, M. E., 1942: 'Saxon Burials at Foxhill, Wanborough, 1941', *Wiltshire Archaeological and Natural History Magazine*, volume 49, pp 542-543

Current Archaeology- online www.archaeology.co.uk

Currie, C. K., 1992: 'Excavations and Surveys at the Roman Kiln Site, Brinkworth, 1986', *Wiltshire Archaeological and Natural History Magazine*, volume 85, pp 27-50

Darvill, T. C., 2001: 'The Roman Ceramic Tile Fabrics' in Anderson, A. S., Wacher, J. S. and Fitzpatrick, A. P., *The Romano-British 'Small Town' at Wanborough, Wiltshire*, Britannia Monograph Series 19, pp 317-319

Dunscombe, H., 1988: 'The Great Landslide' in *Wroughton History, Part 4*, 66, Wroughton History Group

Eames, E., 1991: 'The Tiles' in Saunders. P. and E. (edit), *Salisbury and South Wiltshire Museum Medieval Catalogue, Part 1*, pp 93-138

Ellis, P., (ed), 2000: *Ludgershall Castle, Wiltshire: a report on the excavations by Peter Addyman 1964–72*, Wiltshire Archaeological and Natural History Society, Monograph Series 2

Elrington, C. R., 1974: *Abstracts of Feet of Fines Relating to Wiltshire for the Reign of Edward III*, Wiltshire Archaeological and Natural History Society, Records Branch, Volume XXIX, pp 58, Devizes

Elrington, C. R., 1983: 'Bishopstone', *Victoria County History of the Counties of England*,

Entwhistle, E., 1988: 'Wroughton Manor House' in *Wroughton History, Part 4*, pp 106-124, Wroughton History Group

Farr, B., 1959: *Accounts and Surveys of the Wiltshire Land of Adam de Stratton*, Wiltshire Archaeological and Natural History Society, Records Branch, Volume XIV, Devizes

Farr, B. A., 1966: *The Rolls of the Highworth Hundred 1275-1287. Part 1*, Wiltshire Archaeological and Natural History Society, Records Branch, Volume XXI, Devizes

Farr, B. A., 1968: *The Rolls of the Highworth Hundred 1275-1287. Part 2*, Wiltshire Archaeological and Natural History Society, Records Branch, Volume XXI, Devizes

Fowler, P. J. and Walters, B. 1981: 'Archaeology and the Motorway, 1969-71',

Wiltshire Archaeological and Natural History Magazine, volume 74/75, pp 69-132

Fry, G. S. and E. F., 1908: *Abstracts of Wiltshire Inquisitions Post Mortem, Returned Into the Court of Chancery*, Volume 37

Gingell, C. H. and J. H., 1981: 'Excavations of a Medieval 'Highworth Circle' at Stratton St. Margaret', *Wiltshire Archaeological and Natural History Magazine*, volume 74/75, pp 61-68

Gingell, C., 1989: 'Excavation of an Iron Age Enclosure at Groundwell Farm, Blunsdon St. Andrew, 1976-7', *Wiltshire Archaeological and Natural History Magazine*, Volume 76, pp 33-75

Goddard Documents, Volume 1, Swindon Public Libraries, 1960

Goddard, E. H., 1890: 'Notes on remains of Roman Dwellings at Hannington Wick', *Wiltshire Archaeological and Natural History Magazine* volume 25, pp 232-234

Goddard, E, H., 1895:' Notes on Objects from a Saxon Interment at Basset Down', *Wiltshire Archaeological and Natural History Magazine*, volume 28, pp 104-8

Gover, J. E. B., Mawer, A. and Senton, F. M., 1939: *The Place-Names of Wiltshire*, English Place-Name Society, vol. XVI, Cambridge University Press

G. S. B. Prospection Ltd, 2004: Project 2004/34, Swindon

Hartley, K. F., 2001: 'The Mortaria' in Anderson, A. S., Wacher, J. S. and Fitzpatrick, A. P., *The Romano-British 'Small Town' at Wanborough, Wiltshire*, Britannia Monograph Series 19, pp 220-231

Haslam, J., 1976: *Wiltshire Towns: The Archaeological Potential*, Wiltshire Archaeological and Natural History Society, Devizes

Hayman, R, 2010: *The Green Man*, Shire Publications

Heath, J., unpublished: *Penfold Nurseries, The Planks, Swindon, 1978*, records Wiltshire County Council Archaeological Section, Chippenham

Hills, C., 2003. *Origins of the English*, London

Hoare, R. C., 1821: *The Ancient History of Wiltshire, Volume II, The Roman Aera*, London

Holgate, R. and Mepham, L., 2001: 'The Prehistoric Finds' in Anderson, A. S., Wacher, J. S. and Fitzpatrick, A. P., 2001: *The Romano-British 'Small Town' at Wanborough, Wiltshire*, Britannia Monograph Series 19, pp 37-38

Hutchings, V., 2004: '*Hoare, Sir (Richard) Colt, second baronet (1758–1838)*', online edition 2009

Ireland, C., unpublished report: *Early to Middle Saxon Pottery from Old Town, Swindon*, Wiltshire County Council Archaeological Section, Chippenham

Jones, H. L., (edit), 1917–32: *The Geography of Strabo*, 8 volumes, Loeb Classical Library Jope, E. M., 1953-4: 'Medieval Pottery Kilns at Brill, Buckinghamshire: Preliminary Report on Excavations in 1953', *Records of Buckinghamshire*, volume 16, part 1, pp 39-42

Jope, E. M., 1981: 'Some Early Products of the Brill Pottery, Buckinghamshire',

Records of Buckinghamshire, volume 23, pp 32-38

Keay, S. J., 2001: 'Amphorae' in Anderson, A. S., Wacher, J. S. and Fitzpatrick, A. P., *The Romano-British 'Small Town' at Wanborough, Wiltshire*, Britannia Monograph Series 19, pp 210-219

Larsson, L., 1989: Big Dog and Poor Man, Mortuary Practices in Mesolithic Societies in Southern Sweden, in Larsson, T., B. and Lundmark, H., (edit), *Approaches to Swedish Prehistory: A Spectrum of Problems and Perspectives in Contemporary Research*, BAR International Series 500, pp 211-223, Oxford

Letters, Dr. S., 2005: *Gazetteer of Markets and Fairs in England and Wales to 1516*, volume 1, University of London Centre for Metropolitan History

Linford, P., 1996: *Groundwell Ridge Roman Villa, Blunsdon St Andrew, Swindon, Wiltshire Report on the Geophysical Survey*, Ancient Monuments Laboratory, English Heritage

McCarthy, M. R., 1974: The Medieval Kilns on Nash Hill, Lacock, Wiltshire, *Wiltshire Archaeological and Natural History Magazine*, volume 69, pp 97-160

McCarthy, M. R., and Brookes, C. M., 1988: *Medieval Pottery in Britain AD 900-1600*, Leicester University Press

MacGregor, M. and Simpson, D. D. A., 1963: 'A group of iron objects from Barbury Castle, Wilts', *Wiltshire Archaeological and Natural History Magazine*, volume 58, pp 394-402

McSloy, E. R., et al, 2009: 'Two Anglo-Saxon burials at Abbeymeads, Blunsdon St. Andrew, Wiltshire', *Wiltshire Archaeological and Natural History Magazine*, volume 102, pp 160-174

McWhirr, A and Viner, D., 1978: 'The Production and Distribution of Tiles in Britain with Particular References to the Cirencester Region', *Britannia*, volume IX, pp 359-377

Marshman, L., unpublished report: *Animal Bones from the Excavations in Old Town, Saxon Horizon VII*, records Wiltshire County Council Archaeological Section, Chippenham

Meekings, C. A. F., 1961: *Crown Pleas of the Wiltshire Eyre, 1249*, Wiltshire Archaeological and Natural History Society, Records Branch, volume XVI, Devizes

Mepham, L. and Heaton, M., 1995: 'A Medieval Pottery Kiln at Ashamstead, Berkshire', *Medieval Ceramics* volume 19, pp 29-43

Morris. J., 1979: *Domesday Book – Wiltshire*, Phillimore

Museum of London collection

Musty, J., 1973: 'A Preliminary Account of a Medieval Pottery Industry at Minety, North Wiltshire', *Wiltshire Archaeological and Natural History Magazine*, volume 68, pp 79-88

Myres, J. N. L., 1986: *The English Settlements*, The Oxford History of England, 1986, Clarendon Press, Oxford

Pafford, J. H. P., 1966: *Accounts of the Parliamentary Garrisons of Great Chalfield and Malmesbury*, Wiltshire Archaeological and Natural History Society, Records Branch, Volume II, Devizes

Passmore, A. D., 1899: 'Notes on a Romano-British Building and Interments lately Discovered at Swindon', *Wiltshire Archaeological and Natural History Magazine*, volume 30, pp 217-221

Passmore, A. D., 1913: 'Prehistoric and Roman Swindon' *Wiltshire Archaeological and Natural History Magazine*, volume 38, pp 41-47

Passmore, A. D, 1921: 'Roman Wanborough', *Wiltshire Archaeological and Natural History Magazine*, volume 41, pp 272-280

Passmore, A. P.., 1928: 'Fieldwork in North Wilts 1926-28', *Wiltshire Archaeological and Natural History Magazine*, volume 38, pp 244

Passmore, S., 1998: 'Excavation at Burderop Park in 1995', *Wiltshire Archaeological and Natural History Magazine*, volume 91, pp 57-64

Payne, A., Corney, M. and Cunliffe, B., 2006: *The Wessex Hillforts Project*, English Heritage

Pearce, J. and Vince, A., 1988: *Surrey Whitewares*, London and Middlesex Archaeological Society, Special Paper Number 10

Percival, J., 1976: *The Roman Villa*, 135-136, Batsford

Pettitt, P., Bahn, P. and Ripoll, E., (edit.), 2007: *Palaeolithic Cave Art at Creswell Crags in European Context*, Oxford University Press

Phillips, B., 1981: 'Starveall Farm, Romano-British Villa', *Wiltshire Archaeological and Natural History Magazine*, volume 74/75, pp 40-55

Phillips, B., 1996: *The Romano-British Villa at Abbeymeads, Swindon, Wiltshire, an Initial Survey of the Remains*, report for Wiltshire County Council Archaeological Services

Phillips, B., 1999: *Earlscourt Manor*, client report

Phillips, B., 2001: *The Walled Garden at Lydiard Park, Lydiard Tregoze, Wiltshire*, report for Swindon Borough Council

Phillips, B., 2004a: *Barbury Castle, Wroughton, Wiltshire – A Crouched Burial*, report for Wiltshire County Council Archaeological Services

Phillips, B., 2004b: *The Grange, Blunsdon Saint Andrew, Wiltshire*, client report

Phillips, B., 2004c: *206 Whitworth Road, Swindon, Wiltshire, a Romano-British Cemetery Site*, report for Wiltshire County Council, Libraries and Heritage

Phillips, B., 2005a: *Holy Rood Church, Old Town, Swindon*, report for EH, WCC and SBC

Phillips, B., 2005b: *Access Road, Hreod Parkway School, Rodbourne Cheney, Swindon*, report for Swindon Borough Council and Wiltshire County Council Archaeological Services

Phillips, B., 2007a: *Archaeological Supervised Observation and Salvage at Kingsdown Crematorium, Swindon, Wiltshire*, December 2004 to August 2006, client report BP/KC04/5/6

Phillips, B., 2007b: 'A Romano-British Villa at Stanton Fitzwarren', *Wiltshire*

Archaeological and Natural History Magazine, volume 100, pp 91-103

Phillips, B., 2007c: *Lydiard House, Rear Courtyard Rainwater Drainage – An Archaeological Watching Brief at Lydiard House, Lydiard Tregoze, Swindon, Wiltshire*, report for Swindon Borough Council

Phillips, B., 2008: *Lydiard House, Calor Gas Tank* – Addendum, pp 12-17, report for Lydiard House

Phillips, B., 2012: *Hinton Manor 2012; an Archaeological Watching Brief*, client report, BP/HM2012

Phillips B., unpublished 1: *Lloyd's Bank, Old Town, Swindon, 1976*, records Wiltshire County Council Archaeological Section, Chippenham

Phillips B., unpublished 2: *Britannia Place, Old Town, Swindon, 1976*, records Wiltshire County Council Archaeological Section, Chippenham

Phillips, B., unpublished report 3: *Romano-British Burials at Lower Wanborough (Durocornovium)*

Phillips, B., report in preparation 1: *West Swindon Pottery Industry*

Phillips, B., report in preparation 2: *North Wiltshire Colour-Coated Ware*

Phillips, B., and Boon, R., undated: '*Millbank, Hinton Parva; a Mill Site?*' private publication

Phillips, B. and Henig, M., 2003: 'A Bronze Genius figure from Badbury', *Wiltshire Archaeological and Natural History Magazine*, volume 96, pp 208-210

Phillips, B. and Walters, B., 1977: 'A Mansio at Lower Wanborough, Wiltshire', *Britannia*, volume 8, pp 223-7

Phillips, B. and Walters, B., 1997: *Blunsdon Ridge, An Archaeological Evaluation*, report for Wiltshire County Council Archaeological Services and Swindon Borough Council

Phillips, B. and Walters, B., 1998: *Groundwell House*, report for Swindon Borough Council and Wiltshire County Council Archaeological Services

Phillips, J. R. S., 2004: 'Valance, Aymer de, eleventh earl of Pembroke (d. 1324)', Oxford *Dictionary of National Biography*, Oxford

Phillips, L., 2004: 'An Investigation into the Curious life of A. D. Passmore, 'A Most Curious Specimen', *Wiltshire Archaeological and Natural History Magazine*, volume 97, pp 273-292

Piggott, C. M., 1938: 'Late Bronze Age Urns from Swindon', *Wiltshire Archaeological and Natural History Magazine*, volume 48, pp 353-356

Powell, A. B., 2010: 'Prehistoric, Romano-British and medieval activity at Ridge Green, Shaw, Swindon', *Wiltshire Archaeological and Natural History Magazine*, volume 103, pp 130-141

Public Record Office, 1975: Calendar of Close Rolls: Henry III, 1244-66 (Supplementary), volume 15, Stationery Office Books

Pugh R. B., (edit), 1939: *Abstracts of Feet of Fines relating to Wiltshire for the reigns of Edward I and Edward II*, Wiltshire Archaeological and Natural History Society, Records Branch, volume 1, Devizes

Pugh, R. B., 1970: *Court Rolls of Adam de Stratton's Manors*, Wiltshire Archaeological and Natural History Society, Records Branch, Volume XXIV, Devizes

Pugh, R. B., 1978: *Wiltshire Gaol Delivery and Trailbaston Trials*, Wiltshire Archaeological and Natural History Society, Records Branch, Volume XXXIII, Devizes

Rea, J., 1972:' A lead tablet from Wanborough, Wilts', *Britannia*, volume 3, pp 367-7

Reece, R., 2001: 'Coins' in Anderson, A. S., Wacher, J. S. and Fitzpatrick, A. P., *The Romano-British 'Small Town' at Wanborough, Wiltshire*, Britannia Monograph Series 19, pp 39-40

Reynolds, S., et al, 2014, early Iron Age Settlement and Late Iron Age Burials at the Triangle Site, South Marston, Swindon, *Wiltshire Archaeological and Natural History Magazine*, volume 107, pp 41-49

Rivet, A. L. F. and Smith, C., 1981: *The Place Names of Roman Britain*, London

Robinson, P. R., 1977: 'A local Iron Age coinage in silver and perhaps gold in Wiltshire', *British Numismatic Journal*, volume 47, pp 5-20

Rowbotham, P.A., 2014: A Roman Road in Lydiard Park, Swindon, Wiltshire, *ARA News*, issue 32, The Association for Roman Archaeology

Rudd, C., 2010: *Ancient British Coins*, Aylsham

Sabin, D., and Donaldson, K., 2013: *Swindon Eastern Villages Wanborough Swindon; Magnetometer and Earth Resistance Survey Report*, Archaeological Surveys Ltd.

Schuster, J., 2011: 'A lead Bust of the Goddess Isis from Groundwell Ridge, Swindon, Wiltshire', *Britannia*, volume 42, pp 309-313

Sharp, J. E. E. S., (edit), 1904: *Calendar of Inquisitions Post Mortem, Volume I, Henry III*, entry 564

Swan, V. G., 1984: *The Pottery Kilns of Roman Britain*, Royal Commission on Historical Monuments, Supplementary Series: 5

Swanton, M. J., 1973: *The Spearheads of the Anglo-Saxon Settlements*, London

Swindon Museum Collection

Thamesdown Archaeological Unit, 1994: 'South Swindon Survey' in *Wroughton through the Mists of Time*, pp 108-111, Wroughton History Group

Thomson, T. R., 1956a: The Bounds of Ellandune c. A.D. 956', *Wiltshire Archaeological and Natural History Magazine*, volume 56, pp 265-270

Thomson, T. R., 1956b: 'The Battle of Ellandune AD 825', *Wiltshire Archaeological and Natural History Magazine*, volume 56, pp 270-271

Thomson, T. R., 1959: 'The Early Bounds of Wanborough and Little Hinton- An exercise in topography', *Wiltshire Archaeological and Natural History Magazine*, volume 57, pp 201-211

Turton, A., 1980: 'Highworth in the Civil War' in *A History of Highworth Part 1*, pp 90-95, Highworth Historical Society

Tylden-Wright, D., 1991: *John Aubrey: A Life*, Harper Collins, London

Van Arsdell, R. D., 1994: *The Coinage of the Dobunni*, Studies in Celtic Coinage, no.1, Oxford University Committee for Archaeology, Monograph 38.
Walker, G., 2001: *An Iron Age Site at Groundwell West, Wiltshire – Excavations in 1996*, Cotswold Archaeological Trust Ltd
Walters, B., 2001: 'The Decorated Wall Plaster' in Anderson A. S, Wacher J. S. and Fitzpatrick A. P., 2001: *The Romano-British 'Small Town' at Wanborough, Wiltshire*, Britannia Monograph Series 19, pp 309-312
Walters, B., 2014: The Wanborough, Foxhill Figures: ancient monumental chalk-cut icons in Wiltshire, *Wiltshire Archaeological and Natural History Magazine*, volume 107, pp 28-40
Walters, B. report in preparation: *South Farm Roman Villa*
Webster, G., 1991: *The Cornovii*, (rev, edit,) Allan Sutton
Wessex Archaeology, 2004: Lydiard Park, Swindon, Unit Report number 55380.02
White, R., 2007: *Britannia Prima*, 70-72, Tempus
Whittle, A., Healy, F. and Bayliss, A., 2011: *Gathering Time: Dating the Early Neolithic Enclosures of Southern Britain and Ireland*, Oxbow Books
Wikipedia – online
Wilson, J. M., 1870-72: *Imperial Gazetteer of England and Wales*, Fullerton & Co
Witt, R. E., 1997: *Isis in the Ancient World*, Johns Hopkins University Press, pp7
Wroughton History Group, 2007: 'The Wroughton Hoard' in *Stories from Wroughton*, Wroughton History Group, pp 119-121
Young, D. E. Y., 2008: 'Evidence of 17th century brick-making at Highworth, Wiltshire', *Wiltshire Archaeological and Natural History Magazine*, volume 101, pp 176-192

Notes

1. Cox, Rev. T., 1720-31
2. Tylden-Wright, D., 1991
3. Hutchings, V., 2004
4. Phillips, L., 2004
5. Local museum, Portable Antiquities Scheme or coroner if covered by the 1996 Treasure Act
6. Arkell, W. J., 1945
7. Butler, C., 2005, 57-81
8. British Museum, Research
9. Current Archaeology
10. Current Archaeology, issue 247
11. Butler, C., 2005, 57-81
12. Pettitt, P., 2007
13. Phillips, B., 2012
14. Larsson, L., 1989
15. Butler, C., 2005, 83-118
16. Collins, M. D. H., 1986, 5-7
17. Canham, R. and Phillips B., unpublished
18. Phillips, B., 2007a
19. Wiltshire Archaeological Magazine, volume 104, 151-165
20. Whittle, A., 2011
21. Swindon Museum
22. Phillips, B., 2004a
23. Burl, A., 2004
24. Brett, M. and McSloy, E. R., 2011
25. Arkell, N. T and W. J., 1944
26. Passmore, A. D., 1913
27. Swindon Advertiser 06:11:73 1973
28. Piggott, C. M., 1938
29. Burchard, A., 1970
30. Swindon Museum records
31. Payne, A., Corney, M. and Cunliffe, B., 2006
32. British Museum Blog
33. Jones, H. L., (edit), 1917–32
34. Rudd, C., 2010
35. Robinson, P. R., 1977
36. Rudd, C., 2010, 103-106
37. Payne, A., Corney, M. and Cunliffe, B., 2006
38. Payne, A., Corney, M. and Cunliffe, B., 2006
39. MacGregor, M. and Simpson, D. D. A., 1963
40. Bishop, S., 2004
41. Payne, A., Corney, M. and Cunliffe, B., 2006
42. Walker, G., 2001
43. Gingell, C., 1989
44. Reynolds, S., 2014
45. Askew, P., 2014
46. Powell, A. B., 2010
47. Anderson, A. S., Wacher, J. S. and Fitzpatrick, A. P., 2001
48. Hoare, R. C., 1821
49. Anderson, A. S., Wacher, J. S. and Fitzpatrick, A. P., 2001
50. Browning, E: Excavation notes
51. Phillips, B. and Walters, B., 1977
52. G. S. B. Prospection Limited, Project 2004/34 Swindon
53. Sabin, D., and Donaldson, K., 2013
54. Passmore, A. D, 1921
55. Rivet, A. L. F. and Smith, C., 1981
56. Webster, G., 1991
57. Rivet, A. L. F. and Smith, C.,

NOTES

	1981		1997
58	Holgate, R. and Mepham, L., 2001, 37-38	90	Brickstock, R., et al 2006
		91	Schuster, J., 2011
59	Van Arsdell, R. D., 1994, no. 1, map 19, 24	92	Museum of London collection
		93	Witt, R. E. 1997, 7
60	Anderson, A. S., Wacher, J. S. and Fitzpatrick, A. P., 2001	94	Fowler, P. J. and Walters, B. 1981, 123
61	Phillips, B. and Walters, B., 1977	95	Fowler, P. J. and Walters, B. 1981, 69-132
62	Walters, B., 2001, 309-312	96	Canham, R. and Phillips B., unpublished
63	Passmore, A. D., 1913		
64	Keay, S. J., 2001, 210-219	97	Collins, M. D. H., 1986
65	Swindon Museum Collection	98	Wiltshire Archaeological Natural History Magazine1927, 44
66	Reece, R., 2001		
67	Aubrey, J., 1982		
68	Swindon Museum Collection	99	Phillips, B., report in preparation 1
69	Phillips, B., unpublished report 3		
		100	Anderson, A. S., 1979
70	Cameron, A., Bayley, J. and Keepax, C., 2001, 342-344	101	Hartley, K. F./Bailey, D. M., 2001, 177-178/220-231
71	Rea, J., 1972, 367-7	102	Bailey, D. M., 2001
72	White, R., 2007	103	Anderson, A.S., 1978
73	Fowler, P. J. and Walters, B., 1981	104	Phillips, B., report in preparation 2
74	Phillips, B. and Henig, M., 2003	105	Swan, 1984, 18
		106	Wessex Archaeology, 2004
75	Walters, B. report in preparation	107	Darvill, T. C., 2001, 317-319
		108	McWhirr, A and Viner, D., 1978
76	Phillips, B., 2007b		
77	Phillips, B., 1981	109	McWhirr, A and Viner, D., 1978
78	Percival, J., 1976		
79	Passmore, A. D., 1899	110	Currey, C. K., 1992
80	Passmore, A. D., 1913	111	Rowbotham, 2014, 37
81	Goddard, E. H., 1890	112	Fowler, P. J. and Walters, B. 1981, 69-132
82	Collins, M. D. H., 1992		
83	Swindon Museum collection	113	Phillips, B. and Walters, B., 1998
84	Current Archaeology issue 312, 38-39, March 2016		
		114	Chadwick Hawkes, S., 1961
85	Phillips, B., 2004c	115	Reece, R., 2001, 39-40
86	Linford, P., 1996	116	White, R., 2007, 70-72
87	Corney, M. J., 1997	117	Myres, J. N. L., 1986
88	Phillips, B., 1996	118	Walters, B., 2014, 28-40
89	Phillips, B. and Walters, B.,	119	Burne, A., *1949-1950*, 399-402

120	Ireland, C., unpublished report		1970, 145-148
121	Fowler, P. J. and Walters, B. 1981, 113-115	152	McCarthy, M. R., 1974
		153	Eames, E., 1991, 93-138
122	Brickstock, R., et al 2006	154	Hayman, R, 2010
123	Collins, M. D. H., 1986, 28-32	155	Passmore, S., 1998
124	Canham, R. and Phillips B., unpublished	156	Wilson, J. M., 1870-72
		157	Farr, B., 1966, 13
125	Phillips B., unpublished 1	158	Farr, B., 1966, 2 and 8
126	Chandler, C. and Phillips, B., 1993	159	Crittall, E. and Rogers, K. H. 1970, 175
127	Marshman, L., unpublished report	160	Crittall, E. and Rogers, K. H. 1970, 181 and 184
128	Fowler, P. J. and Walters, B. 1981	161	Crittall, E. and Rogers, K. H. 1970, 177-178
129	Goddard, E, H,. 1895	162	Crittall, E. and Rogers, K. H. 1970, 176-177
130	Cunnington, M. E, and Goddard, E. H., 1912	163	Phillips, B., 1999
		164	Entwhistle, E., 1988, 106-124
131	Cunnington, M. E., 1942	165	Crowley, D. A. (edit.), 1980, 235-252
132	Passmore, A. P.., 1928		
133	Thomson, T. R., 1956a	166	British Listed Buildings
134	McSloy, E. R., et al, 2009	167	Gover, J. E. B., Mawer, A. and Senton, F. M., 1939, 226
135	Swanton, M. J., 1973		
136	Thomson, T. R., 1956b	168	Dunscombe, H., 1988, 66
137	Crowley, D. A., (editor), 1980	169	Crittall, E. and Rogers, K. H. 1970, 78-80
138	Heath, J., unpublished		
139	Canham, R. and Phillips B., unpublished	170	Morris. J., 1979
		171	Phillips, B., and Boon, R., undated
140	British Museum collection		
141	Thomson, T. R., 1959	172	Boon, R., 1999
142	Crowley, D. A. (edit.), 1980, 235-252	173	Crowley, D. A. (edit.), 1980, 235-252
143	Morris. J., 1979	174	Meekings, C. A. F., 1961, 216
144	Creighton, O. H., 2000	175	Pugh, R. B., 1978, 36
145	Crittall, E. and Pugh, R. B., 1955, 147	176	Farr, B., 1968, 312
		177	Pugh, R. B., 1978, 91
146	British Listed Buildings	178	Farr, B., 1966 and 1968
147	Crittall, E. and Rogers, K. H. 197, 48-49	179	Pugh R. B., (edit), 1939, 83
		180	Elrington, C. R., 1974, 58
148	Phillips, B., 2005a	181	Goddard Documents ,no. 402
149	Musty, J., 1973	182	Sharp, J. E. E. S., (edit), 1904, entry 564
150	McCarthy, M. R., 1974		
151	Crittall, E. and Rogers, K. H.	183	Farr, B. A., 1959, 4 and 6

NOTES

184 Fry, G. S. and E. F., 1908, 210
185 Pugh R. B., (edit), 1939, 52
186 Pugh R. B., (edit), 1939, 111
187 Pugh R. B., (edit), 1939, 53 and 71
188 Thamesdown Archaeological Unit, 1994, 108-111
189 Goddard Documents, no. 566
190 British Listed Buildings
191 Pugh, R. B., 1970, 112 and 169
192 Farr, B., 1966, 156
193 Archer, P. J, 11973
194 Fry, A., (edit.), 1908, entry 328
195 Crowley, D. A. (edit.), 1980, 235-252
196 Crittall, E. and Rogers, K. H. 1970, 181
197 Phillips, B., 2004b
198 Wessex Archaeology – online
199 Phillips, B., 2008, 12-17
200 Phillips, B., 2001
201 Crittall, E. and Rogers, K. H. 1970, 105
202 Public Record Office, 1975, entries 249 and 509
203 Phillips, J. R. S., 2004
204 Crittall, E., 1959, 304-313
205 Canham, R. and Phillips B., unpublished
206 Heath, J., unpublished
207 Phillips B., unpublished 1
208 Chandler, C. and Phillips, B., 1993
209 Ellis, P., (ed), 2000
210 Phillips, B. and Walters, B., 1998
211 Crittall, E. and Rogers, K. H. 1970, 81
212 Letters, Dr. S., 2005
213 Letters, Dr. S., 2005
214 Haslam, J., 1976
215 Collins, M. D. H., 1986, 33-36
216 Letters, Dr. S., 2005
217 Farr, B., 1966, 53, 69
218 *Wikipedia* – online 'Black Death'
219 Gover, J. E. B., Mawer, A. and Senton, F. M., 1939
220 Sharp, J. E. E. S., (edit), 1904, entry 564
221 Phillips, B., 2012
222 Coles, S., 2011
223 Gover, J. E. B., Mawer, A. and Senton, F. M., 1939
224 Farr, B. A., 1959
225 Allen, G. W. G. and Passmore, A. D., 1937
226 Gingell, C. H. and J. H., 1981
227 Various – i.e. Crittall, E. and Rogers, K. H. 1970
228 Meekings, C. A. F., 1961, 216
229 Pugh, R. B., 1978, 93
230 Pugh, R. B., 1978, 558
231 Pugh, R. B., 1970, 175, 178 and 181
232 Pugh, R. B., (edit), 1939, 99
233 Gover, J. E. B., Mawer, A. and Senton, F. M., 1939
234 Swindon Museum collection
235 Farr, M. W. (edit), 1959, xxvii
236 Pugh, R. B., 1970
237 Farr, B., 1966
238 Meekings, C. A. F., 1961, 339
239 Mepham, L. and Heaton, M., 1995, 29-43
240 Musty, J., 1973
241 McCarthy, M. R., 1974
242 Jope, E. M., 1953-4, 39-42 and 1981, 32-38
243 Pearce, J. and Vince, A., 1988
244 Barton, K. J., 1963, 95-126
245 Pugh, R. B., 1970, 145 and 146
246 Wikipedia
247 Goddard Documents, no.4
248 Chandler, C. and Phillips, B., 1993

249	Phillips B., unpublished 2		Turton, A., 1980, 90-95
250	Canham, R. and Phillips B., unpublished	258	Pafford, J. H. P., 1966, 20-21
251	Phillips, B., 2005b	259	Pafford, J. H. P., 1966, 27 and 36
252	Wessex Archaeology – online	260	Goddard Documents
253	Phillips, B., 2001	261	Crittall, E. and Rogers, K. H. 1970, 126-128
254	Wessex Archaeology – online		
255	Phillips, B., 2007c	262	Young, D. E. Y., 2008
256	Wroughton History Group, 2009	263	Blackford, B., 1988
		264	Crittall, E. and Rogers, K. H. 1970, 128-130
257	For a fuller account read		

People and Places Index

Illustrations are denoted by page numbers in italics

Abbeymeads, Blunsdon St Andrew 35, 132
Acteon 92
Aethelred, King 135
Akers Garage, Moredon 164
Albinvs (potter) 78
Alexandra 152
Alfred 134
Alfred of Marlborough 154
Allen, Major G.W.G. 174
Ambrose (Saint) 150, 151
Ambrosius Aurelius 151
Amesbury 196
Anatolia, Turkey 83
Anderson, Scott 70, 111
Andrews and Dury's map 1773 156, 181,*182*, *184*, *188*, *192*
Angles 118
Anglo-Saxon 68
Anglo-Scandinavian 135
Annales Cambriae 122
Anted 57
Apollo 83, *83*
Apsley House 18, *19*
Archer, quarrier 191
Argoges, Thomas de 180
Artemis 92
Arthur 120, 122
Arwillis, Thomas de 180
Ashdon, Essex 136
Ashdown (battle of) 136
Ashingdon, Essex 136
Ashmead Brake, Blunsdon St Andrew 174
Ashmolean Museum 16, 47, 164
Ashton Keynes 194, 196
Ashton Keynes kiln site 194, *194*
Ashton Keynes parish records 193
Assandun (battle of) 134
Athelwolf 133,
Atrebates 57, 66, 67, 68
Atrebatic 57
Aubrey, John 16, 69, 80, 189, 191
Augustinian 150

Avenel, Christine 157
Avenel, Robert 157
Avon 57
Avon Archaeological Unit 18, 191
Aylmer, William, Sevenhampton 158

B&Q warehouse, Stratton 63
Badbury (*Baddeburri*) 15, 17, 26, 85, 86, *86*, 114, 120, 121, 136
Badbury Hill 120
Badbury Mill 155
Badbury Wick (*Baddenham Wyke*) 173, 193
Badbury Wick House 174
Badon Hill 120
Bagendon, Gloucestershire 57
Bagsecg 134
Baldred, King 133, *133*
Baldwin, Earl of Devon 166
Balle, Thomas 170
Barbury Castle 41, 50, 58, 59, 109, 119, 122. 133
Barbury Down 50
Barnsley Park, Gloucestershire 112
Basingstoke 197
Bassett Down House, Lydiard Tregoze 131
Bath 123
Bath Road brickworks, Kingshill, Swindon 192
Bath Road, Swindon 18, *19*
Bayonne, France 163
Belgae 69
Beliatus 81
Bellevue Terrace, Swindon 192
Bendry's Allotment, Perry's Lane, Wroughton brickworks *193*
Benedictine 150
Beornwulf, King 133
Beranburh (Barbury Castle) (battle of) 122
Berde, Isabel la 157
Berde, John 157
Bernard, Joan 158
Bernard, John 158

Berricot Lane, Badbury 86
Berry Mill, Hinton 157
Bicknoll 145
Bicknoll Castle 144, *144*, 145
Bishop of Milan 151
Bishopstone 15, 26, 89, 171, 173, 178
Bishopstone Church 40, 146, 149
Bishopstone Downs 25, 65
Black Death 171
Black Horse brickworks, Wroughton 193
Blackford Lane, Castle Eaton 187
Blagrove Farm, West Swindon 110
Blakengrove Hundred Rolls 163
Blunsdon 39, 71, 160, 179
Blunsdon Abbey Stadium 178
Blunsdon Bypass 35, 47
Blunsdon Gay (*Bluntesdon Gay*) 158
Blunsdon Mill 155
Blunsdon Ridge 174
Blunsdon St Andrew (*Bluntsesdon Sant Andreu*) 15, 25, 35, 41, 65, 130, 161
Blunsdon St Andrew Church 146
Bodvoc 57
Boon, Mogs 148, 149, 173, 186
Boon, Jonathon 149
Bordars (smallholders) 142
Borough of Swindon 57
Bosworth Field (battle of) 181
Bouverie Avenue, Swindon 48
Bow 195
Boxgrove, West Sussex 28
Bradenstoke, Wiltshire 150
Braydon Forest 154
Brewery Street, Highworth 168
Brill/Boarstall (pottery) 180
Brimble Hill, Wroughton 131, 132
Brinkworth 115
Bristol 194, 195, 196, 197
Britain 29, 49, 56, 78, 84, 103, 117, 118, 134, 195
Britannia Maxima 84
Britannia Place 183
Britannia Prima 84, 117, 122, 123
Britannia Secunda 84
British Museum 55
Broad Blunsdon (*Brodebluntesdon*) 15, 25, 60, 158, 159, 161, 174
Broad Blunsdon Church 146
Broad Blunsdon Manor House 153
Broad Hinton 145
Broad Street, Swindon 51
Broken Street (*Tobrokene Strata*) 68, 71, 86, 87, 96, 115
Bromesdon, Adam de 159
Bromesdon, Agnes de 159
Bronze Age 44, 122
Broome 42
Broome Manor (*Brome*) 95, 96, 162
Broome Manor Lane 42
Broseley, Shropshire 197
Brunel 197
Buckland, Thomas 193
Burderop Camp 64
Burderop, Chiseldon 150, 192
Burderop Down, Chiseldon 45, 47, 49, 50, 109, 114
Burderop Farm, Chiseldon 30
Burderop House, Chiseldon 150
Burderop Park, Chiseldon 65, 192
Buredrud 137
Burhs 134
Burma Oil., Piper's Corner, Swindon 46
Bury, quarrier 191
Burytown Farm (*Buribluntesdon*) 174
Bydemill Brook 23, 34, 35

Caerleon 78
Caesar 56
Callas Hill, Wanborough 16, 131
Calley Arm's, Wanborough 161
Camlann (battle of) 122
Canham, Roy 18
Canute 136
Cary, John de Babbe 157
Castle Eaton 15, 25, 137, 144, 160, 187
Castle Eaton Church, St Mary's 35, 146, 160
Castle Eaton Mill 155
Castle Hill 60
Catalonian, Spain 194
Catholic Church, West Swindon 110, 113, 114
Catti 57
Catuvellauni 57, 67
Caughly 195
Ceawlin 122
Celtic 84, 117, 137
Central Gaul 83
Ceres 83
Cerne, Henry de 158
Challow, Oxfordshire 112
Chamberlain of the Exchequer 180
Chandler, Chris 18, 182
Chapel Farm, Blunsdon St Andrew 174

INDEX

Chaperlin, Giles pipe maker 196
Charlbury Hill, Bishopstone 133
Charles I 187, 188, 195
Chauler, Thomas 157
Chelworth 159, 160
Cherry Orchard, Highworth 168
Cherry Orchard Court, Glebe Place, Highworth 184, 192
Chichester 67
China 171
Chippenham, Wiltshire 134
Chiseldon (*Cyseldene*) 15, 26, 34, 54, 61, 66, 136, 143, 158, 177
Chiseldon Church 139, 146, 149, *149*, 150
Chiseldon Mill 155
Christ Church, Swindon 148
Christian(s) 152, 169
Christianity 152
Church Street, Stratton St Margaret 165
Church Well, Swindon 33, 125, 158
Chuseldun, Richard de 158
Cirencester (*Corinium Dubonnorum*) 57, 68, 84, 112, 123, 188, 196
Cistercian ware 194
City Corner, Little Hinton 50, 105
Claudian 68
Claudius 67
Clefard, John (pipe maker) 196
Close Rolls 163
Cloverlands, Haydon Wick 163
Clyffe Pypard 145
Coarse Border ware 180
Coate 17, 24, 35, 42, 50, 51
Coate Water, Swindon 34, 39, 42, 46, *46*, 51
Coffin Close, Highworth 169
Colchester (*Camulodunum*) 67, 78
Colcote, Robert de 157
Colcote, Maud de 157
Cold Court, Lower Wanborough 150, 151, 152, 176
Cole, Henry of Broome 175
Cole (*Smita*), River 23, 137
Collins, Mike 107
Commodus 80
Common Farm, Highworth 174
Commonhead 48
Commonhead, Moor Leaze Farm 51
Commux 57
Constantine I 81, 104
Constantine III 117
Constantinian 94

Coombe House, Liddington 177
Corio 57, 66
Cornovii 73, 84
Cornwall 68, 73
Costow Farm 174
Cotswold Archaeological Trust 18, 48, 61, 115
Cottar(s) (cottagers) 141
Court Book, Swindon 191
Court Rolls of Adam de Stratton 159, 178
Covingham Farm 177
Covingham School, Swindon 113
Cox (quarrier) 191
Cox, Reverend Thomas 15
Creswell Craggs 29
Cricklade 135, 179
Cricklade Street, Swindon 51
Crimea 171
Croft Campus, Swindon 39
Cue's Lane, Bishopstone 35
Cullems, The, Highworth 169
Cumbria 41
Cunnington, Maud E 131
Cuttle Mill, Hinton 157
Cvtts, Richard pipe maker 196
Cynric 122

Dammas Lane 125, 181, 182, *183*, 191
Danes 136
Danish 135, 136
Darrivs (potter) 78
Dartford, Kent 29
Day House Farm 42, 46, 50
Day House Lane 41
Deane, Sir Drew 195
Deceangii 84
Demetae 84
Denmark 135, 136
Deorham (battle of) 122
Devereux, Robert Earl of Essex 189
Devizes 196
Devizes Museum 16, 161
Devizes Road 106, 183
Devon 67
Digby, H. 18
Diocletian 84
Dobunni 57, 66, 67, 68, 84
Dobunnic 57, 66, 73
Dogridge, Purton 97
Doinvs (potter) 78
Domesday Book 143, 145, 155, 157, 163
Dorcan (*Dorca*), River 34, 67, 73, 77, 78,

83, 137, 177
Dorchester 123
Dorset 78
Downs Barn, Bishopstone 50
Draycot Foliate 15, 23, 26, 158
Draycot Foliate Church 146
Drove Road, Swindon 192, *192*
Dumnonii 84
Durocornovium (see Lower Wanborough)
Durotriges 67, 84
Dyrham, Gloucestershire (*Deorham*) 122

Ealhstan, Bishop of Sherborne 133
Earlscourt, Wanborough 136, 150, 152
East Anglia 123, 134
East Leaze Farm, West Swindon 110, 111
East Swindon 181
East Wiltshire tribe 57, *57*, 66, 73
East Woodhay, Hampshire 196
Eastcott (*Estcote*) 15, 157, 162
Easton Pierse 16
Eastrop 174
Edington, Wiltshire 134
Edmund II 136
Edward the Confessor 136, 140
Edward the Elder 135
Edward I 136, 158, 177, 180
Edward IV 177
Edward VI 187
Egbert, King 133
Eisu 57
Elcombe, Wroughton 51, 159, 174
Eleye, atte Geoffrey 176
Eleye, atte William 176
Elizabeth I 187
Ellandune (battle of) 133
Ellandune (part of Wroughton) 132, 139
Emelote, Richard 176
England 134, 136, 163
English Civil War 187, *189*, 190
English Heritage 58, 101
Ermin Street 68, 71, 72, 76, 77, 78, 81, 82, 83, 85, 115,116, 165, 177
Ethandun (battle of) 134
Ethelwulf, King 152
Europe 55, 171
Evelyn Street, Swindon 39, 131
Even Swindon (*Theveneswyndon*) 62, 162
Ewen (quarrier) 191
Exeter 68

Fairfax, Thomas 188

Farleigh, Somerset 150
Farmer (quarrier) 191
Farnham, Hampshire 78, 112
Feet of Fines of Edward I 158
Fery, William (pipe maker) 196
Fir Clump 42
Fishbourne 67
Fishere, Hugh le 176
Fitzgerald, Margaret 151, 167
Fitzgerald, Warin 167
Fitzmaurice, Maurice 151
Flavia Caesariensis 84
Flaxlands Cottage, Lydiard Tregoze 51
Flaxlands Quarry, Swindon 190
Foliate, Sampson 158
Ford, Bill 18
Forest Hill, Marlborough 57
Forty Acre Barn, Castle Eaton 65, 131
Fosse Way 68, 74, 112
Foundation Archaeology 18, 115, 152
Fox, Purton, The 131
Foxbridge, Wanborough 35, 172
Foxhill 122, *131*
Foxhill House, Wanborough 65
Foxhill Stud, Wanborough 131
France 78, 109, 163, 167
Fresden, (*Fersedon*) 40, 133, 158, 172
Fresden Manor, Highworth 172
Freshbrook, West Swindon 110
Furnese, Anne 154

Gallienus 81
Garinges Priory 158
Gaul 56, 117, 151
Gaulish 66, 118
Genius 86, 87
Geoffrey of Chiseldon 179
Geophysics 20, 58, 60, 63, 77, 89, 90, 104, 115
George II 183
George III 183
George V 183
Germanic 117, 118, 119
Germany 78, 109
Gilbert of Breteuil 145
Gildas 118
Gingell, Chris 47, 50, 62, 175
Glebe Place, Highworth 192
Gloucester (*Glevum*) 68
Gloucester Abbey 154
Gloucestershire 15, 57, 123
Goddard Arms, Swindon 164

INDEX

Goddard, E. H. 94, 131
Goddard Estate map 1763 159
Goddard, Richard, Lord of the Manor of Swindon 190
Goddard, Thomas 159
Godhyne, William 157
Godhyne, Margery 157
Gore, Charles H. 18
Gore Lane Farm, Bishopstone 40
Goring, Lord George 195
Gorse Hill brickworks, Swindon 192
Grange, The, Blunsdon St Andrew 161
Gratian 117
Great Moor Leaze 96, 176, 178
Great Western Hospital 46
Great Western Railway 46, 183, 192
Great Western Railway brickworks 192
Greater Thames estuary 36
Green Man 149
Greendown, West Swindon 110, 113
Greenfield, Ernest 70
Greenland, John (pipe maker) 196
Groundwell Farm, Blunsdon St Andrew 35, 61, *61*, 62, *62*, 71, 115, 176
Groundwell House (*Grundewylle*), Blunsdon St Andrew 46, 136, 162, 165
Groundwell Ridge, Blunsdon St 6, 35, 99, *99*, 100, 102, 103, *103*, 115, 123
Groundwell West 61
Grove Hill, Highworth 109
Grubenhaus 124
Guthrum 134
GWR 46, 183, 192
Gypsy Lane, Chiseldon 50

Hadrian's Wall 77
Half Moon Plantation, Wanborough 130
Halfdan 134
Hall Place, Wanborough 150, 151
Ham Green, Somerset (pottery) 180
Hammel, Leonard 196
Hampshire 123
Hampton (*Hantone*) 25, 123, 174
Hampton Hill, Highworth 47, 64
Hannington *(Hanindone)* 15, 25, 161, 169, 176
Hannington Church 146
Hannington Mill 155
Hannington Wick 25, 94, 179
Hannington Wick, Manor Farmhouse 153
Happisburgh, Norfolk 27

Haradrada, King 140
Hardecanute 136
Haresfield Estate, Highworth 107, *108*
Harlstone House, Bishopstone 130, 133
Harold I 136
Harold Godwinson 140
Harold, son of Ralph, Earl of Hereford 154
Hastings (battle of) 140
Havelock Square, Swindon 197
Haydon (*Haydone*) 16, 162, 164
Haydon Wick (*Heydonwyk*) 25, 114, 130, 162, 164
Headlands School, Swindon 107
Heath, Julian 18, 186
Hendy, Rose 185
Henne, Major Henry 188
Henry of Hannington 179
Henry II 167
Henry III 163, 167, 169, 177
Henry V 177
Henry VI 177
Henry VII 181
Henry VIII 181
Hermitage, Swindon 39, 163
Hermitage Surgery, Swindon 125, 181
High Street, Highworth 153, *153*, 168
High Street, Swindon 196, 163, 181
High Street, Wroughton 152
High Swindon 163
Highworth (*Wrde*) 15, 24, 25, 116, 135, 143, 145, *146*, 159, 167, 169, 170, 179, 180, 181, 184, 187, 188, *188*, 189, 190, 191, 192, 196
Highworth Church, Saint Michael and All Angels 145, *146*, *168*, *187*, 188, 189
Highworth Hill 33, 39, 107, 169
Highworth Historical Society 16, 107
Highworth Hundred 175
Highworth Hundred Rolls 150, 157, 179
Highworth Parish Register 188
Highworth Rural District 15
Hill Farm, Liddington 64
Hills brickworks 193
Hinton Downs, Bishopstone 50, 65, 66, 105, 131
Hinton Marsh Farm 156, 157, 172
Hinton Parish 156
Hoare, Sir Richard Colt 16, 50, *68*, 69
Hodson, Chiseldon 15, 40
Holy Rood Church, Swindon 146, *147*, 148, 157, 162, 181

Holy Well, Little Hinton 105
Home Farm, Blunsdon St Andrew 39
Honda, Stratton 63
Honorius 107
Hopkins, Guy (quarrier) 191
Horders, Old Town 183
Horne, Richard 191
Horus 103
Hospitallers 150
House of Commons 188
Humphries, quarrier 191
Hunt Street, Swindon 192
Hunt, Thomas (pipe maker) 196
Hyams, Peter 55, 80, 131
Hyde Abbey, Hampshire 150

Icknield Way 26
Inamn 57
Inglesham (*Inggenshamme*) 15, 25, 136, 138, 173, 190, *190*
Inglesham Church, St John the Baptist 137, 149
Inquisition Post Mortem 172
Insula, Baldwin de 169, 172
Ireland 117
Iron Age 54
Isabella, Countess of Devon 180
Isis 103, *103*, 104
Isle, Baldwin de 158
Isle of Man 135
Isle of White (*Vectis*) 67, 68
Italy 109
Ivar the Boneless 134

James I 185, 87, 195
Jefferies, Richard 42
John, King 167
John of Stanton Fitzwarren (miller) 157
John Moore Heritage Services 18
Jones (quarrier) 191
Jubilee Copse 94
Jutes 118

Kemble, William (baker) 157, 158
Kempsford, Gloucestershire 66, 137
Kempsford Church 66
Kempsford House 187
Kennet, River 23, 57
Kennet Valley pottery 180
Kent 123
King's Arms Hotel 160
King's Works, Westminster 180

Kingsdown 40, 192
Kingsdown brickworks, Stratton 192
Kingsdown Crematorium 30, 34, *34*, 39, 45, *45*, 47
Kingsdown Nursery 35
Kingshill, Swindon 192
Kite Hill, Wanborough 95
Knowlands, Highworth 108

Lacock, Wiltshire 149
Lambourne 175
Latch, Sir John 195
Lawn Lane, Hannington 174
Lawns, Swindon 125, 147, 148, 157, 158, 162, 181
Legio II 67
Lennox Drive, Walcot 51
Lewisham Castle, Aldbourne Chase 144
Liden 136
Liddington (*Lidentune*) 15, 17, 26, 40, 136, 142, 143, 153
Liddington Castle 30, 42, 51, 52, 58, *58*, 59, 60, 61, 66, 119, 120, *120*
Liddington Church 146
Liddington Hill 38, 40, 122, 123
Liddington Manor 157
Liddington Mill 155
Liddington Upper Mill 157
Liddington Warren 36
Liddington Warren Farm 177
Liddington Wick (*Ludeemewyke*) 162, 184, 185
Liddington Wick Farm 185
Liftlot, Johannes 180
Lincoln 68
Little Crouch Hill 174
Little Hinton 15, 26, 30, 130, 137, 155, *156*, 172
Little Hinton Church, St Swithun's 138, 148, 149
Little Rose Lane, Blunsdon St Andrew 64
Littlecote, Wiltshire 112
Liverpool 195
Lloyd's Bank, Old Town, Swindon 39, *39*, 106, *107*, 125, *125*, 126, 129, 163, 183
Locarno, Swindon 163
London (*Londinium*) 84, 103, 194, 196
Longespée, Emily 151, 152
Longespée, Stephen 169
Lotmead Farm, Wanborough 72, 177
Louis XIV of France 185
Lower Mill, Liddington 157

INDEX 221

Lower Tadpole Farm, Blunsdon St Andrew 35
Lower Wanborough (*Durocornovium*) 16, 68, *68*, 69, 71, *71*, 72, 73, 74, *74*, 76, 78, 79, 80, *80*, 81, 82, *83*, 84, 85, 95, 105, 107, 112, 113, 114, 115, 117, 118, 137, 177
Ludgershall, Wiltshire 164, 196
Lus Hill Mill 155
Luttrell Psalter 155, *160*, 175
Lydiard House 154, *186*
Lydiard Park, West Swindon 110, 113, 115, 176
Lydiard Tregoze (*Lidgerd*) 136, 154, 161, 179
Lydiard Tregoze Church 146, 154
Lydiard Tregoze House 154, *154*, 185
Lydiard Tregoze Mill 157
Lyncroft Estate 71

Madonna and Child 137, *138*
Magnus Maximus 81, *81*, 117
Malmesbury 135, 196
Mannington (*Mehandun*) 136, 162, 165
Mannington House 165, 166, 178
Marcus 117
Marcus Martiannius Pulcher 103
Mariner, Bartholomew le 157
Market Square, Old Town, Swindon 39, 124, 162, *162*, 163, 181
Marlborough 24, 57, 196
Marlborough Downs 26
Marlborough Road, Swindon 35, 130
Marsh, The, Wanborough 190
Marsh Farm, Lydiard Tregoze 51
Mary Magdalene 169
Mary, Queen 187
Maryz, John 176
Masonic Hall, Old Town 48
Maxentius 81, 152
Maxim Caesariensis 84
Mays Lane, Chiseldon 51
Medbourne, (*Medeburne*) 105, 123, 130, 136
Medieval *141*
Mediterranean 171
Medway, River 67
Melvs (potter) 78
Mendip 29
Mercia 123, 134, 135
Mercian(s) 133, 135
Mercury 82, *82*

Mesolithic 32, 39
Michelmersh, Hampshire 136
Milan, Italy 151
Mildenhall (Cvnetio) 57
Mill House, Perry's Lane, Wroughton 159
Mill Lane, Stanton Fitzwarren 144
Mill Lane, Swindon 29, 30, 33, *33*, 93, *93*, 159, 177
Millbank, Little Hinton 155
Milvian Bridge, Italy 81
Minety 148, *179*, 180
Mohun, John de 159
Moledino, Nicholas De 159
Moon Plantation, Wanborough 41, 65
Moore Leaze, Liddington 177
More, William de la 177
Moredon (*Mordun*) 16, 25, 136, 162, 164, 184
Moredon Bridge 35, 63
Morinic 66
Motorway (M4) 17, 42, 64, 86, 104, 105, 115, 130
Mount Badon (*Monte Badonis*) 120, *120*
Mount Pleasant Farm, Wanborough 66. 80
Mulle, Philip atte 158
Mulle, Richard atte 159

Namnetes 66
Nash Hill, Wiltshire 148, 180
Nene Valley Pottery 78
Nennius 120
Neolithic 37, 122
Nero 104
Neronian 68
Nether Swindon 181
Nethercott (*Neyerkote*) 157, 162, 175
Nethercott, Maud's de 176
New Forest Pottery 78
New Minster, Winchester 139
New Pond, Lydiard Park 185
New Swindon 197
Newbury (battle of) 189
Newport Street, Swindon 163, 181
Nidum 69
Nightingale Farm 115, 192
Norfolk 27, 29
Norman 138, 145, 146, *146*
Normandy 136
Norse 134, 135
North Africa 78, 109
North Lease Farm, Highworth 174

North Leaze Farm, Moredon 184, 185
North Somerset 57
North View Hospital, Purton 97
North Wales 41
North Wroughton Park (brickworks) 193
Northamptonshire 78
Northumbria 123, 134
Northeast Wiltshire 15
Norwood Castle, Oaksey 144
Nottingham 194
Nuremberg 184
Nythe (*Niweam*) 177

Oak Drive, Highworth 94
Oaksey 115
Oare, Wiltshire 112
Odin the Chamberlain 157
Offa 123
Office Campus, West Swindon 110
Og, River 23
Okus, Swindon 107
Okus Quarry, Swindon 51, 65
Okus Road, Swindon 191
Old Mill, Baker's Road, Wroughton 159
Old Mill Lane, Swindon 181
Old Pond, Lydiard Park 185
Old Swindon 162
Old Town, Swindon 18, 38, 65, *117*, 118, 122, 123, 124, *124*, 125, *126*, 127, *128*, 129, 148, 195
Olde Quarre, Old Town, Swindon 107. 190
Old's Close, West Swindon 110
Ordnance Survey Map 184, 185
Ordovices 84
Over Swindon 181
Overtown (*Wervetone*) 174
Oxford 136, 179
Oxford Archaeology 18
Oxford University 60
Oxfordshire 15, 78, 135

Palaeolithic 28
Park Farm, Haydon Wick 185
Park Farm, Moredon 164
Parliamentarian(s) 188, 189
Passmore, A.D. 16, 41, 47, 48, 50, 69, 90, 91, 93, 94, 107, 109, 152, 160
Penfold Nurseries, Swindon 39, 107, 136, 163, 183
Philip, Queen Mary and 187
Picardy, France 163

Pickett's Copse, Highworth 174
Pictish 117
Piper's Corner, Swindon 192
Planks, Old Town 47, 48, 163, 181
Plautius, General 67
Plough Hill, Chiseldon 41
Plymouth 195
Polo Ground, Swindon 95
Polton, Edith 151, *151*
Polton, Thomas 151, *151*
Pomeroy-Kellinger, Melanie 18
Popplechurch, Wanborough 40, 130
Pre Construct Archaeology 18
Prince Rupert 188
Priory Green, Highworth 33, 107, 124
Priors Hill, Wroughton 152
Purton 99
Pytheas 53

Queen's Park, Swindon 93, 192
Quenington 150
Quidhampton 153
Quidhampton Wood 153

Raeran, Germany salt glazed wares 194
RAF 185
Rainer Close, Stratton St Margaret 165
Ralph Earl of Hereford 154
Ralph, John (brickmaker) 192
Ray, River 23, 34, 41, 104, 109, 159
Red Barn, Castle Eaton 64, 66
Red Barn Field, Wroughton 51
Red Lion Inn, Castle Eaton 160
Redlands House, Old Town 182
Redvers, Baldwin de, 7th Earl of Devon 167
Reid's Piece, Purton 97
Restall, Henery (tobacconist) 196
Richard I 167
Richard III 181
Richborough, Kent 67
Rickfield House, Liddington 130
Ridge Green, Shaw 46, 63
Ridgeway 50, 55, 65, 109, 120, 134
Ridgeway Farm, Common Platt 63
River Cole (*Smita*) 23, 137
River Dorcan (*Dorca*) 34, 67, 73, 77, 78, 83, 137, 177
River Kennet 23, 57
River Medway 67
River Og 23
River Ray 23, 34, 41, 104, 109, 159

INDEX 223

River Thames 23, 25, 35, 49, 57, 65, 66, 94, 135, 137, 144, 176, 187, *190*
Robert Hitchin Associates Ltd 99
Robert of Highworth (miller) 157
Robert of Lydiard Tregoze (miller) 157
Robert of Sevenhampton (miller) 158
Robert of Stanton (blacksmith) 179
Robert of Stratton (miller) 157
Robert Pont de l'Arche 148
Rodbourne 25
Rodbourne Cheney (*Redborne*) 16, 98, 162
Rodbourne Cheney Church 98, 139
Roger of Widhill (miller) 157
Roman 117, 123, 137, 148, 149
Roman Britain 83
Romano-British 70, 123
Rome 67
Rossi, Joe 80, 87
Rotton Row, Wanborough 184
Royal Air Force 185
Royal Commission for Historical Monuments 60
Royalists 187
Rufus, Simon 175
Rushey Platt, Swindon 160
Russely Down, Bishopstone 34, 64
Russley Park, Bishopstone 94
Rycher, Walter 176
Rycher, William 176

St. Albans (*Verulamium*) 78
St. Amand, Amauri de 160
St. Andrew's Court, Wroughton 30
St. John, John Viscount 154
St. Katherine 151
St. Katherine's Chapel 151, *151*, 152
St. Margaret 169
St. Mary 174
St. Mary's Church, Castle Eaton 160
St. Michael 167
St. Peter ad Vincula 167
St. Pol, Marie de 163
Salisbury 149, 196, 197
Salisbury Museum 38
Salisbury Plain 16
Salthrop House (*Salteharpe*) 174
Savernake 112
Savernake Forest, Wiltshire 57, 78
Savernake pottery 78
Saxon(s) 118, *121*, 148, 149
Saxon Court, Old Town, Swindon 22, *105*, 106, *106*, 124, 127

Scandinavian 135
Schultes, Hans 184
Selsley Common, Gloucestershire 180
Seven Bridges 116
Sevenhampton (*Suvenhamtone*) 15, 25, 158, 174, 178
Shaw (*Shaghe*) 16, 109, 111, 130, 162
Shaw Ridge, West Swindon 113
Shaw Ridge Primary School 64
Sheep Street, Highworth 167
Shepherd's Rest, Wanborough 174
Shipley Bottom, Liddington 50
Shrivenham Road, Swindon 46
Silchester (*Calleva Atrebatum*) 68
Silk Road 171
Silures 84
Simmons (quarrier) 191
Smita stream 155, 156
Snodd's Hill (*Snodeshelle*) 136, 162
Somerset 122, 123, 134
Somerton 123
South Farm, Chiseldon 21, 87, *87*, 118
South Herefordshire 57
South Marston 15, 25, 63, 97, 150, 179
South Marston Church 146
South Marston Industrial Park 97
South Wales 41
South Warwickshire 57
Southwick Augustinian Priory, Hampshire 148
Spa Spring, Highworth 33
Spackman, John 193
Spain 78, 109
Sproet, Maud of *Haydon Wyke* 157
Staffordshire potters 194
Stamford Bridge 140
Stanley Close, Wroughton 96
Stanton Fitzwarren 15, 25, 88, *88*, 89, 115, 116, 131, 144, 179
Stanton Fitzwarren Church 146
Stanton Water, Blunsdon 97, 116
Starveall Farm, Bishopstone 25, 89, *90*, *91*, *92*, 93
Stone, Mike 105
Stone, Ray 177
Strabo 56
Stratton 150, 192
Stratton, Adam de 158, 180
Stratton Green, Swindon brickworks 192
Stratton Park 175
Stratton Park Cross, Swindon brickworks 192

Stratton St Margaret (*Margrete Stratton, Muchelesratton*) 16, 25, 130, 137, 150, 162, *163*, 165, 169, 170, 178, 179, 180
Stratton St Margaret Church 146
Stratton St Margaret Mill 155
Stubbs Hill, Blunsdon 97
Suetonius 67
Sugar Hill, Wanborough 176
Surrey green-glazed white ware 136
Svein Forkbeard 136
Swindon (*Swindone*) 15, 16, 25, 30, 42, 58, 63, 66, 113, 135, 143, 160, 162, 163, 169, 181, 189, 190, 191, 194, 196, 197
Swindon and District Directories 185
Swindon Archaeological Society 16, 18, 35, 71, 86, 88, 89, 91, 94, 95, 105, 109, 177, 185
Swindon Borough 15, 67, 135, 143, 144, 150
Swindon Borough Archaeological Advisory Committee 18
Swindon Borough Council 89, 99, 185
Swindon College 122
Swindon Council 191
Swindon Hill 23, 24, 30, 33, 39, 46, 48, 66, 71, 77, 82, 93, 106, 107, 109, 115, 124, 172, 178, 190, 197
Swindon House 124, *129*, 136, 183
Swindon Mill, Old Town 155, *158*
Swindon Museum and Art Gallery 16, 18, *19*, 95
Swindon New Town 191
Swindon Road, Highworth 192
Swindon Windmill 159, 160
Thames, River 23, 25, 35, 49, 57, 65, 66, 94, 135, 137, 144, 176, 187, 190
Thames Valley 23, 45, 65
Thames Valley Archaeological Services 18
Thamesdown 15
Thamesdown Archaeological Unit 18
The Cullems, Highworth 169
The Fox, Purton 131
The Grange, Blunsdon St Andrew 161
The Marsh, Wanborough 190
The Willows, Highworth 33
Thermodon 83
Thompson, Luigi 99
Thorne, George (baker) 159
Tincommius 66
Toothill Farm (*Mehandun*), West Swindon 65, 110, 111, *166*, *167*, 167

Tostig 140
Tower of London 180
Town Gardens, Swindon 190
Tregoze, Robert, Sheriff of Wiltshire 154
Trier 151
Trublevill, Hawyse 169
Trublevill, Henry 169
Tudor Dynasty 181
Turner Street, Swindon 192
Turner, Thomas 192, *193*
Turner's brickworks, Drove Road, Swindon *192*, 195
Tutty, Thomas 175

Ubbe Ragnarsson 134
Upper Burytown Farm, Broad Blunsdon 51, 130
Upper Mill, Liddington 157
Upper Shaw Farm, West Swindon 110, 115
Upper Stratton 16, 25, 162
Upper Thames 104
Upper Thames Valley 36
Upper Wanborough 85, 130

Valance, Almer de 159, 163
Valence, William de 162, *162*
Venus 83
Verwood Potteries, South Dorset 194
Vespasian 67, 107
Victoria 183
Victorian 182
Villa Regia 123
Villeins (villagers) 140, 141, 142, 143

Wacher, John 70
Walcot (*Walecote*) 162
Wales 74
Wallingford, Oxfordshire 135
Walter of Highworth 179
Walter of South Marston (miller) 157
Walters, Bryn 87, 100, 122
Wanborough (*Wenbeorgan*) 15, 24, 26, 40, 66, 136, 137, 150, 160, 169
Wanborough Church, St Andrew's 146, 151, *151*
Wanborough Marsh 151
Wanborough Mill 152, 155, 176
Wanborough Plain Farm 66, 104
Wantage, Oxfordshire 134
Warneage Manor 152
Waryn, William Fiz 158
Water Eaton Copse, Blunsdon St Andrew

INDEX

174
Waterfall House, Wroughton 187, *187*
Wayte, Walter le 159
Webb, William (tobacconist) 196
Webb's Wood, Lydiard Tregoze 176
Wedgwood, Josiah 194
Wessex 123, 133, 134, 135
Wessex Archaeology 18, 55, 63, 113, 186
Wessex School (tile makers) 149
West Country Sgraffito Red Ware 194
West Hill, Highworth 65
Westhill House, Highworth 94
West Leaze (*Wichelestote*), West Swindon 158, 172
West Oxfordshire 57
West Saxon 133
West Swindon 114, 165, 181
West Swindon Field Quarry 190, 191
West Swindon Ware (pottery) 78, 111, 114, 115
West Widhill (*Westwydyhull*) 159
Westcott (*Westcot*) 162
Westcott Place, Swindon 192
Westlea Down, West Swindon 110
Westlecott Mill 155, 159
Westlecott Road, Swindon 48
Westlecott Quarry, Swindon 190
Westminster Abbey 140, 163
Westrop, Highworth 94, 167
White Walls 112
Whitehill Farm, West Swindon 16, 17, 109, 110, *110*, 111, *111*, *112*, 113
Whitheved, William, North Widhill 157
Whitting, John 185
Whitworth Road, Swindon 98, *98*
Wichelestote, Swindon 159, 172
Wick Farm (*La Wik*), West Swindon 165
Widhill (*Widehille*) 174
Widhill Farm, Blunsdon St Andrew 174

Widhill Mill 155
William I (Duke of Normandy) 140, 143
William of Hampton (miller) 157
Williams, F J, Swindon (brickmaker) 192
Williams, W 184
Willows, The, Highworth 33
Wilson, Peter 101
Wilton 123
Wilts and Berks canal 191, 197
Wiltshire 15, 123, 135
Wiltshire Archaeological Society Magazine 16, 17
Wiltshire County Council 15
Wiltshire County Council's archaeological unit 18, 106
Wiltshire Inquisitions Post Mortems 159
Winchester (*Venta Belgarum*) 69, 136
Winchester, Church of St Peter and Paul 152
Windmill Quarry 190
Wood Street, Swindon 106, 160, 163, 164, 181
Woodland Farm, Lydiard Tregoze 176
Woodward, John 16, 95
Woollard, Gerald 120
Worcester 195
Wrde Hill, Highworth 94
Writel, Roger le 159
Wroughton (*Ellendun*) 15, 25, 58, 130, 186, 143, 152, 159, 192
Wroughton Airfield 64
Wroughton Church 139, 146
Wroughton mills 155
Wroughton Parish 64
Wroxeter (*Viroconium Cornoviorum*) 73
Wulffierd 133

York 134

Ingram Content Group UK Ltd.
Milton Keynes UK
UKHW051307120623
423300UK00010B/44